W9-ARG-573

A GOOD OLD AGE?

THE PARADOX OF *SETTING LIMITS*

EDITED BY PAUL HOMER
AND MARTHA HOLSTEIN

AFTERWORD BY
DANIEL CALLAHAN

A TOUCHSTONE BOOK
Published by Simon & Schuster Inc.
New York • London • Toronto • Sydney • Tokyo • Singapore

Simon and Schuster/Touchstone

Simon & Schuster Building
Rockefeller Center
1230 Avenue of the Americas
New York, New York 10020

Designed by Sheree L. Goodman

Manufactured in the United States of America

1 3 5 9 10 8 6 4 2

1 3 5 9 10 8 6 4 2 Pbk.

Library of Congress Cataloging in Publication Data

A Good old age? : the paradox of setting limits / edited by Paul Homer
and Martha Holstein ; afterword by Daniel Callahan.
p. cm.
"A Touchstone book."
Includes bibliographical references.
1. Aged—Medical care—Moral and ethical aspects. I. Homer,
Paul. II. Holstein, Martha.
RA564.8.G63 1990
362.1'9897'001—dc20   90-9852
                                             CIP
ISBN 0-671-68439-6
0-671-70739-6 Pbk.

ACKNOWLEDGMENTS

I want to express my deepest thanks and appreciation to the following: my friends and former colleagues at the American Society on Aging, which has been my "home" for over thirteen years, for listening to me and providing critical readings, for their moral support, their encouragement, and even their cheers; La Patisserie, the warmest and most welcoming café in San Francisco, for offering a hospitable place to read and write; my daughters—Jenny and Julie—for their pride and their love; my friends, who simply understood and who enrich my life immeasurably; Meredith Minkler and Charles J. Fahey, two authors in this collection, who said this was important and must be done and whose faith in me and this project consistently renewed my energy; all the authors, who not only took our suggestions but welcomed them; Lands End and the Pacific Ocean for never letting me forget that there was a world beyond my desk; Dan Callahan for sparking something important in me; and Paul Homer—one couldn't ask for a better coeditor.

MARTHA HOLSTEIN

I was very fortunate to be a part of the Hastings Center from 1985 to 1989, and to witness the birth and development of *Setting Limits*. Being so close to the project and the author afforded me a special glimpse into the process by which a philosopher brings his ideas to the public arena. I have much admired Dan Callahan's integrity, for he never let the overwhelming, and sometimes undeserved, response to *Setting Limits* dampen his enthusiasm for and commitment to discussion and debate. I have learned a great deal from him and because of him, and I want to thank him for giving me the opportunity to be a part of the Hastings Center and his work. His encouragement and trust over the years and during this project will forever be appreciated.

Coediting a book, I am told, can be more arduous than editing one, especially when the collaborators live and work 3,000 miles apart. Martha Holstein was a wonderful partner—creative, diligent, and always supportive. I am grateful that our efforts produced a book and a friendship.

The authors who either wrote essays for this volume or agreed to have their work reprinted here also deserve credit. Like Dan Callahan, they have our admiration for their belief in the importance of dialogue on these issues.

The Hastings Center is a place where no one works alone—by design or by choice—and I want to thank the whole staff for their support. Special thanks to Marna Howarth for her patience; Courtney Campbell for his many excellent suggestions on the manuscript; Amy McGranahan and Bette-Jane Crigger for lending their immense typing and editing skills; Bart Collopy for his insights and humanity; Virginia Wells, my administrative assistant, who saw this project through each and every step with great loyalty and care; and Lauri Posner, whose contributions all along the way and to all hours of the night cannot be measured.

I want also to thank my family. Having a publisher's dead-

ACKNOWLEDGMENTS

line and wedding day coincide made for more excitement than anyone ought to endure, but my new wife, Karen, was always there to help and forgive. And, finally, I thank my mother, Monica. As I reflect on my life, I realize she was my first and best teacher.

PAUL HOMER

CONTENTS

CONTENTS

10

CONTENTS

11

Contents

FOREWORD: STANDING AT THE CROSSROADS

Many of the deepest and, simultaneously, some of the most practical problems of our time focus on the meaning and significance of old age, the proper goals of medicine, and the devising of a just system for allocating health-care resources. In a society with a sparse cultural context for growing old and facing death and dying, the ability of technology to re-define medical need on an almost daily basis raises very special questions about medical treatment at the edges of life. Some, like Daniel Callahan and former Colorado Governor Richard Lamm, worry about the ominous consequences of open-ended health care for the elderly on children and other areas of social needs. Others, including many elders, worry that they will be allowed to live too long, and that they will lose control over treatment decisions. And more and more people worry about the obligations of generations toward one an-other and, above all, worry that we have lost the ability and the will to talk as a community about these issues.

Blunt talk about the explicit rationing of health care can unsettle even the toughest pragmatist. Nevertheless, we have begun to ask tough questions about the costs of medicine, suggesting that the continuation of the *status quo* is an unacceptable option. For many, explicit rationing is preferable to the implicit rationing that exists today: rationing based primarily on the ability to pay. Perhaps, says Daniel Callahan, in taking the argument beyond cost questions, limits are essential not only to halt obsessive spending on an unwinnable war against death but, most important, because limits are what elders ought to want.

The idea of setting age limits on health-care dollars has received applause as well as piercing criticism from philosophers, theologians, policy analysts and policymakers, attorneys, and physicians; from elders, gerontologists, and aging advocates. It has been labeled everything from compassionate to callous, welcome to dangerous, insightful to muddied, communitarian to individualistic, proeuthanasia to antieuthanasia; from premodern to timely to prophetic.

Standing at the crossroads of moral reflection and practical decision-making, Callahan, a leading medical ethicist, was certainly not the first to propose setting limits to health care. He went further, however, than any of his predecessors in justifying and developing a specific plan for implementing limits. Now irrevocably etched in the public consciousness, his long-range goal to categorically deny Medicare reimbursement for life-extending therapies to those older people who have lived a "natural life span" has led to cries of outrage as well as to unabated applause.

The contributors to *A Good Old Age?* were chosen to represent the many diverse fields and disciplines with an interest in the issues. Distinguished figures in their fields as well as those who are beginning to establish themselves as the next generation of leaders, these individuals reflect the range of thinking that has emerged and articulate the direction that future debate is likely to take.

Parts I–IV of *A Good Old Age?* sum up the earliest responses to the multiplicity of ideas that *Setting Limits* raises.

14

The writers—theologians, ethicists, gerontologists, policy analysts, journalists, and physicians—cover the entire range of response, both laudatory and critical. They also provide a quick take on the issues and background for the more detailed essays in Parts V–VIII from authorities who accepted our invitation to probe many of the most wrenching and complex questions of our time. They remind us that not all competing goals can be met, that not all goods can be realized. In Part IX Daniel Callahan responds to these critics and commentators.

Daniel Callahan wrote in *Setting Limits* that its first and fundamental purpose was to stimulate a public discussion of the future of health care for the aged. In that he has clearly succeeded. That discussion is the task before us. The essays that follow are the first comprehensive examination of the elements of that public discourse.

Despite differences in approach, virtually all the contributors to this collection, and others who have responded to *Setting Limits,* share Callahan's vision that a morally just society rests on mutual reciprocity among generations, on a collective concern for the good of all, and on the human enterprise of caring. Yet these are the very values that may be the most profoundly difficult to translate into public policy in contemporary America.

While none of the authors featured here unequivocally approves of Callahan's age-disentitlement proposals, each underscores the urgency of the moral and political problems that we, as a society, face. Together, in both their critiques and their proposed alternative visions, they call to mind the reflections of Isaiah Berlin, the noted British social and political theorist, who suggests that "human nature . . . generates values, which though equally sacred, equally ultimate, exclude one another. . . . Moral conduct therefore may involve making agonizing choices, without the help of universal criteria between incompatible but equally desirable values."[1]

Moral anguish is integral to life in a free society, and contemporary America is no exception. Never before in our history have questions of ethics so dominated public discussion. Rarely have the stakes been so high and the opportunities for the language of dialogue so slim. Despite these obstacles, bridges between ethics and public policy are implicitly constructed every day.

Before the bridges narrow, before the choices inflict grave harm, we offer this exploration of alternative answers to the questions of meaning in old age and the goals of medicine and health care for the old. We offer it because joining in a quest with thoughtful people is an adventure worthy of mind and spirit. We offer it because the exchange of ideas will help each of us to think differently about our own lives, about making choices wisely—about medicine and a just society, about communal well-being and personal responsibility, about radical and incremental policy options, about dying, and also about living. We offer this collection because its range sparks ideas that a less interdisciplinary perspective would inhibit. And, lastly, we offer it because in public forums, in our own hearts and minds, with intellectual rigor and moral passion, we each have the task to pursue the ancient Athenian ideal: to join moral reflection with practical policymaking, to engage in substantive ethical discussion, to be unafraid to speak the unpopular ideas, and to listen closely to the views of those who disagree with us.

Each of us, then, has a personal as well as an intellectual task. We must first articulate our own values, particularly about the extent of personal and societal obligation to assure the common good. And second, we must grapple with how, after examining our own beliefs in light of the following arguments, we would resolve the issues raised, for these issues

16

will undoubtedly govern debate about health care and aging for the foreseeable future.

PAUL HOMER
MARTHA HOLSTEIN

NOTES

1. Aileen Kelly, "Introduction," in Isaiah Berlin, *Russian Thinkers* (New York: Pelican Books, 1979), p. xv.

A GOOD OLD AGE?

PART I

FRAMING THE DEBATE ON *SETTING LIMITS*

"*My primary purpose in writing* Setting Limits *was to stimulate discussion and debate. Of course, debate means criticism, and that is as it should be,*" *observes Daniel Callahan.*

A Good Old Age? *gives every reader a chance to hear all sides of the debate and to evaluate the arguments from a personal perspective. In this section, Dr. Callahan sums up his position that society should ration health care at the end of life's journey. Then Martha Holstein, evoking the voices of our elders, provides a context and a starting point for confronting the emotional and intellectual reactions that* Setting Limits *has engendered.*

WHY WE MUST SET LIMITS

DANIEL CALLAHAN

DANIEL CALLAHAN is Director and cofounder of the Hastings Center in Briarcliff Manor, New York.

IN OCTOBER 1986 Dr. Thomas Starzl of Presbyterian University Hospital in Pittsburgh successfully transplanted a liver into a seventy-six-year-old woman, thereby extending to the elderly patient one of the most technologically sophisticated and expensive kinds of medical treatment available (the typical cost of such an operation is more than $200,000). Not long after that, Congress brought organ transplants under Medicare coverage, thus guaranteeing an even greater range of this form of life-saving care for older age groups.

That is, on its face, the kind of medical progress we usually hail: a triumph of medical technology and a newfound benefit provided by an established health-care program. But at the same time those events were taking place, a government campaign for cost containment was under way, with a special focus on Medicare. It is not hard to understand why.

In 1980 people over age sixty-five—11 percent of the population—accounted for 29 percent of the total American health-care expenditures of $219.4 billion. By 1986 the elderly accounted for 31 percent of the total expenditures of

23

$450 billion. Annual Medicare costs are projected to rise from $75 billion in 1986 to $114 billion by the year 2000, and that is in current, not inflated, dollars.

Is it sensible, in the face of rapidly increasing health-care costs for the elderly, to press forward with new and expensive ways of extending their lives? Is it possible to hope to control costs while simultaneously supporting innovative and costly research? Those are now unavoidable questions. Medicare costs are rising at an extraordinary pace, fueled by an increasing number and proportion of the elderly. The fastest-growing age group in the United States is comprised of those over age eighty-five, increasing at a rate of about 10 percent every two years. By the year 2040, it has been projected, the elderly will represent 21 percent of the population and consume 45 percent of all health-care expenditures. How can costs of that magnitude be borne?

Yet there is another powerful reality to consider that moves in a different direction: Medicare and Medicaid are grossly inadequate in meeting the real and full needs of the elderly. The system fails most notably in providing decent long-term care and home care. Members of minority groups, and single or widowed women, are particularly disadvantaged. How will it be possible, then, to provide the growing number of elderly with even present levels of care, and also rid the system of its inadequacies and inequities, and yet at the same time add expensive new technologies?

The straight answer is that it will be impossible to do all those things and, worse still, it may be harmful even to try. The economic burdens that combination would impose on younger age groups, and the skewing of national social priorities too heavily toward health care, would themselves be good reasons to hesitate.

BEYOND ECONOMICS: WHAT IS
GOOD FOR THE ELDERLY?

My concern, however, extends beyond the crisis in health-care costs. "I want to lay the foundation for a more austere thesis: that even with relatively ample resources, there will be better ways in the future to spend our money than on indefinitely extending the life of the elderly. That is neither a wise social goal nor one that the aged themselves should want, however compellingly it will attract them. . . . Our affluence and refusal to accept limits have led and allowed us to evade some deeper truths about the living of a good life and the place of aging and death in that life" (*SL,* 53, 116).[1]

The coming economic crisis provides a much-needed opportunity to ask some fundamental questions. Just what is it that we want medicine to do for us as we age? Other cultures have believed that aging should be accepted, and that it should be in part a time of preparation for death. Our culture seems increasingly to dispute that view, preferring instead, it often seems, to think of aging as hardly more than another disease, to be fought and rejected. Why does our culture have such difficulty with this question?

Let me start by saying that "the place of the elderly in a good society is a communal, not only an individual, question. It goes unexplored in a culture that does not easily speak the language of community and mutual responsibility. The demands of our interest-group political life constitute another obstacle. . . . It is most at home using the language of individual rights as part of its campaigns, and can rarely afford the luxury of publicly recognizing the competing needs of other groups. Yet the greatest obstacle may be our almost utter inability to find a meaningful place in public discourse for suffering and decline in life. They are recognized only as enemies to be fought: with science, with social programs, and with a supreme optimism that with sufficient energy and imagination they can be overcome. We have created a way of life that can only leave serious questions of limits, finitude, the proper ends of human life, of evil and suffering, in the realm of the private self or of religion; they are thus treated as incorrigibly subjective or merely pietistic" (SL, 220).

In its long-standing ambition to forestall death, medicine has reached its last frontier in the care of the aged. Of course children and young adults still die of maladies that are open to potential cure, but the highest proportion of the dying (70 percent) are over sixty-five. If death is ever to be humbled, that is where endless work remains to be done. This defiant battle against death and decline is not limited to medicine. Our culture has worked hard to redefine old age as a time of liberation, but not decline, a time of travel, of new ventures in education and self-discovery, of the ever-accessible tennis court or golf course, and of delightfully periodic but thankfully brief visits from well-behaved grandchildren. That is, to be sure, an idealized picture, but it arouses hopes that spur medicine to wage an aggressive war against the infirmities of old age.

As we have seen, the costs of such a war would be prohibitive. No matter how much is spent, the ultimate problem will still remain: People will grow old and die. Worse still, by pretending that old age can be turned into a kind of endless middle age, we rob it of any meaning.

THE MEANING AND SIGNIFICANCE OF OLD AGE

There are various sources of meaning and significance available for the aged, but it is the elderly's particular obligation to the future that I believe is essential. "Not only is it the most neglected perspective on the elderly, but it is the most pertinent as we try to understand the problem of their health

26

care. The young—children and young adults—most justly and appropriately spend their time preparing for future roles and developing a self pertinent to them. The mature adult has the responsibility to procreate and rear the next generation and to manage the present society. What can the elderly most appropriately do? It should be the special role of the elderly to be the moral conservators of that which has been and the most active proponents of that which will be after they are no longer here. Their indispensable role as conservators is what generates what I believe ought to be the *primary* aspiration of the old, which is to serve the young and the future. Just as they were once the heirs of a society built by others, who passed on to them what they needed to know to keep going, so are they likewise obliged to do the same for those who will follow them.

"Only the old—who alone have seen in their long lives first a future on the horizon and then its actual arrival—can know what it means to go from past through present to future. That is valuable and unique knowledge. If the young are to flourish, then the old should step aside in an active way, working until the very end to do what they can to leave behind them a world hopeful for the young and worthy of bequest. The acceptance of their aging and death will be the principal stimulus to doing this. It is this seemingly paradoxical combination of withdrawal to prepare for death and an active, helpful leave-taking oriented toward the young which provides the possibility for meaning and significance in a contemporary context. Meaning is provided because there is a purpose in that kind of aging, combining an identity for the self with the serving of a critical function in the lives of others—that of linking the past, present, and future—something which, even if they are unaware of it, they cannot do without. Significance is provided because society, in recognizing and encouraging the aged in their duties toward the young, gives them a clear and important role, one that both is necessary for the common good and that *only* they can play" (*SL*, 43).

It is important to underscore that while the elderly have an obligation to serve the young, the young and society have a duty to assist the elderly. Before any limits are imposed, policies and programs must be in place to help the elderly live out a "natural life span," and beyond that to provide the means to relieve suffering.

A "NATURAL LIFE SPAN" AND A "TOLERABLE DEATH"

Earlier generations accepted the idea that there was a "natural life span"—the biblical norm of threescore and ten captures that notion. It is an idea well worth reconsidering and would provide us with a meaningful and realizable goal. Modern medicine and biology have insinuated the belief that the average life span is not a natural fact at all, but instead one that is strictly dependent on the state of medical knowledge and skill. And there is much to that belief as a statistical fact: Average life expectancy continues to increase, with no end in sight.

There are, moreover, other strong obstacles to the development of a notion of a "natural life span." This notion "requires a number of conditions we seem reluctant to agree to: (1) that life has relatively fixed stages—a notion rejected on the ground that we are free to make of our different stages of chronological age whatever we want; biology presents no unalterable philosophical and moral constraints or any clear pointers; (2) that death may present an 'absolute limit' to life—an idea repudiated because of the ability of medicine to constantly push back the boundary line between life and death; life is an open-ended possibility, not a closed circle; (3) that old age is of necessity marked by decline and thus requires a unique set of meanings to take account of that fact—a viewpoint that must be rejected as part of the political struggle against ageism, which would make of the old a deviant, marginal, and burdensome group; and (4) that 'our civilization' would be better off if it shared some common view of 'the whole of life'—rejected as a politically hazardous notion, more congenial to authoritarian and collectivist cultures than to those marked by moral and religious pluralism and individualism" (*SL,* 40–41).

I want to argue that we can have and must have a notion of a "natural life span" that is based on some deeper understanding of human needs and possibilities, not on the state of medical technology. I offer a definition of the "natural life span" as "one in which life's possibilities have on the whole been achieved and after which death may be understood as a sad, but nonetheless relatively acceptable event.

"Each part of that definition requires some explanation. What do I mean when I say that 'one's life possibilities have on the whole been accomplished'? I mean something very simple: that most of those opportunities which life affords people will have been achieved by that point. Life affords us a number of opportunities. These include work, love, the procreating and raising of a family, life with others, the pursuit of moral and other ideals, the experience of beauty, travel, and knowledge, among others. By old age—and here I mean even by the age of 65—most of us will have had a chance to experience those goods; and will certainly experience them by our late 70s or early 80s. It is not that life will cease, after those ages, to offer us some new opportunities; we might do something we have never done but always sought to do. Nor is it that life will necessarily cease to offer us opportunities to continue experiencing its earlier benefits. Ordinarily it will not. But what we have accomplished by old age is the having of the opportunities themselves, and to some relatively full degree. Many people, sadly, fail to have all the opportunities they might have: they may never have found love, may not have had the income to travel, may not have gained much knowledge through lack of education, and so on. More old age is not likely to make up for those deficiencies, however; the pattern of such lives, including their deprivations, is not likely to change significantly in old age, much less open up radically new opportunities hitherto missing" (*SL*, 66–67).

A longer life does not guarantee a better life. No matter how long medicine enables people to live, death at any time— at age 90 or 100 or 110—would frustrate some possibility, some as-yet-unrealized goal. The easily preventable death of a young child is an outrage. Death from an incurable disease of someone in the prime of young adulthood is a tragedy. But death at an old age, after a long and full life, is simply sad, a part of life itself, what I would call a "tolerable death."

This notion of a "tolerable death" helps illumine the concept of a "natural life span," and together these two notions set the foundation for an appropriate goal for medicine in its approach to aging. "My definition of a 'tolerable death' is this: the individual event of death at that stage in a life span when (a) one's life possibilities have on the whole been accomplished; (b) one's moral obligations to those for whom one has had responsibility have been discharged; and (c) one's death will not seem to others an offense to sense or sensibility, or tempt others to despair and rage at the finitude of human existence. Note the most obvious feature of this definition: it is a biographical, not a biological, definition" (*SL*, 66).

THE PRINCIPLES AND PRIORITIES
OF A PLAN

How might we devise a plan to limit the costs of health care for the aged under public entitlement programs that is fair, humane, and sensitive to their special requirements and

30

dignity? Let me suggest three principles to undergird a quest for limits:

"1. Government has a duty, based on our collective social obligations, to help people live out a natural life span, but not actively to help extend life medically beyond that point. By life-extending treatment, I will mean any medical intervention, technology, procedure, or medication whose ordinary effect is to forestall the moment of death, whether or not the treatment affects the underlying life-threatening disease or biological process.

2. Government is obliged to develop, employ, and pay for only that kind and degree of life-extending technology necessary for medicine to achieve and serve the end of a natural life span; the question is not whether a technology is available that can save a life, but whether there is an obligation to use the technology.

3. Beyond the point of a natural life span, government should provide only the means necessary for the relief of suffering, not life-extending technology" (*SL,* 137–38).

What would the actual policy look like? "A full policy plan would include detailed directions, for example, for determining priorities within basic biological research, within health-care delivery, and between research and delivery. That I will not try to provide. I can only sketch a possible trajectory— or, to switch metaphors, a kind of likely general story. But if that at least can be done in a coherent fashion, avoiding the most flagrant contradictions, it might represent some useful movement" (*SL,* 141–42).

Three elements of health policy emerge from my position: "The first is the need for an antidote to the major cause of a mistaken moral emphasis in the care of the elderly and a likely source of growing high costs of their care in the years ahead. That cause is constant innovation in high-technology medicine relentlessly applied to life-extending care of the el-

31

derly; it is a blessing that too often turns into a curse. . . . No technology should be developed or applied to the elderly that does not promise great and inexpensive improvement in the quality of their lives, no matter how promising for life extension. Incremental gains, achieved at high cost, should be considered unacceptable. Forthright government declarations that Medicare reimbursement will not be available for technologies that do not achieve a high, very high, standard of efficacy would discourage development of marginally beneficial items" (*SL*, 142, 143).

"The second element is a need to focus on those subgroups of the elderly—particularly women, the poor, and minorities—who have as yet not been well served, for whom a strong claim can be entered for more help from the young and society more generally. . . . The elderly (both poor and middle-class) can have no decent sense of security unless there is a full reform of the system of health care. It may well be that reforms of the sweeping kind implied in these widely voiced criticisms could more than consume in the short run any savings generated by inhibitions of the kind I am proposing in the development and use of medical technology. But they would address a problem that technological development does nothing to meet. They would also reassure the old that there will be a floor of security under their old age and that ill health will not ruin them financially, destroy their freedom, or leave them dependent upon their children (to the detriment of both)" (*SL*, 142, 147).

"The third is a set of high-priority health and welfare needs—nursing and long-term care, prevention—which would have to be met in pursuit of the goals I have proposed. . . . Beyond avoiding a premature death, what do the elderly need from medicine to complete their lives in an acceptable way? They need to be as independent as possible, freed from excess worry about the financial or familial burdens of ill health, and physically and emotionally positioned to seek whatever meaning and significance can be found in old age. Medicine can only try to maintain the health which facilitates that latter quest, not guarantee its success. That facilitation is enhanced by physical mobility, mental alertness, and emotional stability. Chronic illness, pain, and suffering are all major impediments and of course appropriate targets for medical research and improved health-care delivery. Major research priorities should be those chronic illnesses which so burden the later years and which have accompanied the increase in longevity" (*SL*, 142, 149).

EUTHANASIA AND ASSISTED SUICIDE

Some might view my position as an endorsement of euthanasia and assisted suicide. My position "is exactly the opposite: a sanctioning of mercy killing and assisted suicide for the elderly would offer them little practical help and would serve as a threatening symbol of devaluation of old age. . . . Were euthanasia and assisted suicide to be legalized, would there be a large and hitherto restrained group of elderly eager to take advantage of the new opportunity? There is no evidence to suggest that there would be, in either this country or in any other. But even if there might be some, what larger significance might the elderly in general draw from the new situation? It would be perfectly plausible for them to interpret it as the granting of a new freedom. It would be no less plausible for them to interpret it as a societal concession to the view that old age can have no meaning and significance if accompanied by decline, pain, and despair. It would be to come close to saying officially that old age can be empty and pointless and that society must give up on elderly people. For the young it could convey the message that pain is not to be endured, that community cannot be found for many of the old, and that a life not marked by good health, by hope and vitality, is not a life worth living. . . .

"What do we as a society want to say about the elderly and their lives? If one believes that the old should not be rejected, that old age is worthy of respect, that the old have as valid a social place as any other age group, and that the old are as diverse in their temperaments and outlooks as any other age group, an endorsement of a special need for euthanasia for the old seems to belie all those commitments. It would be a way of legitimizing the view that old age is a special time of lost hopes, empty futures, and personal pointlessness. Alternatively, if it is believed that old age can have a special value, that it can—with the right cultural, economic, and political support—be a time of meaning and significance, then one will not embrace euthanasia as a special solution for the problem of old age, either for the aged as individuals or for the aged as a group. It would convey precisely the wrong symbolism. To sanction euthanasia as a special benefit for the aged would signal a direct contradiction to an effort to give meaning and significance to old age" (*SL*, 194, 196, 197). We as a society should instead guarantee elderly persons greater control over their own dying—and particularly an enforceable right to refuse aggressive life-extending treatment.

CONCLUSION

The system I propose would not immediately bring down the cost of care of the elderly; it would add cost. But it would set in place the beginning of a new understanding of old age, one that would admit of eventual stabilization and limits. The elderly will not be served by a belief that only a lack of resources, better financing mechanisms, or political power stands between them and the limitations of their bodies. The good of younger age groups will not be served by inspiring in them a desire to live to an old age that maintains the vitality of youth indefinitely, as if old age were nothing but a sign that medicine has failed its mission. The future of our society will not be served by allowing expenditures on health care for the elderly to escalate endlessly and uncontrollably, fueled by the false altruistic belief that anything less is to deny the elderly their dignity. Nor will it be aided by the pervasive kind of self-serving argument that urges the young to support such a crusade because they will eventually benefit from it.

We require instead an understanding of the process of aging and death that looks to our obligation to the young and to the future, that recognizes the necessity of limits and the acceptance of decline and death, and that values the old for their age and not for their continuing youthful vitality. In the name of accepting the elderly and repudiating discrimination against them, we have succeeded mainly in pretending that with enough will and money the unpleasant part of old age can be abolished. In the name of medical progress we have carried out a relentless war against death and decline, failing to ask in any probing way if that will give us a better society for all.

"There is little danger that the views I advance here will elicit such instant acclaim (or any acclaim, for that matter) that the present generation of the elderly will feel much of their effect. That could take two or three decades if there is any merit in what I say, and what I am looking for is not any quick change but the beginning of a long-term discussion, one that will perhaps lead people to change their thinking, and most important, their expectations, about old age and death" (*SL,* 10).

In the articles that follow, you will hear many penetrating practical and theoretical objections to these ideas, as well as vigorous affirmations. I have requested the right to the last word in this volume in the final response to my critics. But the debate is only beginning, and all of us in this society will bear the responsibility for the ultimate outcome.

NOTES

1. Daniel Callahan, *Setting Limits: Medical Goals in an Aging Society* (New York: Simon and Schuster, 1987). References may appear in this text with the notation "*SL.*"

VOICES OF THE OLD

....

MARTHA HOLSTEIN

MARTHA HOLSTEIN, formerly with the American Society on Aging, San Francisco, California, is currently with the Center for Ethics and Social Policy, Berkeley, California.

IN HER eighty-fifth year, Florida Scott Maxwell wrote, "... inside we flame with a wild life that is almost incommunicable ... it is a place of fierce energy...."[1] Later she adds that age gives one "ample time to face everything one has had, been, done; we have time at last to make them truly ours."[2]

In reflections about his old age, Theologian D. Elton Trueblood, in his 90s, notices his ability to assemble his memories in some semblance of order, the chance not to hurry, to "savor each step of the journey."[3] He reminds us of the blessing of grace, of the conscious and deliberate habit of finding somebody to thank, and affirms that "the greatest blessing of maturity is that gratitude may transcend the single occasion, to become both habitual and continuous."[4]

Gertie, at 89, observed: "I might be eighty-nine years old. I feel good. I feel like I could fly the coop. I do. I feel younger, like I'm forty-five or fifty. I want to doll up, and I like to fuss.

37

Oh, golly, I can break the mirror. I don't know I'm old. I feel like I'm going to live for a long time."[5]

And in his 90s, Supreme Court Justice Oliver Wendell Holmes, on catching sight of a pretty "girl," lamented, "Oh, to be eighty again!"[6]

For many who are very old, death becomes an everyday fact, something to be noted and filed away; instead of dwelling on death, they celebrate the "central miracle of being alive."[7] They also change, adapt to new situations. Millie, an 80-year-old nursing home resident, after a lifetime of acquiescence chose a new style, that of self-determination, to allow her to survive emotionally in the institution.[8]

But there are fears and acceptance as well as celebration. Many elders describe their restricted vision of the future, living from day to day, acknowledging that they have no unfinished business, no desire to do more.[9] One 92-year-old woman remarked, "I don't want to live much longer. It seems that I've had the best that life can give me already."[10] The old often worry about "declining into simplified versions of themselves, of being reduced from the complexity of adult life into a single characteristic. . . . It is frightening to think that one might end as a caricature of oneself."[11]

The downside of being old most seriously affects those whose health restricts their ability to do things, to be busy. A 92-year-old woman, still able to drive and do errands, cook and clean nonetheless comments, ". . . the late afternoon drags on slowly until it's time to prepare a dinner. . . . Recently, when I went to the park, I was so exhausted that I decided such outings were no longer in the cards."[12]

An 81-year-old retirement community resident's pain emerges when she says, "It's a terrible ending to live so long without having something specific to do, or being needed."[13]

And the old also fear protracted periods of dependency, of being a burden on their families, of not being able to do for themselves. "My only fear about death is that it will not come soon enough. Life still interests and occupies me. Happily I am not in such discomfort that I wish for death. I love and am loved, but please God may I die before I lose my independence."[14] Few wish to become dependent, to be kept alive beyond the period of sentient life. And a number simply fear living for too long, no matter the circumstances.

These are the infinitely diverse people for whom a policy of "setting limits" would apply. For some the choice may be a relatively simple one, to discontinue treatment or not initiate treatment for a person beyond the point of sentience. However, the idea of setting limits, of categorically stopping Medicare reimbursement for life-extending treatment does not focus only on those who are near death, comatose, or cognitively impaired. The policy would include Florida Scott Maxwell and D. Elton Trueblood and Gertie. It would include those who are busy remembering, untangling their lives, creating the coherent pattern in the only life they have lived. It would include those who face their end with calm acceptance, having no dreams for the future. Setting limits may have the salubrious effect of forcing closure, demanding that the last word be written, the final sentence spoken. But would it? Would it instead fuel resentment or anger? Would it devalue, even further, those who are "drab on the outside" by implying that they had nothing more to contribute?

Among one Indian tribe on the shores of Lake Winnipeg, if an old person deserved special honor, they held a tribal feast for him. The old man sang a death song and danced, if he could. While he was still singing, his son came from behind and brained him with a tomahawk.[15] Is this an even more humane policy than simply denying treatment? The line between caring and curing or treating and not treating is often tenuous. Is it just to deny treatment and provide comfort when suffering is inevitable? A natural death is not always peaceful, humane, and dignified. "Refusing treatment [may make] dying too hard."[16]

Many American families today face anguishing choices about the withdrawal of treatment for their elderly parents or spouses. In a recent *New York Times* feature, correspondent Andrew Malcolm described his own struggle to let his mother die. He asks, "How could I, the only child of my only surviving parent, know when to say when? How could I live with my decision?"[17] A policy of categorically denying life-extending therapy would have eased his struggle (unless he chose to pay privately for care at whatever cost). Is that the way we want such decisions to be made? What is the line between personal choice and public commitment to support that choice? In whose hands should such decisions rest? Does a public rather than a private choice support the good of society? Are decisions about life-extending therapies the way to subordinate the individual to society?

Most family choices are like Andrew Malcolm's. Some must fight to have their wishes to terminate treatment honored. Others find that it just happens; the directives of the dying person were clear or the hospital permitted and encouraged surrogate decision-making. Where it is less clear are cases like the following.

An 82-year-old woman, with intractable pain from arthritis but otherwise a vigorous participant in a life constrained only by her disability, suffers kidney failure. Should Medicare cover dialysis treatments or the possible costs of a kidney transplant? Who should decide and how should that decision be made?

A 78-year-old grandfather, busily engaged in writing his memoirs, has a massive stroke. Rehabilitation facilities, though overcrowded, are available in his community. Because he is otherwise healthy he is considered a good candidate for treatment. Should he receive intensive rehabilitation therapy? Who should decide and on what basis?

An 80-year-old woman, content with the life she has led and fearing dependency and the loss of her treasured independence, develops colon cancer. This is the second diagnosis of cancer. The first was many years ago. Otherwise she is in good health. Preliminary studies do not detect metastases. What treatment plan should be offered to her? On what basis should the decision be made?

A 79-year-old nursing home resident, a former college professor, lives with mild cognitive impairment, serious hypertension, and an inability to bathe and dress herself. She is much loved by her family and the staff. She goes into cardiac arrest. Although she left no advance directives (living wills or durable power of attorney for health care), she has often spoken of her unwillingness to be subject to aggressive treatment. What decision is appropriate? Who should make it? What if her wishes were unknown?

If indeed there is an ageless self, a capacity to live dynamic, vital lives often within private worlds of thought and feeling, "drab on the outside" but burning with a fierce energy within, what are appropriate goals of medicine and of public policies for the elderly? How can we, through such policies, facilitate a "good old age"? How can we design policies that nourish community and connectedness? How can we create a society "so that in his last years a man might still be a man?"—that is committed to pursuing ends that give life meaning through love, friendship, indignation, compassion.[18] Can a policy of setting limits at the end of life contribute to this vision of a good old age? Is a policy acceptable that applies despite differing individual wishes? Should a policy of limits be imposed even if there is no guarantee that the money saved would be applied to other forms of health care for other individuals or groups? How does one decide?

From the 144th and 90th Psalms, we are told:

Man is like a breath
His days are as a fleeting shadow
In the morning he flourishes and grows up like grass,

41

In the evening he is cut down and withers.
So teach us to number our days,
That we may get us a heart of wisdom.[19]

On the path to wisdom, the question before us is how to number our days: by acceptance of limits imposed by public policy or by choosing when and how we wish to die.

NOTES

1. Florida Scott Maxwell, *The Measure of My Days*, (New York: Penguin Books, 1979), pp. 32–33.
2. Maxwell, p. 41.
3. D. Elton Trueblood, "The Blessings of Maturity," in Philip Berman, ed., *The Courage to Grow Old*, (New York: Ballantine Books, 1989), p. 295.
4. D. Elton Trueblood, p. 300.
5. Sharon Kaufman, *The Ageless Self*, (New York: New American Library, 1989), p. 12.
6. Cowley, *The View from Eighty*, p. 29.
7.. Cowley, p. 29.
8. Kaufman, *The Ageless Self*, p. 48.
9. Kaufman, p. 111.
10. Kaufman, p. 111.
11. Cowley, *The View from Eighty*, p. 56.
12. Kaufman, *The Ageless Self*, p. 105.
13. Kaufman, p. 108.
14. Maxwell, *The Measure of My Days*, p. 75.
15. Cowley, *The View from Eighty*, p. 1.
16. M. Pabst Battin, "The Least Worst Death," in Robert Weir, ed., *Ethical Issues in Death and Dying*, (New York: Columbia University Press, 1986), p. 209.

17. Andrew Malcolm, "The Ultimate Decision," *The New York Times Magazine*, December 3, 1989, Section 6, p. 50.

18. Simone de Beauvoir, *The Coming of Age*, (New York: Putnam's Sons, 1972) pp. 541, 542.

19. Barbara Meyerhoff, *Number Our Days*, (New York: Simon & Schuster Inc, 1978), p. 215.

PART II

FIRST IMPRESSIONS: PROPHET OR PIED PIPER?

When Daniel Callahan's Setting Limits: Medical Goals in an Aging Society *appeared, the reaction was immediate, widespread, and varied: enthusiastic, warmly praising, troubled, accusatory, and sharply critical. Book reviews, interviews with Callahan, review essays, discussion groups, and finally entire conferences centered around its themes.*

These excerpts from early commentaries in major newspapers and professional journals represent, in a microcosm, the scope and intensity of the first response.

They also provide a case study of the promises and pitfalls of discussing complex ethical, social, legal, and economic issues. As such, they offer an opportunity for self-reflection. We must ask ourselves: Have we responded in a way that allows for public debate or has our reaction foreclosed that possibility? We might learn much about the possibilities for moral dialogue by listening to the tone of our own voices and to the words we speak.

LONGER LIVES, HARDER CHOICES

....

DAVID BLUMENTHAL

DAVID BLUMENTHAL is Senior Vice President, Brigham and Women's Hospital, Boston, Massachusetts.

CALLAHAN'S ANALYSIS offers no true short-term or even middle-term solution to the demographic avalanche and its health-care consequences. For the foreseeable future, we are left, as always, to muddle through.

This realization should not diminish, however, either the importance of this book, or the motivated reader's enjoyment of it. As Callahan pushes his main argument toward its conclusion, he pauses to consider any number of side-issues that are both important and fascinating. What are the obligations of the young to the old, of children to parents? How should we think about intergenerational conflict and equity? Under what circumstances can we withhold nutrition and hydration from dying elderly? Do euthanasia and assisted suicide have a special legitimacy in the care of the dying aged? (Interestingly, Callahan opposes them.)

David Blumenthal's "Longer Lives, Harder Choices" excerpted from *The Washington Post* (October 11, 1987). Reprinted by permission of the author and *The Washington Post*.

47

Even those who find Callahan's central message unsatisfying or distasteful will gain much from his examination of these special topics. He explores as thoroughly and compassionately as I can imagine both the strengths and the weaknesses of an approach that many of us, in our innermost thoughts, will repeatedly consider as health-care expenditures for the elderly escalate. Finding a warm hearth for the nation's elders will not be easy, but certainly, silence on the tough issues will not in the end make their homecoming any easier.

SETTING LIMITS: FROM RATIONING TO RATIONALIZING HEALTH CARE

T. PATRICK HILL

T. PATRICK HILL is Director of Public Information, Citizens Committee on Biomedical Ethics, Inc., Summit, New Jersey.

PERHAPS, after all is said and done, the finest compliment to be paid to *Setting Limits* is that it has arrived not a moment too soon to save us from ourselves. It is, above all else, a prophetic book, a tract for the times, reading as it does so clearly the signs of a society poised upon a watershed. And since it is prophetic, it should surprise no one that only with great difficulty, if at all, will it be received by those who stand to gain the most from its message. . . .

To share Dr. Callahan's insight at its most radical and cogent level, it is essential to see that his language has allowed him to recognize that rationing medical care just for its own sake can be detrimental to society. Simply put, rationing under these terms makes everyone a competitor for a scarce commodity. Clearly, Dr. Callahan is prepared to use what ethicists call the principle of utility to achieve a greater bal-

T. Patrick Hill's "*Setting Limits:* From Rationing to Rationalizing Health Care" excerpted from *Medical Ethics for the Physician* 3(3) (July 1988). Reprinted by permission of the author and the KSF Group, New York.

49

ance for good over bad allocation of medical care for an aging society. But he will not use the principle on its own, insisting that the principle of justice must also be applied so that beneficence tempers usefulness.

Precisely because history has placed us at a watershed, Dr. Callahan observes, we have to decide what we want old age to be. For this reason, a just allocation is more important than a useful allocation of medical care. To his enormous credit, Dr. Callahan shows us that we can do the former without compromising the latter. In other words, he shows us where we can set limits while showing us how to set the standards.

THE PIED PIPER RETURNS
FOR THE OLD FOLKS

....

NAT HENTOFF

NAT HENTOFF is a Columnist, *The Village Voice* and *The Washington Post,* and staff writer, *The New Yorker.*

I EXPECT that the sardonic Dean of Dublin's Saint Patrick's Cathedral, Jonathan Swift, would appreciate Daniel Callahan's *Setting Limits*—though not in the way he would be supposed to. Swift, you will recall, at a time of terrible poverty and hunger in Ireland, wrote *A Modest Proposal.* Rather than having the children of the poor continue to be such a burden to their parents and their nation, why not persuade the poor to raise their children to be slaughtered at the right, succulent time and sold to the rich as delicacies for dining?

What could be more humane? The children would be spared a life of poverty, their parents would be saved from starvation, and the overall economy of Ireland would be in better shape.

So, I thought, Callahan, wanting to dramatize the parlous and poignant state of America's elderly, has created his modern version of *A Modest Proposal.*

Nat Hentoff's "The Pied Piper Returns for the Old Folks" excerpted from *The Village Voice* (April 26, 1988). Reprinted by permission of the author and *The Village Voice.*

I was wrong. He's not jiving. . . .

Callahan sees "a natural life span" as being ready to say goodbye in one's late seventies or early eighties. He hasn't fixed on an exact age yet. Don't lose your birth certificate.

If people persist in living beyond the time that Callahan, if not God, has allotted them, the government will move in. Congress will require that anybody past that age must be denied Medicare payments for such procedures as certain forms of open heart surgery, certain extended stays in an intensive care unit, and who knows what else.

Moreover, as an index of how human the spirit of *Setting Limits* is, if an old person is diagnosed as being in a chronic vegetative state (some physicians screw up this diagnosis), the Callahan plan mandates that the feeding tube be denied or removed. (No one is certain whether someone actually in a persistent vegetative state can *feel* what's going on while being starved to death. If there is a sensation, there is no more horrible way to die.)

What about the elderly who don't have to depend on Medicare? Millions of the poor and middle class have no other choice than to go to the government, but there are some old folks with money. They, of course, do not have to pay any attention to Daniel Callahan at all. Like the well-to-do from time immemorial, they will get any degree of medical care they want.

So, *Setting Limits* is class-biased in the most fundamental way. People without resources in need of certain kinds of care will die sooner than old folks who do not have to depend on the government and Daniel Callahan. . . .

Callahan reveals that once we start going down the slippery slope of utilitarianism, we slide by—faster and faster—a lot of old-timey ethical norms. Like the declaration of the Catholic bishops of America that medical care is "indispensable to the protection of human dignity." The bishops didn't say that dignity is only for people who can afford it. They know that if you're 84, and only Medicare can pay your bills but says it won't pay for treatment that will extend your life, then your "human dignity" is shot to hell. . . .

It must be pointed out that Daniel Callahan does not expect or intend his design for natural dying to be implemented soon. First of all, the public will have to be brought around. But that shouldn't be too difficult in the long run. I am aware of few organized protests against the court decisions in a number of states that feeding tubes can be removed from patients—many of them elderly—who are not terminally ill and are not in intractable pain. And some of these people may not be in a persistently vegetative state. (For instance, Nancy Ellen Jobes in New Jersey.)

So, the way the Zeitgeist is going, I think public opinion could eventually be won over to Callahan's modest proposal. But he has another reason to want to wait. He doesn't want his vision of "setting limits" to go into effect until society has assured the elderly access to decent long-term home care or nursing home care as well as better coverage for drugs, eyeglasses, and the like.

Even if all that were to happen, there still would be profound ethical and constitutional problems. What kind of society will we have become if we tuck in the elderly in nursing homes and then refuse them medical treatment that would prolong their lives?

And what of the physicians who will find it abhorrent to limit the care they give solely on the basis of age? As a presumably penitent former Nazi doctor said, "Either one is a doctor or one is not."

On the other hand, if the Callahan plan is not to begin for a while, new kinds of doctors can be trained who will take a utilitarian rather than a Hippocratic oath. ("I will never forget that my dedication is to the society as a whole rather to any individual patient.") Already, I have been told by a physician who heads a large teaching institution that a growing number of doctors are spending less time and attention on the elderly. There are similar reports from other such places.

Meanwhile, nobody I've read or heard on the Callahan proposal has mentioned the Fourteenth Amendment and its insistence that all of us must have "equal protection of the laws." What Callahan aims to do is take an entire class of people—on the basis only of their age—and deny them medical care that might prolong their lives. This is not quite *Dred Scott,* but even though the elderly are not yet at the level of close constitutional scrutiny given by the Supreme Court to blacks, other minorities, and women, the old can't be pushed into the grave just like that, can they?

Or can they? Some of the more influential luminaries in the nation—Joe Califano, George Will, and a fleet of bioethicists, among them—have heralded *Setting Limits* as the way to go.

Will you be ready?

LETTING INDIVIDUALS DECIDE

....

TERRIE WETLE AND RICHARD W.

BESDINE

RICHARD W. BESDINE is Director, Travelers Center on Aging, and Professor of Geriatrics and Gerontology, University of Connecticut Health Center, Farmington, Connecticut. TERRIE WETLE is Director of Research, Institute of Living, Hartford, Connecticut.

SETTING LIMITS is disturbing in several ways. First, there is the premise that we are justified in setting public policy that determines a "natural life span" for an entire cohort of the population. Referring to the Nazi concept of the *Untermensch,* Callahan notes the evils that result from the political determination that a life is dispensable, but he sets aside the concern far too easily that the elderly—or any other age group, for that matter—would interpret his "natural life span" policy as devaluation of life in old age.

A second concern is whether the program could be applied consistently and fairly. Noting that a policy to limit public payment for life-sustaining care on the basis of age would lead to a two-tiered system in which wealthy older people

Terrie Wetle and Richard W. Besdine's "Letting Individuals Decide" excerpted from an untitled book review from the *New England Journal of Medicine* 319(7) (August 18, 1988): 452–53. Reprinted by permission of the authors and the *New England Journal of Medicine.*

could still buy such care, Callahan still does not believe that "a society would be made morally intolerable by that kind of imbalance." It was just such an imbalance between those who could pay for care and those who could not that led to the enactment of Medicare and Medicaid 25 years ago.

Many distinctions on which the proposed program would depend are not made clearly or reliably. For example, the distinction between interventions that prolong life and those that relieve suffering is perhaps easy to make conceptually and in situations, but not at the bedside or in that vast middle ground where the majority of cases are found. An 80-year-old man with excruciating abdominal pain and fecal vomiting due to adhesions obstructing his small bowel will have his suffering relieved quickly and best by surgery to release the obstruction. In the process, his life may also be saved. We wonder whether Callahan would urge morphine rather than surgery for such a patient.

Callahan uses the treatment of diabetes to define the rules of his game further. Considering insulin a life-prolonging rather than a symptom-relieving treatment, he states that a diabetic using insulin before the end of his policy-defined natural life span would be "grandfathered" into a continuation of that medication, whereas the person who acquires diabetes after the cutoff age would not be provided such treatment. Similarly, dialysis would be continued indefinitely if it was initiated before the cutoff date, but it would not be provided for late-onset renal disease. Thus, the patient whose diabetes or renal failure develops before the cutoff age and who begins treatment promptly is given preference over the person healthy at that age but in whom illness develops later. This is a peculiar logic.

Much of the book, it seems, is based on the premise that such a policy would save the taxpayer money and allow a reallocation of resources. It is not clear, nor is evidence provided, that the policy actually would accomplish these goals.

In fact, it is possible that certain "life-prolonging" interventions also improve function, resulting in the decreased use of other expensive forms of care.

Certainly, the book is worth reading, but with a critical eye. Care must be taken to avoid facile applications of its arguments in support of negative views of older people. Although Callahan has warned against the tyranny of individualism throughout his career, perhaps aging and health care are one arena in which an acute focus on the individual is most appropriate. The decision to provide or withhold life-prolonging interventions may still be best left to the individual patient, family, and care provider.

Seek Vision, Not Limits

STEVEN MILES

STEVEN MILES is Associate Director, Center for Clinical Medical Clinics, University of Chicago, Pritzker School of Medicine.

It is a perverse irony that in a rich country where one person in five has inadequate access to health care, medical ethics has become identified with stopping treatment. *Setting Limits* will etch this perception deeper. It proposes that the cost of health care for the elderly is so high that we should stop giving life-prolonging therapy to the old. . . .

The book gives an inadequate account of the postindustrial demographic transition. Health care costs are treated as a loss and an expense, rather than as an integral and contributing part of a service economy. Noting only the fact of an increasingly aged population, Dr. Callahan does not present data on the remarkable functional capacity of persons in their 60s and 70s and thus does not consider how dated and prejudiced views generate social policies or indexes that assume de-

Steven Miles's "Seek Vision, Not Limits" excerpted from an untitled book review from the *Journal of the American Medical Association* 259(19) (May 13, 1988): 2765. Copyright 1988, American Medical Association. Reprinted by permission of the author and the American Medical Association.

pendency and deny the well old the possibility of economic productivity. . . .

There is truth in the proposal that our death-denying, youth-glorifying, technologically acquisitive society has great difficulty addressing the compelling and repulsive fact of mortality. But the relentless overtreatment of some of the dying and Dr. Callahan's proposal for a moratorium on life-prolonging care are but two facets of the same fear of death and depersonalization of aging. The inadequacies of our allocation of human services are less a distortion induced by the high cost of dying than a result of a lack of vision of our duty to address the human needs of the whole community. Denying treatment to the old is unlikely to lead to greater charity to the dispossessed or young. After all, savings from diagnosis-related groups went hand-in-hand with decreased support for prenatal care in the service of military spending and a tax cut for the affluent.

This century gives sordid testimony to the corrosive effect of using "natural" differences to restrict public goods. The destructive impact of Dr. Callahan's biologic argument may well be ameliorated by the democracy of aging. His argument that medical care be denied to those with socially defined "completed" biographies threatens the stigmatized or dispossessed of any age.

PART III

IN OUR COMMON HUMANITY: ARE WE GOING TOO FAR OR NOT FAR ENOUGH?

The responses in this section probe larger philosophical and ethical issues that age-based rationing raises. At the same time, they propose alternative answers to questions that we as a society must confront if the next decades are not to deteriorate into the famous Hobbesian war of all against all. Defining ourselves as a community may become the most important task before us.

SETTING MEDICAL LIMITS

....

JOSEPH FLETCHER

JOSEPH FLETCHER is Professor Emeritus, School of Medicine, University of Virginia, Charlottesville, Virginia.

DO WE OLDSTERS (I am myself an octogenarian) have a moral obligation to die—an obligation based on distributive justice and a cost-benefit calculation?

This position is for most people a much harder one to take than the one lying behind the right-to-die movement. The right to choose to die rather than suffer further treatment, especially in terminal illnesses, is . . . a far cry from claiming that if people are elderly they ought to die whether they want to or not, as a matter of social obligation. The difference is between saying we "may" choose death and we "ought" to choose it.

The right-to-die movement poses a microethical problem on a one-by-one choice basis of decision making, but what Callahan is talking about is macroethical, on the basis of impersonal demographic data and a sense of social justice. It

Joseph Fletcher's "Setting Medical Limits" is excerpted from the *Loma Linda University Ethics Center-Update* 4(1) (June 1988). Reprinted by permission of the author and the Loma Linda University Ethics Center.

is this difference between being free as an individual to choose to die, on the one hand, and being morally obliged to die, on the other, which makes the demographic basis so radical—that makes it such a wrenching break from the conventional wisdom.

Advocates of the right-to-die will not automatically or quickly turn into ought-to-die advocates. Far from it. Even if they endorse it as a principle of social ethics, they will fall back from acting on it, especially in cases where the lives of their own parents or kin are at stake. The general run of people love being alive too much to give it up, no matter what they may think logically about the "tyranny" of the wish to survive. They may gladly give life up when the flame is no longer worth the candle, when it's better to be dead, but not for reasons of abstract social justice.

Survival is a "gut" matter; distributive justice is an abstract principle, much weaker motivationally. Survival is an instinctual demand and, indeed, the fundamental dynamic of the evolutionary process, whereas principles of social justice are only matters of intellectual or rational reflection. As a question of philosophy I am convinced, as Callahan is, that personal morality is properly spelled out within the context of social ethics. Moreover, we (he and I) agree that the social interest has priority over private interests—if and when they come into tension or conflict. Hence, the principle of eminent domain in the law, for example. The case for not extending the life of older people may be strong cerebrally, but it is not strong "intentionally." It is therefore without culture or popular force. . . .

To toy with the thought of [allocating and limiting medical care to the elderly] reveals an inordinate scheme of values, a value system gone awry, a distorted pondering of what we prize and value. It fails to render our obligations to our elderly parents and neighbors the high-order value they should have. A test of our humanity is what we are willing to sacrifice for them. They are disadvantaged through no fault of their own, even though some of them may be culpable in part because of their habits and lifestyle.

I propose, therefore, that we drop the idea that we can or should apply the concept of moral obligation for the category "old age." Let us apply it instead to cases. In short, we ought to decide whether there is an obligation to die in terms of particular individuals in particular situations, not in terms of generalized categories of human beings.

This, of course, is the approach of situation ethics. Situation ethics is, as Webster-Merriam defines it, a "system" of ethics "based on love . . . by which acts are judged within their context instead of by categorical principles." When the families and physicians of our old men and women perceive that life has become irreversibly a sore burden for them, then out of loving concern let them "go" by stopping treatment and withholding resuscitative measures and artificial medical life-support systems—in short, welcome death.

Only if the patient is hopelessly incompetent and no longer able to choose for or against dying should we decide for him. This is what the courts call "substituted judgment," and even in such cases it's still really the patient's own choice, reasonably presumed.

Putting it bluntly, we should be case-centered, not rule-centered. Let us hope we will never adopt an undiscriminating age limit, such as the British National Health Service once set *de facto* on renal dialysis for patients over 55, although without any formally stated policy or provision in the law. The practice ended because England's elderly protested vigorously, as well as their friends in the younger generations. Even the Eskimos used to let their decrepit elderly go out of the igloo in freezing weather to die by hypothermia, often said to be a "good way to go." This was on a diagnostic basis, not a birthdate basis.

I can, I believe, take comfort in the knowledge that patients and their families, like people in general, are open more and more to giving death a welcome. I recall how old Dr. Logan Clendendenning once remarked that the natural world blundered on to the form of energy called life but having so blundered, if there is any creative intelligence behind it all, death was "a real stroke of genius" (*The Human Body,* 1941).

The statistic and demographic data, even in terms of a lay grasp, are already generating changes in popular sentiment. Out of a combination of rational self-regard and loving concern for the sick and old, we see that families, physicians and patients themselves are pulling out of the old outmoded notion that life is an absolute value or end in itself and that dying is outside any human initiatives—taboo and untouchable. Quality of life steadily transcends the absolutism of the "sanctity" of life doctrine.

We should continue to provide the funds for medical care of the old even though it uses up resources we could have used for other things. We should provide it as a matter of love and loyalty, not as a "sacrifice," revising if necessary the way we rank-order our relative values. The "squeeze" of medical costs for the elderly which falls on younger people will constantly be lightened by the elderly themselves, as they exercise their right to die. Our ability to improve cost-effectiveness can help. . . .

We should repair disabilities only if the patient chooses treatment, and only after a careful assessment has been made and interpreted to the patient of how much promise it gives of continued quality of life. We should be clinically realistic; physicians should be candid with all involved, but willing to treat except where it is patently useless. Society should be willing to spend all that is needed for the elderly's medical needs. The free and competent consent should be all we require for either treating them or withholding treatment.

All this adds up to dropping any notion of setting impersonal and categorical limits on medical treatment for the aged.

It turns us instead to a policy of respect for the aged's choice, doing all we can meanwhile to encourage a choice of death whenever it is in the patient's own best interest. By this route we will avoid giving what somebody recently called a bumpersticker answer to a bubblegum question. . . .

Physicians accept the reality and inevitability of death. It takes very little clinical experience to learn the desirability in certain situations of stopping treatment if that is the patient's wish, or a surrogate's. The common law has always regarded involuntary treatment as a tort. The courts, especially at the appellate level, constantly uphold the right of all patients to choose to die by stopping treatment for sufficient rational cause. Resuscitation and medical life-support systems are being turned off every day in our hospitals.

Facing the problems posed by a steadily increasing population of elderly people, we will have to face the fact that "stopping treatment" really means ending the lives of those who exercise their right to die voluntarily. To avoid ending the lives of senior citizens en bloc by the indirect strategy of limiting funds for their medical care we should, as I propose, turn to a plan of voluntary living and dying for the old. Let me offer a description of what it will mean, not in legal terms but in terms of basic ethical principles.

Causing people to die—whether young, middle-aged, old or old old—is repugnant. In the case of the elderly, if their numbers cost the rest of us more than it used to cost, we shall meet the problem by a new allocation of funds, perhaps entailing a cut in other things and even a revised definition of "need" and "luxury." As to medical costs in particular we will not try to eliminate the elderly by indirect maneuvers such as limiting funds for care and treatment. (None of this is inconsistent with the fact that triage selections are sometimes necessary. This is a heart-breaking choice situation due not to policy but to insufficiencies of supplies which come about for various reasons, not intended or wanted.)

Categorical discriminations for the purpose of reducing the numbers of the old are unethical. Patients of any age are persons. In a genuine democracy the Kantian principle is basic—persons are ends in themselves, not means to the ends of others. Our social ethics allocates common resources on the principle of equal worth and our personal resources on the principles of loving concern, loyalty, and gratitude.

Our cultural attitude toward dying by choice becomes more favorable all the time. Between 1973 and 1985 those Americans opposing euthanasia fell from 52 percent to 35 percent, according to a poll by Louis Harris and Associates; those favoring rose from 38 percent to 62 percent. This is really active euthanasia, not passive. It does not wait for death to come. The ethical assumption is that patients in such straits are terminally ill, but "terminal" is a loose word meaning hopelessly ill. The courts are still conflicted. On one hand they uphold the principle of self-determination and the personal freedom to stop treatment, but on the other hand they still disapprove of euthanasia and decry suicide, even though the latter has been granted legal status.

Euthanasia, in fact, is being decriminalized as suicide has already been. By such voluntary decisions, such free choices, the effect is that the costs of medical treatment are being reduced. That is the way they should be reduced, not by picking out the elderly to be finished off no matter what their personal health might be like—just because they are old.

To arrange to have the elderly die because they cannot get medical help due to a purposive lack of funds is a policy of involuntary euthanasia. Ethically it is ignoble, just as voluntary dying can be noble and right, depending on the situation and without invidious distinction.

THE RETURN OF
EUGENICS

....

RICHARD JOHN NEUHAUS

RICHARD JOHN NEUHAUS is Director, Rockford Institute Center on Religion and Society, New York, New York.

DRAWING ON THE work of Leon Kass of the University of Chicago, Daniel Callahan urges our accepting the idea that there is such a thing as "a natural life span." In this respect Callahan sets himself against the eugenics project with its delusory dream of immortality through technological control. Yet he simultaneously subscribes to a quality-of-life index by which "natural" limits, such as severe disability, are not accepted but taken to be signs of a life not worth living. Callahan is well aware of the Nazi doctrine of *lebensunwertes Leben* and notes that, in the light of the Nazi experience, "there has been a justifiable reluctance to exclude borderline cases from the human community." That reluctance can be overcome, however, if we keep it firmly in mind that the Nazis "spoke all too readily of 'a life not worth living,' " and if we ourselves are very careful when we speak the same way.

Richard John Neuhaus's "The Return of Eugenics" excerpted from *Commentary* (April 1988). Reprinted by permission of the author and *Commentary*.

Callahan clearly wants to distance himself from the proponents of euthanasia, assisted suicide, and other such measures. But he also argues that "artificial" feeding is a medical treatment and should be discontinued in the case of patients suffering from severe quality-of-life deficiency. Lacking any ethical framework other than liberal individualism, Callahan stresses respect for the patient's decision, or, as it turns out, those who decide for the patient when the patient is "incapable." What it comes down to is bluntly stated: "At stake is how far and in what ways we are emotionally prepared to go to terminate life for the elderly."

The sentence is typical of the logic of the eugenics project and interesting in several respects. For instance, it is said that we are terminating life "for" other people, rather than terminating the life "of" other people, it being assumed by the "reasonable-person standard" that we are doing them a favor. As important, we are told that what is at stake is what we are "emotionally prepared" to do. For many people, that is a slight barrier indeed. In this way of thinking, the accent is on freedom, voluntarism, and choice. Nobody is allowed to "impose his values" on others. You are free to decide not to terminate your elderly parent or handicapped child, but you must also agree not to interfere with my decision to "terminate life for" the incapacitated who fall within my decision-making authority. . . .

Daniel Callahan is a spirited opponent of the slippery-slope metaphor, insisting that one thing does not necessarily, or even probably, lead to another. But his own emotional preparedness with respect to the treatment of the dependent and incapable has undergone a remarkable development. In the October 1983 issue of the *Hastings Center Report* he wrote forcefully against withdrawing food and water. "Given the increasingly large pool of superannuated, chronically ill, physically marginal elderly, it could well become the nontreatment of choice." He added, "Because we now have become sufficiently habituated to the idea of turning off a respirator, we are psychologically prepared to go one step further." In 1983 Callahan was convinced that "the feeding of the hungry, whether because they are poor or because they are physically unable to feed themselves, is the most fundamental of all human relationships. It is the perfect symbol of the fact that human life is inescapably social and communal. We cannot live at all unless others are prepared to give us food and water when we need them. . . . It is a most dangerous business to tamper with, or adulterate so enduring and central a moral emotion." Four years later Callahan invites us, not to tamper with or adulterate, but to discard that moral emotion. It is, after all, but an emotion. One may perhaps be forgiven for thinking that Callahan dramatically illustrates the slippery slope that he so vigorously denies.

To be sure, there is nothing wrong with changing one's mind, and people like Daniel Callahan may simply say that they have thought things through more carefully. As he himself suggests, however, this is not a matter of thinking one's way through but of feeling one's way through. We need no longer think about the unthinkable when, in time, it has become emotionally tolerable, even banal. A useful term in this connection is primicide, the first murder. When it is first suggested that we do a murderous deed, we may respond, "But that would be murder!" After we have done it once, or maybe twice, that response loses something of its force of conviction.

As a barrier to evil, novelty is a one-time thing; it cannot be reinstated. In the 1930s a hit man for Murder Inc. was on trial. The prosecutor asked him how he felt when committing a murder. He in turn asked the prosecutor how he felt when he tried his first case in court, to which the prosecutor allowed that he was nervous, but he got used to it. "It's the same with murder," observed the hit man, "you get used to it."

Champions of the eugenics project are deeply and understandably offended when it is said that they are advocating murder. For some reason they do not take offense when the statement is amended to say that they are advocating what used to be called murder. . . .

Is There Any Future in
Being Old?

....

THOMAS H. MURRAY

THOMAS H. MURRAY is Director, Center for Biomedical Ethics, Case Western Reserve University School of Medicine, Cleveland, Ohio.

DANIEL CALLAHAN'S *Setting Limits* means to be provocative; it succeeds. Most readers will likely fix on Callahan's tentative explorations into policy, especially his suggestion that life-extending treatment be withheld from the very elderly. That would be doubly unfortunate. For one thing, his discussions of specific policies are of secondary importance; his critique of the "modernist" view of aging is far more significant and every bit as provocative as his remarks about withholding treatment. For another, he is mistaken about the kinds of policies required by his attack on contemporary understandings of aging. . . .

Setting Limits puts forth a number of specific proposals. It urges us to be generous in sparing from economic ruin all those who suffer already from disease or disability. I agree wholeheartedly: any minimally decent society with our level

Thomas H. Murray's "Is There Any Future in Being Old?" excerpted from *Christianity and Crisis* (February 15, 1988). Copyright Feb. 15, 1988, Christianity and Crisis, New York. Reprinted by permission of the author and *Christianity and Crisis*.

of affluence ought to do this. Two other proposals, however, are more controversial because they run afoul of deepseated cultural assumptions.

The first concerns technology development: "No technology should be developed or applied to the elderly that does not promise great and inexpensive improvement in the quality of their lives, no matter how promising for life extension." The practical difficulties this proposal would encounter are enormous. Merely identifying the technologies will be perplexing: technologies are rarely age-specific. Those most used for the aged include the various paraphernalia of the intensive care unit, most dramatically, the mechanical ventilator, kidney dialysis and transplantation, and, increasingly, prostheses such as artificial hip implants. While the elderly are most likely to use these technologies, they are often employed by other age groups as well. We could try to prevent their use by the elderly. But how far would we be willing to go to enforce such a policy? Altering the funding priorities at the National Institutes of Health would have little effect. What would we do to a company or individual who attempted to apply new technologies to the aged: fines? censure? jail? Voluntary compliance would be the best, but ludicrously ineffective unless we already accepted the underlying principles.

Callahan's most striking proposal faces similar difficulties. After living out a normal life span (roughly 80 years), medical care "should no longer be oriented to resisting death"; instead it should be "limited to the relief of suffering." Careful to insist that this is a tentative exploration, he nonetheless addresses a range of circumstances and technologies—not always consistent with his own premises. He acknowledges making an exception for the physically vigorous elderly because he does not think "anyone would find it tolerable to allow the healthy person to be denied lifesaving care." Besides, they have not yet demonstrated that they are in the grip

74

of decline and death, although "a second and further incident will be a different matter."

Public revulsion at denying care to persons who, however old, are likely to benefit from it is a certain, and fatal, liability for the policy Callahan suggests *unless* profound changes were to occur in our shared social understanding of aging and death along the lines he suggests in the first part of the book. Callahan recognizes a comparable problem with justice. Either we try to enforce such a policy by denying public support for life-extending treatment for the elderly, or we erect more strenuous prohibitions. If we merely refuse to pay, then those who nevertheless desire it and can afford it will simply buy it. Those who can less afford it will either die, or inflict financial ruin on themselves and their families. If we prohibit a legal market in such care, we face the horrendous prospect of an underground market in life-prolonging treatment. Imagine trying to enforce such a policy: will we have "Respirator cops" raiding disguised clinics? Underground-market penicillin?

Either way we incur unbearable social costs: on the one hand we would confront a flagrant correlation between wealth and life; on the other, organized state coercion designed to shorten lives. Callahan recognizes the dilemma, and suggests a third option: if physicians could agree that such treatment should not be given, then we would achieve most of our objectives without having to resort to onerous and coercive alternatives. He goes further, asserting that such policies "can be morally acceptable only within a context that accords meaning and significance to the lives of the individual aged and recognizes the positive virtues of the passing of the generations." In other words, Callahan acknowledges that the policies advocated in the second part of the book depend upon a widespread acceptance of his diagnosis of our social ills laid out in the first part. Ironically, however, he fails to recognize the consequences of his assumption.

Unless our thinking about the meaning of aging and the ends of medicine corresponds at least roughly with the sorts of ideas Callahan describes, the policies he suggests have scant chance of being adopted. Even if they were, defiance of them would be rampant—and heartily applauded! But, if we were to think about aging and medicine as he counsels, coercive policies would be unnecessary. The aged, their families, and their caregivers would have a clear sense of what was right to do—and not to do. We would not need the policies on withholding treatment that Callahan proposes. To put it succinctly: without the conception of aging and medicine Callahan advocates, the policies are infeasible; with those conceptions, they are superfluous.

In part, this is true because the test of a policy is not absolute or universal success, but rather how close it comes to its goal, and at what cost—symbolic, economic, or other. If most people accepted the inevitability of death, and embraced an obligation to act as conservators for future generations, then the savings Callahan believes are necessary would come about without coercive public policies and without the dreadful symbolic costs they would inflict.

I have other reasons for thinking that we will not require such policies. Callahan's critique of the "modernist" views of aging and medicine are cogent and insightful. But his alternative vision is terribly austere. In his effort to counter the implacable optimism and narrow individualism of the prophets of modernist aging, he seems to leave little room for the possibility that a morally responsible old age could include a good measure of joy, growth, and accomplishment. Yet nothing in his analysis requires such renunciation.

More important, the way we actually live—and die—is less in thrall to modernism than Callahan supposes. Without question, our public discourse is couched in the moral vocabulary bequeathed by modernist individualism. We look no further than Callahan's (and my) own field—bioethics.

Discussions of the right to refuse life-prolonging treatment, for example, typically end with an assertion that such decisions belong to the affected individual. Rarely do we even raise the question of whether the individual's decision is a morally responsible one. Nor do we inquire into the motives for refusing treatment. Many people who refuse life-extending treatment do so, I suspect, only in part out of their distaste for compromised life. Most of us would want to spare our families the melancholy task of caring for us half-alive, and the physical, financial, and emotional toll such care commonly exacts. The same impulse—to see that one's family is provided for—lies behind the purchase of life insurance—by definition, a thing for which we know only the burdens and none of the benefits while we live, unless we count as a benefit the satisfaction of having done what we could for those we love.

Despite the shrunken moral language of public discourse, we lead lives of considerable moral depth, or at least try to do so. This, I take it, is the central theme of *Habits of the Heart:* we are better than we can say. Our task, then, is to recapture a richer language of moral discourse, and to revivify public discussions of public policies. For the most part, we will find that language in our religious traditions, although there are fruitful resources in our secular traditions as well.

Recovering a more resonant moral language will not be easy in a society intoxicated with superficial understandings of autonomy and liberty. The danger always exists that our core beliefs and actions will be diluted by the thin gruel of our moral vocabulary. The type of argument Callahan tries to make in the first part of his book is an essential step towards reordering public debate; I am certain, however, that it is not sufficient. Those of us who believe the stakes are indeed high must insist on keeping the larger issues in view. One of the ways we can do this is to point out repeatedly where people's moral commitments are in fact more profound than their customary descriptions suggest. We need to assure as well that our public policies permit us to act with a sense of our individual limitations and of our bonds with others.

Daniel Callahan's fundamental purpose in writing *Setting Limits,* he tells us, is "to stimulate a public discussion of the future of health care for the aged." If readers are not distracted by his specific policy proposals, he will have accomplished that and more. He will have enhanced the quality of our public conversation about the meaning and significance of aging, of medicine, of health policy, of the several stages of life, and of what Erik Erikson calls the "cogwheeling of generations." He will also have emboldened us to treat questions about the content of the good life, finitude, suffering, and mutual responsibilities as essential parts of this culture's social conversation. For his efforts, he has my gratitude; for his purpose, my support.

Daniel Callahan's
Public Problem

....

JAMES P. WIND

JAMES P. WIND is Director of Research and Publications, the Park Ridge Center, Chicago, Illinois.

I WANT TO CALL attention to an important problem pointed out in Callahan's book: our national public meaning crisis. If we take seriously the author's social location (director of the Hastings Center) and his experience (as one of the most active participants in our nation's public policy debates over health issues), Callahan's diagnosis of this deep culture-wide problem should give us pause. Yet, this part of his argument has received much less attention than have his specific proposals. If he is right about our national malady, then we have a much more serious situation on our hands than we thought, one affecting our public policies on aging, but also spilling over into many other areas of modern life.

Consider these lines from *Setting Limits*.

> We lack, as a people, any common coherent vision of the wellsprings of moral obligation toward the elderly in general

James P. Wind's "Daniel Callahan's Public Problem" excerpted from the *Bulletin of the Park Ridge Center* (September/October 1988). Reprinted by permission.

and our elderly parents in particular. We do not have a shared understanding of the moral significance of pain and suffering, or any clear notion of how we ought to support one another's private griefs and burdens. We do not provide strong encouragement for those personal virtues which enable people to endure in the face of adversity. All of these communal deficits can come to a high intensity in the demands that vulnerable elderly parents can make upon their children (pp. 97–8).

No common coherent vision. No shared understanding. Communal deficits. These are the deep problems that make decisions about appropriate care for aging people intractable. Far more is needed to meet our health care needs in the future than fine-tuning our national budget or finding one more magic bullet to keep death at bay a little longer. We need to arrive at publicly shared understandings of death, aging, medicine, and the obligations between parents and children.

Read on with Callahan. Asserting that our traditional moral language of rights and obligations "does not seem to fit" the current situation of many parents and children, he concludes that "our secular morality (though perhaps not our religious traditions) provides few resources for living lives of unchosen obligations" (p. 96). I will say more below about Callahan's parenthetical comment. For now the main thing to note is that Callahan's big problem is our culture's operative moral tradition. It is, he claims again and again, inadequate for our new needs.

Beneath the reigning "medical needs" model of determining health care strategies and what Callahan calls our "spend down" approach to the illness of elderly people (policies that require the elderly to spend their life savings before receiving financial aid) is a thin but powerful cultural mind-set that puts its hopes in technology and its priorities on defeating death. We need, says Callahan, "a full reform" of our health care system. But he is quick to say that such a reform is not likely. "Many years will be required to bring about the kind of shift in values needed to change attitudes and practices pertinent to the provision of life-extending technologies to the elderly" (p. 147). . . .

But Callahan provides little help in creating, sustaining, and shaping the debate he believes we so desperately need. His book sets forth an issue and a point of view that cannot be ignored and calls for a debate to begin. So far so good. But more needs to be said than that we need to talk. Here I would return to his parenthetical comment noted above. Perhaps to create the kind of ongoing public debate our society needs we must move it beyond the walls of our legislatures and the editorial pages of our newspapers. Not that senators, commentators, and other experts should keep quiet. On the contrary, they must participate in the discussion Callahan wants. But most such discussions use the "secular morality" language of rights and obligations that Callahan has doubts about.

His tentative admission that there might be better resources elsewhere ("perhaps" in "our religious traditions") suggests that many debates need to take place—and not just between society's elites. What if each of the more than 300,000 religious congregations in our land began to stimulate discussion about these basic questions—first within themselves and later with members of the surrounding communities? What if they began to host these debates rather than passively waiting for them to begin and then, when things seemed to be taking a wrong turn, demanding to be heard? These religious communities have answers—even if underused and contradictory—to meaning questions about death, aging, family obligations, and justice different from those that dominate our television screens and political rhetoric. Do those communities have a public duty to offer their resources to a society searching for answers? Callahan did not extend a direct invitation to the religious communities to join the debate, yet it seems apparent that help is needed and that a serious reckoning with our pluralism of beliefs and practices must occur for consensus to emerge.

Just as Callahan was hesitant in making his proposal about changing medicine's goals, so am I in suggesting that the religious traditions join the discussion. We will only further our confusion if various traditions try to cancel each other out with exclusive positions. Only if various religious communities can muster a deep commitment to the good of a diverse public can anything more than a cacophony result. Only if each religious community is willing to confront the fact that there are as Paul Tillich once reminded us "sick traditions" not just in everybody else's way of life but also in our own, can there be the possibility of new insight and agreement. Only if each group searches not for the way it can prevail, but for what its special contribution could be, can we hope to find new approaches to our problems. The track record of religious communities in public debate is pronouncedly mixed—suggesting that our various religious communities need to prepare themselves for the kind of debate that Callahan and others think we need. Such preparation is far from being optional. The magnitude of the decisions we face in health care and public policy may make failure to prepare for this debate hazardous to our societal and individual health.

PART IV

IF NOT "SETTING LIMITS," THEN WHAT?

These experts not only examine Callahan's assumptions and his policy proposals, they propose alternative choices—based on differing public policies and new research agendas. For example, would a policy of age-based rationing actually conserve society's resources? Are there other, more appropriate, ways to address the inflationary spiral in health-care costs? How can we deny life-extending therapies to older Americans while simultaneously subsidizing the tobacco industry? What do such choices tell us about our values as a society?

MEDICAL CARE—AND CARING

....

EZEKIEL J. EMANUEL

EZEKIEL J. EMANUEL is a Fellow, Program in Ethics and the Professions, Kennedy School of Government, Harvard University, Cambridge, Massachusetts.

MR. CALLAHAN'S specific proposals reveal important difficulties in his own vision. An underlying but unsubstantiated claim behind his argument is that future demographic changes increasing the number of elderly will dramatically raise health-care costs. This claim appears to be false. According to leading health-policy experts, over the next few decades increases in the proportion of older people are expected to boost health-care costs by a small amount, much less than either general population growth or general inflation in hospital input—prices, wages and supplies. Further, the entire cost of lifesaving care is a very small fraction of all Medicare expenditures, around 3 percent to 4 percent. Eliminating these services for the elderly will hardly reduce medical care costs.

More important, however, if we adopt Mr. Callahan's proposal, medical costs are likely to rise, not fall. Medical services

---

Ezekiel J. Emanuel's "Medical Care—And Caring" excerpted from *The Wall Street Journal* (January 7, 1988). Reprinted by permission of the author and *The Wall Street Journal*.

that improve the elderly's quality of life, such as long-term nursing-home care, rehabilitation for stroke victims, new devices for those with failing eyesight and hearing, are extremely costly. For instance, one year in a quality nursing home can cost in excess of $25,000 for a single patient; a cochlear-implant treatment for hearing loss costs about $13,000. And the demand for such services is, in Mr. Callahan's own words, "open-ended." It is estimated that more than one million Americans might benefit from cochlear implants alone. Thus, adopting his "cost cutting" proposals could prove very, very costly.

Mr. Callahan recognizes this, but in so doing changes the rationale for his scheme. Instead of justifying the proposed policies for their economy, he argues that the new perspective would give the elderly security, a guarantee that ill health would not leave them impoverished, dependent and socially isolated. By the end of his book, it seems Mr. Callahan's objective is not to propose ethical policies to control medical-care costs but to change society's attitudes toward aging and death regardless of the effect on costs. While this new attitude toward aging may be more humane and compassionate, it is not likely to be cheap.

A TOUGH CHOICE ON
HEALTH CARE COSTS

···

WILLIAM B. SCHWARTZ AND HENRY J.

AARON

WILLIAM B. SCHWARTZ is Vannevar Bush University Professor and Professor of Medicine, Tufts University School of Medicine, Boston, Massachusetts; HENRY J. AARON is Senior Fellow, the Brookings Institution, Washington, D.C.

DANIEL CALLAHAN, an ethicist and author of the book *Setting Limits,* has stirred sharp debate over his proposal for slowing the rise in health care costs by eliminating life-extending care for most people over the age of 75.

Mr. Callahan's recommendation has attracted attention because other vaunted panaceas for soaring health care costs, such as health maintenance organizations and other competitive mechanisms, are having little effect.

But Mr. Callahan's proposal suffers from two major shortcomings. First, it almost certainly would not be acceptable to patients, health care providers, or, one suspects, anyone else. Second, it would do almost nothing to slow the rise in costs of medical care.

Mr. Callahan's idea is something less than thoroughly reasoned. He provides no analysis of current costs and offers no estimate of the savings he hopes to achieve. In fact, the impact on costs would be minimal.

In 1986, people aged 75 or older constituted less than 5 percent of the United States population. Because per capita medical costs for the very old run about three times the national average, such costs account for about 15 percent of annual health care spending. Abruptly eliminating half of the services used by this group—a Draconian cut, because even Mr. Callahan has not proposed denying routine care or ignoring life-threatening illness in the aged who are otherwise healthy—would reduce total spending by only about 7 percent.

In recent years, health care spending has risen by 5.5 to 6 percent annually after adjusting for inflation. Thus, a sudden cut in services to the elderly would reduce current outlays by no more than the costs typically grow in a little more than a year—a significant amount but not enough to materially slow the steady climb in health care costs.

Most of the growth in health care spending results from scientific advances—open heart surgery, organ transplants, magnetic resonance imaging, clot-dissolving agents to prevent heart attacks—that are applied to the general population, not just the few who are 75 or older.

Indeed, a simple calculation shows that even if all fruits of future medical progress were denied to the elderly, the nearly 5 percent annual growth rate in medical costs would be slowed by less than half a percentage point.

If cutting care to the elderly won't contain health care costs, what will? The United States is not the first developed country to face this question. The British health care system, which has rationed health care for years, shows that age is only one of many social, medical and economic factors invoked to contain costs.

For example, visible suffering commands far more resources than private pain. The grotesque swollen joints and massive bleeding of hemophiliacs have caused the British to reject all restrictions on therapy. But because angina pectoris, or chest pain from coronary artery disease, causes silent and invisible suffering, Britain spends less than one-fifth as much as the United States does on coronary artery surgery.

Many other basic societal values also determine what services the British withhold. Services dependent on equipment allocated by bureaucrats located far from the point of treatment are rationed far more than are those dependent on resources readily available in hospitals. A case in point: many major British hospitals lack a CAT scanner, now widely acknowledged to be vital in modern diagnosis.

Simple fear also shapes rationing decisions. The dread of cancer has led the British not to stint on radiotherapy or chemotherapy even for cases in which the treatment is designed only to relieve pain rather than to prolong life.

Aggregate costs of therapy is a further key factor. Bone marrow transplants, averaging $50,000 to $100,000 a patient, are provided as often in Britain as in the United States, largely because only a few patients require them.

In contrast, some British patients must wait five years for hip replacements because the thousands of people with arthritic hips would impose burdensome costs on the health care system if all were treated.

One British expert, asked what would happen if a high-cost curative drug became available for a common form of metastatic cancer, responded, "I wake up screaming at such a prospect" and expressed the opinion that many people would go untreated.

If the American public ever gets serious about containing health care costs, rationing of treatment will likely proceed along lines similar to those in Britain, not simply on the basis of age. But Americans are unlikely to be as willing as the

British to accept reduced quality of care. Americans, promptly informed by the media of each new medical advance, are quick to demand the new treatment.

How will we resolve the conflict in the basically incompatible goals of controlling costs while maintaing quality? Some real economies can be achieved by increased efficiency, but no matter what, a significant reduction in the growth of medical spending will require the sacrifice of beneficial services not by just the very old but by all of us.

AIM NOT JUST FOR LONGER LIFE, BUT EXPANDED "HEALTH SPAN"

....

DANIEL PERRY AND ROBERT N. BUTLER

DANIEL PERRY is Executive Director, Alliance for Aging Research, Washington, D.C.; and ROBERT N. BUTLER is Brookdale Professor of Geriatrics and Adult Development, Mount Sinai School of Medicine, New York, New York.

MOST AMERICANS instinctively recoil at the thought that their government would try to save money by pulling the plug on life-sustaining care when it is needed by older people. In this case, their instincts are correct.

To determine a person's access to medical care solely on the basis of that person's age is clearly unfair, unworkable and unnecessary. It is wrong to blame the elderly for rising hospital expenses and physicians' fees that are driven principally by other factors or to require older Americans to pay for the failure of government and industry to find a more humane and workable policy to curb health care costs.

President Reagan signed into law the most sweeping Medicare expansion in that program's 22-year history, indicating the nation's strong commitment to providing health care to the elderly. The new catastrophic care program will cost

Daniel Perry and Robert N. Butler's "Aim Not Just for Longer Life, but Expanded 'Health Span' " from *The Washington Post* (December 20, 1988). Reprinted by permission of the authors and *The Washington Post*.

about $31 billion over five years. Even that amount will seem small when compared to proposals for insuring Americans against the costs of long-term care, the next major health care issue to face Congress and the Bush presidency.

As the curtain rose on Congressional debate over long-term care, some came forward to argue that the United States could save billions by simply denying lifesaving medical interventions to people over a certain age—say 65 to 75. But there is a better way to control costs of providing health care to the elderly: work to eliminate the very afflictions of old age, which are costing billions in health care, long-term care, and lost productivity. By attacking diseases associated with aging—such as Alzheimer's disease, stroke, osteoporosis, arthritis and others—the need for many costly medical procedures, lengthy hospital stays and financially draining long-term care could be ended or reduced.

Why not start with a real commitment to scientific research that could extend the healthful middle years of life and compress the decline of aging into a very short time?

Why not redirect federal research efforts to aim for scientific and medical discoveries to reduce frailty, improve health status and increase independence in older people? It's a far better goal—and more realistic—than rationing medical treatment.

At present, however, aging research is not where the U.S. government is placing its biggest bets. Most people don't believe much can be done to change aging. Therefore, research funds generally go elsewhere.

There is every reason to fear spiraling health costs if effective ways to lengthen healthy years and delay the onset of debilitating age are not found before the baby boomers become the biggest Medicare generation in history.

Americans already are paying billions because medical science lacks the ability to cure, prevent or postpone many chronic maladies associated with aging. And national investment in research to avoid these costs is minuscule when compared to the billions spent for treatment.

Of the $167 billion a year spent on health care for people over age 65, far less than one half of 1 percent of that amount is reinvested in research that could lead to lower health care costs for chronic diseases and disabilities. That is a poor investment strategy for a nation soon to experience the largest senior boom in history.

Tinkering with changes in the health care delivery system can save some money, but these savings will not equal the long-term benefits of dramatic medical and scientific changes that alter the way people experience old age.

If scientists do not find a way to treat Alzheimer's, for instance, by the middle of the next century, there will be five times as many victims of this disease as there are now simply because of the demographic shift that is occurring. Incontinence, memory loss and immobility are the main factors driving long-term care and high health costs to the elderly. If no advances occur in these and other conditions of aging, up to 6 million older Americans will be living in nursing homes, instead of the 1 million who are there today.

Unfortunately, there may be no way to prevent aging per se. However, there are conditions that occur only as a person ages. Many of these can be prevented. The risk of suffering a chronic disease such as arthritis or osteoporosis is very slight at middle age. But from the forties onward, that risk doubles exponentially about every five years until someone in the mid-eighties has about a one-in-three chance of having dementia, immobility, incontinence or other age-related disabilities.

If medicine could delay the beginning of decline by as few as five years, many conditions and the costs they incur could be cut in half. The ability to re-set biological clocks to forestall some of the decline of aging may be closer than anyone realizes, thanks to new knowledge in immunology and in the molecular genetics of aging.

Answers may be near. Help for immobility, osteoporosis and incontinence can be achieved with only a modest extension of present technologies. If the U.S. doubles its present meager $30 million for osteoporosis research, by the year 2010 this condition could be eliminated as a major public health problem, which now affects 90 percent of all women over 75.

Learning how to postpone aging could help lower health care costs and improve the health of older Americans at the same time. The goal here is not just longer life span but extended "health span," with fewer problems caused by chronic disease.

SPARE THE OLD, SAVE THE YOUNG

AMITAI ETZIONI

....

AMITAI ETZIONI is University Professor, George Washington University, and Director of the Center for Policy Research, Washington, D.C.

IN THE COMING YEARS, Daniel Callahan's call to ration health care for the elderly, put forth in his book *Setting Limits,* is likely to have a growing appeal. Practically all economic observers expect the United States to go through a difficult time as it attempts to work its way out of its domestic (budgetary) and international (trade) deficits. Practically every serious analyst realizes that such an endeavor will initially entail slower growth, if not an outright cut in our standard of living, in order to release resources to these priorities. When the national economic "pie" grows more slowly, let alone contracts, the fight over how to divide it up intensifies. The elderly make an especially inviting target because they have been taking a growing slice of the resources (at least those dedicated to health care) and are expected to take even more in the future.

Old people are widely held to be "nonproductive" and to constitute a growing "burden" on an ever-smaller proportion of society that is young and working. Also, the elderly are viewed as politically well-organized and powerful; hence "their" programs, especially Social Security and Medicare, have largely escaped the Reagan attempts to scale back social expenditures, while those aimed at other groups—especially the young, but even more so future generations—have been generally curtailed. There are now some signs that a backlash may be forming. . . .

Those opposed to Callahan but who also favor extending the frontier of life must answer the question, where will the resources come from? One answer is found in the realization that defining people as old at the age of 65 is obsolescent. That age limit was set generations ago, before changes in lifestyles and medicines much extended not only life but also the number and quality of productive years. One might recognize that many of the "elderly" can contribute to society not merely by providing love, companionship and wisdom to the young but also by continuing to work, in the traditional sense of the term. Indeed, many already work in the underground economy because of the large penalty—a cut in Social Security benefits—exacted from them if they hold a job "on the books."

Allowing elderly people to retain their Social Security benefits while working, typically part-time, would immediately raise significant tax revenues, dramatically change the much-feared dependency-to-dependent ratio, provide a much-needed source of child-care workers and increase contributions to Social Security (under the assumption that anybody who will continue to work will continue to contribute to the program). There is also evidence that people who continue to have meaningful work will live longer and healthier lives, without requiring more health care, because psychic well-being in our society is so deeply associated with meaningful work. Other policy changes, such as deferring retirement, modifying Social Security benefits by a small, gradual stretching out of the age of full-benefit entitlement, plus some other shifts under way, could be used readily to gain more resources. Such changes might be justified prima facie because as we extend life and its quality, the payouts to the old may also be stretched out.

Beyond the question of whether to cut care or stretch out Social Security payouts, policies that seek to promote intergenerational equity must be assessed as to how they deal with another matter of equity: that between the poor and the rich. A policy that would stop Federal support for certain kinds of care, as Callahan and others propose, would halt treatment for the aged, poor, the near-poor and even the less-well-off segment of the middle class (although for the latter at a later point), while the rich would continue to buy all the care they wished to. Callahan's suggestion that a consensus of doctors would stop certain kinds of care for all elderly people is quite impractical; for it to work, most if not all doctors would have to agree to participate. Even if this somehow happened, the rich would buy their services overseas either by going there or importing the services. There is little enough we can do to significantly enhance economic equality. Do we want to exacerbate the inequalities that already exist by completely eliminating access to major categories of health care services for those who cannot afford to pay for them?

In addition to concern about slipping down the slope of less (and less) care, the *way* the limitations are to be introduced raises a serious question. The advocates of changing the intergenerational allocation of resources favor rationing health care for the elderly but nothing else. This is a major intellectual weakness of their argument. There are other major targets to consider within health care, as well as other areas, which seem, at least by some criteria, much more inviting than terminating care to those above a certain age. Within the medical sector, for example, why not stop all interventions for which there is no hard evidence that they are beneficial? Say, public financing of psychotherapy and coronary bypass operations? Why not take the $2 billion or so from plastic surgery dedicated to face lifts, reducing behinds and the like? Or require that all burials be done by low-cost cremations rather than using high-cost coffins?

Once we extend our reach beyond medical care to health care, if we cannot stop people from blowing $25 billion per year on cigarettes and convince them to use the money to serve the young, shouldn't we at least cut out public subsidies to tobacco growers before we save funds by denying antibiotics to old people? And there is the matter of profits. The high-technology medicine Callahan targets for savings is actually a minor cause of the increase in health care costs for the elderly or for anyone—about 4 percent. A major factor is the very high standard of living American doctors have, compared to those of many other nations. Indeed, many doctors tell interviewers that they love their work and would do it for half their current income as long as the incomes of their fellow practitioners were also cut. Another important area of saving is the exorbitant profits made by the nondoctor owners of dialysis units and nursing homes. If we dare ask how many years of life are enough, should we not also be able to ask how much profit is "enough"? This profit, by the way, is largely set not by the market but by public policy.

Last but not least, as the United States enters a time of economic constraints, should we draw new lines of conflict or should we focus on matters that sustain our societal fabric? During the 1960s numerous groups gained in political consciousness and actively sought to address injustices done to them. The result has been some redress and an increase in

the level of societal stress (witness the deeply troubled relationships between the genders). But these conflicts occurred
in an affluent society and redressed deeply felt grievances. Are
the young like blacks and women, except that they have not
yet discovered their oppressors—a group whose consciousness should be raised, so it will rally and gain its due share?

The answer is in the eye of the beholder. There are no
objective criteria that can be used here the way they can be
used between the races or between the genders. While women
and minorities have the same rights to the same jobs at the
same pay as white males, the needs of the young and the aged
are so different that no simple criteria of equity come to mind.
Thus, no one would argue that the teen-agers and those above
75 have the same need for schooling or nursing homes.

At the same time, it is easy to see that those who try to
mobilize the young—led by a new Washington research
group, Americans for Generational Equity (AGE), formed to
fight for the needs of the younger generation—offer many
arguments that do not hold. For instance, they often argue
that today's young, age 35 or less, will pay for old people's
Social Security, but by the time they come of age they will
not be able to collect, because Social Security will be bank-
rupt. However, this argument is based on extremely far-
fetched assumptions about the future. In effect, Social Security
is now and for the foreseeable future overprovided, and its
surplus is used to reduce deficits caused by other expenditures,
such as Star Wars, in what is still an integrated budget. And,
if Social Security runs into the red again somewhere after the
year 2020, relatively small adjustments in premiums and payouts would restore it to financial health.

Above all, it is a dubious sociological achievement to fo-
ment conflict between the generations, because, unlike the
minorities and the white majority, or men and women, many
millions of Americans are neither young nor old but of in-

termediate ages. We should not avoid issues just because we face stressing times in an already strained society; but maybe we should declare a moratorium on raising new conflicts until more compelling arguments can be found in their favor, and more evidence that this particular line of divisiveness is called for.

SETTING LIMITS OR PROMOTING HEALTH?

....

ANNE R. SOMERS

ANNE R. SOMERS is Adjunct Professor, Department of Environmental and Community Medicine, University of Medicine and Dentistry of New Jersey–Robert Wood Johnson Medical School, Piscataway, New Jersey.

ONE OF THE disappointing elements in the Callahan thesis is the failure to recognize many self-correcting trends that can already be discerned. For example, there is some evidence that the long period of nonproductive and expensive disability that blights the lives of so many elderly today may be giving way to a new phenomenon, variously known as "Productive Aging" (Butler), "Successful Aging" (Rowe and Kahn), "Compression of Morbidity" (Fries) or "Extension of the Adult Prime" (Pifer and Bronte). The related concept of Preventive Gerontology (Hazzard) reflects professional recognition and encouragement of this potential.

There is also evidence that heart attacks are not only less often fatal than they used to be but occur later in life. The general decline of cardiovascular disease and the improve-

Anne R. Somers's "Setting Limits or Promoting Health?" from *Health Management Quarterly* (First Quarter 1988). Reprinted by permission of the author and *Health Management Quarterly*, a publication of The Baxter Foundation.

ment in control of many erstwhile disabling or incapacitating conditions—including cataracts, deafness, osteoporosis, some forms of cancer, even incontinence—suggest that many elderly are living not only longer but healthier and more active lives than in the past.

At the same time, the rate of increase in life expectancy, so dramatic during the past two decades, has slowed markedly. Between 1971 and 1976, for example, life expectancy at birth increased by 1.8 years; between 1981 and 1986, it was only 0.7 years, less than half as fast. At 65, the increase dropped from 0.9 to 0.2. One decade is too brief to be sure of this new trend, but it suggests that Callahan may have been much too quick in accusing the American people of an "insatiable appetite for a longer life no matter what the expense" (*New York Times,* September 25, 1987). On the contrary, there is reason to believe that many, if not most, elders seek just the opposite—the longest possible healthy and productive life, followed by the briefest possible period of disability and dependency, and the quickest possible death.

The rapid spread of living wills and other forms of "advance directives," adoption of laws legalizing such documents in 39 states, establishment of ethics committees in the majority of U.S. hospitals, and a striking series of court decisions that expand the right to patient self-determination all attest to the strength of the "right-to-die" movement. Callahan and his organization, The Hastings Center, have led in many of these developments. It is both ironic and sad to find him now emphasizing governmental limits on medical treatment rather than greater patient/family and institutional responsibility. While some might argue that Medicare-imposed limits could help to reinforce the push for self-determination, I believe the result would be just the opposite. If treatment decisions were made on the basis of age—however defined—and by some external authority, what incentive would there be for individuals to assume responsibility for their own advance directives?

The alternative I propose accepts much of the Callahan critique of U.S. health care inadequacies and inequities. However, the thrust is positive rather than negative, and it builds on the concepts cited above. Rather than thwarting normal pro-life instincts, professional ethics and provider technology, it calls for redirection toward prevention and rehabilitation. It calls for more, rather than less, responsibility and risk-taking on the part of individuals and institutions. It emphasizes health maintenance and productive work rather than termination of treatment and a hopeless wait for death.

Progress in this direction will require simultaneous action in at least five different areas. The following is barely an outline of needed changes in existing policies and practices.

One—Health promotion/disease prevention for the elderly. The primary goal of all national health policies should be maintenance of the best possible health status for all people, including the elderly. This would mean a basic shift in Medicare policy, which now specifically excludes preventive services from reimbursement. It would mean better definition of such services than is now available and their incorporation into mainstream health insurance programs, public and private. It would also mean a gradual change in Social Security, private pension and employment policies to reflect increasing life expectancy and the need of the elderly to continue productive activity as long as possible.

Two—Long-term care for the chronically disabled and elderly. The elderly and chronically disabled who can work should be assisted to do so with mechanical and personal aids, if necessary, as well as flexible employment policies. When no longer able to work, they should receive needed long-term health care, either through amendment of Medicare, mixed public-private insurance or both. Essential quality

103

and cost controls, including patient cost-sharing, should be built into the program(s).

Three—Patient/family responsibility, autonomy and risk-sharing in treatment decisions. Some degree of risk is inseparable from life. This applies to patients as well as providers. Recent progress in expanding patient rights must be balanced with equal expansion in patient responsibilities, including more emphasis on individual health maintenance and wider use of advance directives.

Four—Basic health services for all Americans. To correct existing imbalances in resource allocation, steps should be taken promptly to define essential or basic health services for all, regardless of age, and to write such definitions into national and state legislation. Such definitions should be incorporated into all approved health insurance programs, public or private, and adequate payment provided therefor—even if this involves some transfer from existing programs.

Five—Hospital policies. Hospitals and other health care institutions could and should play a crucial role in helping to move U.S. policies in the direction of greater individual and institutional responsibility as opposed to more government regulation. They and their professional staffs should devote more attention and resources to health promotion/disease prevention, rehabilitation and long-term care. They could develop health-maintenance contracts with local business organizations and community groups, as well as long-term care programs, on an insurance basis where possible. Risk-contracts with Medicare, Medicaid and/or private insurers could be explored.

Providers should incorporate advance directives of some sort into all adult admissions procedures and patient files, and establish ethics committees to assist patients, families and physicians with difficult treatment decisions.

Hospitals should not wait to be dragged into a new era of more equitable resource allocation. By making sure that they are meeting basic community obligations in terms of prevention, primary care and long-term care, before further investment in acute care, they can help to redress current imbalances more effectively and far less traumatically than under any radical rationing proposal. Failure to act may well result in some such rationing program within a decade or so.

PART V

In Search of a Model

What types of values do and should inform our reflections on health care and aging in our society? The
following contributors set out to answer that question
by examining the philosophical foundations of Setting
Limits and its major themes.

Larry R. Churchill asks us to explore how contemporary American political language shapes the way we
see problems and prevents us from making sense of
themes rooted in a different communal perception. He
believes it foolhardy to pretend that the problem of
resource scarcity will simply disappear. Yet, he recognizes the difficulties that a society dedicated to the
"moral sovereignty of the individual" may have with
the achievement of equity in resource allocation. He
challenges the assumptions of traditional liberalism and
suggests that we need a more accurate, rich, and nuanced
language to address these issues.

Theologian Stanley Hauerwas examines why answers
to the question of what ends medical skill should serve
are so profoundly difficult in contemporary society. He
describes life as narrative—a process of discovery and

not creation in which death is part of the pattern that gives purpose to our lives.

Dan W. Brock, by contrast, finds it philosophically and politically necessary to accommodate the arguments for setting limits and age-based rationing to liberalism. In seeking an alternative basis to the "natural life span" for public policy, Brock examines the approaches of John Rawls and Norman Daniels to resource distribution and argues instead for empowering patients to choose limits to their own health care.

Getting from 'I' to 'We'

....

Larry R. Churchill

LARRY R. CHURCHILL is Professor of Social Medicine and Religious Studies, University of North Carolina at Chapel Hill.

Questions of how best to allocate scarce health-care resources to the elderly, or to the rest of us, face two obstacles to a fair hearing. The first is a denial of scarcity, a conviction that the problem of limits is not a real one, or if it currently exists, is remediable. The remedies proposed are usually variations on greater efficiency, technological innovation, or budgetary re-alignments. They are typically proposed in sincerity and with good will, but they are essentially distractions.[1] No society has ever devised a way to meet all the health needs of its citizens. The allocation of relatively scarce health-care resources is a present fact and it promises to become increasingly difficult as American society ages.

The second obstacle is more difficult, and it is the one I address here. It involves more than psychological predispositions of denial and problem avoidance. Rather, it involves problems of how we talk, think, and imagine the problem of scarce resources. This set of problems is more intransigent, for even when we acknowledge the problem of scarcity, we have few moral idioms to grasp it, and those we do possess

109

appeal to an orientation that distorts the problem. The issue is, how can a culture committed to the moral sovereignty of individuals cope with a problem that arises because of our efforts to achieve equity in social life? This can be expressed in a variety of ways, but it is essentially a question of individuals finding their social voice.

For earlier societies—less committed, if at all, to tolerance for diversity, pluralism, and the protection of individual freedoms—this question was not a pressing one. Superordinate cultural hierarchies of religion or the state, or both, supplied the language and meaning of life in society. For good and for ill, such encompassing linguistic and meaning structures are no longer available to late-twentieth-century Americans. I assume that although many of the concepts of religious traditions will have relevance for our situation, their force is equivocal across a population as diverse as this one. We cannot begin with an assumption that, for example, traditional Christian theological concepts will be easily applicable. I think Jeffrey Stout has rightly characterized our task as one of *bricolage,* that is, an eclectic and pragmatic use of a variety of traditions, theories, and approaches adapted to current problems.[2] Whether we can rediscover or invent idioms of affiliation is an open question. There is currently no more dramatic scene for the playing out of that question than health-care resource allocation, especially as it affects the elderly.

I turn now to two tasks. The first is diagnostic, that is, a fuller explication of the absence of social moral discourse. Rehearsing this absence will help us see the extent to which we are captured by individualistic paradigms. It will also help us to see why the proposals of Daniel Callahan in *Setting Limits* are frequently misunderstood and necessarily incomplete.

The second task is corrective, namely, attention to those dimensions of human experience that are neglected by our current moral repertoire. Some human experiences of moral importance are irreducibly social. Thus, I am not trying here to invent a language *and* invent a domain of experience, but to construct (or revive) moral idioms adequate to the experience we all know but do not sufficiently appreciate. The problem is that our experience outruns our conceptual ability; we have more experiences than we have adequate terms to describe them. Moreover, we seem to rely on a moral vocabulary that actually cloaks our sociality, rather than displays it. Our task, then, is to imagine and give moral voice to what we know.

ATOMISM: BEGINNING WITH 'I'

Amitai Etzioni claims that "the celebration of individualism has been carried too far, beyond the challenge of authoritarian and totalitarian doctrines, to undercutting the legitimation of the community and of the public realm."[3]

His response is not a return to community in a simplistic sense, but to what he terms, following Martin Buber, 'I and We', or the "Open Community." Etzioni sees traditional conservative conceptions of the community as closed and inimical to individual rights, and traditional liberal conceptions as noncommunal, and sometimes anticommunal. The Open Community configuration is one in which communal and individual forces both have standing and in which the tension between them is valued as a healthy dynamic rather than a problem to be solved. The moral force of each is anchored in its response to its opposite. Traditional conservative and liberal positions, the "closed community" and "no community" options, collapse the tension and force this dynamic into a rigid (and thereby unstable) resolution.

It is something very close to Etzioni's model that I want to endorse here. Yet, most of our moral language steers away from this sort of dynamic synthesis of the multiple sides of our moral selves in favor of more simplistic formulations of both the problem and its possible solutions. The predominant American cultural ethic is liberal, or "no community" in orientation, with a heavy emphasis on individual rights and liberties, a suspiciousness that all forms of affiliation are authoritarian and repressive, and consequently, an impoverished concept of community.

There is no more telling evidence for the accuracy of this thesis than the images of self and society that emerge from contemporary political philosophy, for here we find that the two chief rival schools of thought are both deeply indebted to a view of the self as atomistic and a view of society as a derivative construction of solitary selves.[4] Rawls and Nozick are the most prominent and vivid examples. Rather than rehearse their arguments here, I want to focus on *why* an individualistic view has such a captive presence over us, for the real problem may be not the intellectual appeal of individualistic models, but the emotional appeal of this portrait of the self. My argument here follows a line of thinking suggested by Charles Taylor.[5] The pull and staying power of moral atomism has to do with the seductive force of the portrait of the person it conveys. The portrait emphasizes vast kinds of freedom, dignity, and power; in short, it portrays persons as atomic moral sovereigns who may choose social relationships, or community affiliation, but whose moral structures are not essentially changed by such choices.

This portrait goes roughly like this:

In the beginning (or "in the state of nature," or "behind the veil of ignorance," or "in the Garden") were individuals, and these individuals were essentially complete unto themselves and self-sufficient with regard to their needs and aims. For reasons of convenience and mutual self-interest, these individuals decided to form social compacts. Included in these compacts were moral provisos indicating how each individual would relinquish enough sovereignty for collective activity. Yet these social compacts were optional and provisional, and in no way changed the essential and antecedent freedom, dignity, or power of each individual over him/herself. Each individual remained free to disengage from any particular social compact, or from all social compacts whatever, when the balance of self-interest over the sacrifice of restrictions was not served.

This formulation, frequently in modified form, has dominated our thinking for at least three hundred years, and arguably longer. We could use the publication of Locke's *Second Treatise on Government* in 1690 as a convenient benchmark. This portrait is hardly ever painted in such bold colors, but I have presented it in an unqualified form to display, not its logical persuasiveness or its realism (of which there is little), but its emotional appeal. Whether presented as history or as hypothetical vignette, as fact or as argumentative stipulation, it carries the same appeal to our psyche. The message is one of grandeur, freedom, dignity, and power. It is a portrait of a sovereign. Individual existence is essential to human beings, social existence optional. Individuals constitute the moral unit of meaning worthy of study. Social relations, being derivative, are ethically uninteresting except as they form an occasion for, or the setting of, individual moral choice. Social relations, much less communal existence, are not constitutive of persons, or of the morally important aspects of persons. This, of course, tilts the study of ethics in a certain way. But what I want to draw attention to is not the theoretical skewing of a discipline but the flattering and grandiose picture of the self we are given to work with here.

MOVING FROM 'I' TO 'WE'?

It should not be surprising that modern political philosophy should begin with atomism and move to a construction of society based on individual choice. Modern epistemology had already cut the path. Descartes put it definitively in the *Meditations*, Part IV, in his assertion *"Je pense, donc je suis"*—"I think, therefore I am."[6] The impact of this pronouncement for our view of knowledge has been, of course, enormous. Of equal importance is the form of the assertion for our moral self-understanding. Descartes did not say, from the solitariness of his Dutch oven, *"Nous pensons, donc nous existons"*—"We think, therefore we are,"—or better *"Nous existons, donc je pense"*—"We are, therefore I think." He said 'I', not as Etzioni would have had it, 'I and We', just 'I'—a sovereign, essentially asocial 'I'. Descartes said that in matters of knowledge the mind begins with itself and proceeds to the outside world through inference and construction. Modern political philosophy, following suit, begins with moral atomism and proceeds to the social world through choice and construction.

In the best of all worlds we might hope for a reformulation something like *"Nous existons, donc je peux penser"*—"We are, therefore I am able to think"—to signal the roots of individual self-awareness in the soil of sociality. And acknowledging this, we could then assert, *"Je pense, donc nous existons"*—"I think, therefore we are"—to signal the crucial way that individuals must sustain communal activity.

I do not gainsay the importance of individual liberation, historically, from repressive collectivities or tyrannical political hierarchies. But I believe we can still maintain individual freedoms while embracing social affiliations. The solution is to situate the dignity, power, and freedom we wish to ascribe to individuals socially, rather than reject them altogether. Yet, a good deal of current thinking portrays individual freedom and social relatedness as mutually exclusive, as if one must choose between them.

Following the Cartesian portrait of moral atomism, contemporary bioethical analysis is preoccupied with the concept of autonomy—its meaning, its centrality in the moral life, and how best to safeguard it. Our concern with autonomy is important and proper—even vital—but our preoccupation with it damaging. Bioethics must be more than the analysis and safeguarding of autonomy and encouragement of respect for autonomy, for autonomy is the chief issue only in situations in which individuals are threatened by coercion, infringement, or diminishment. It is not the chief issue when individuals are disengaged from each other and when matters of policy and social well-being are at stake. To evoke autonomy in the context of resource allocation is to stretch it beyond its proper sphere of application and to succumb to the flattering portrait of individual moral sovereignty discussed above. An autonomy ethic fits all-too-easily with an atomistic picture of the moral life. If atomism is the beginning point, an autonomy ethic of a very myopic sort will likely be the result.

In short, if one begins with Cartesian certainty and Lockean self-sufficiency as the definitive picture of moral selfhood, one cannot get from 'I' to 'We', for this 'I' is a disengaged and essentially completed entity; it has no need to say 'We'. That such a portrait is false, or at best only partially true, and that we must *begin* with 'I and We', as Etzioni would have us say, is my point here. We cannot begin with a premise of asocial individualism and arrive at a viable social ethic. If there is to be a social ethic of any force, it must be discovered as a necessary complement to an individual ethic. The 'I' must locate its saying of 'I' in a 'We', or as Merleau-Ponty puts it, we must discover that "the social is already there when we come to know it or judge it."[7]

SOCIALITY: LOCATING 'I' IN 'WE'

If Charles Taylor is right, as I believe, and the modern self conceives of itself as a disengaged consciousness, then this discovery of social embeddedness will not be simple or pain-

115

less. It will seem like asking a sovereign to give up power, when in fact it is more than showing a would-be sovereign that his grandeur is delusional and that the potential for true freedom and dignity lies in social relatedness. The move from 'I' to 'We' can be made less painful if it can be shown that this movement is not a virginal voyage, but a trip home. The 'I' can say 'We' because the 'We' is seen to underlie the ability to say 'I' in the first place.

Merleau-Ponty has put it well, claiming that it is one of the tasks of philosophy to help us recover the social world that exists as a permanent, though often out-of-focus, dimension of personal existence. While we may reject particular social relationships, we never fail to be situated relative to some form of social life:

> Our relationship to the social is, like our relationship to the world, deeper than any express perception or any judgment. It is as false to place ourselves in society as an object among other objects as it is to place society within ourselves as an object of thought, and in both cases the mistake lies in treating the social as an object. We must return to the social with which we are in contact by the mere fact of existing, and which we carry about inseparably within us before any objectification.[8]

Our inability to think seriously about resource allocation lies precisely in the effort to "place society within ourselves as an object of thought"—a thought, a possibility, or an option for the sovereign individual chooser. And while particular social arrangements may, and should, become objects of our critical scrutiny, to make the social dimension of moral life itself a choice is a *reductio ad absurdum*. The existence of a self that can formulate such a choice is testimony to the social, and forecloses on atomism, or any form of individualism that believes it can generate the social *ab original* from its own reason and will. We are in the social world as fish are in water, as a sustaining ecology without which moral life would be impossible. We cannot focus on the social dimension as a discrete object any more than a fish can focus on the water in which it swims.

What is required is a consideration of resource allocation in health care that acknowledges the irreducibly social dimension of life and attends to it as morally significant, rather than as optional or accidental. Moral thinking cannot neglect the fact of our interdependence in a social world that precedes and nourishes the individualism we so highly praise.

Callahan's *Setting Limits* offers a solution to a problem we do not wish to face. The problem is scarcity and if we are to face it, we must first understand why it is distasteful to us. I have tried to locate some of that distaste in our embrace of a seductive and flattering portrait of ourselves as discrete mini-sovereigns. And I have suggested, following others, some of the sources of that portrait in the solitary certitude of Descartes and the presocial self-sufficiency of Locke. It should not be surprising that a moral sensibility nourished by these figures would find little interest in issues of resource allocation. Resource allocation, in health care or any area of endeavor, becomes a problem only after we identify with a social network, only after we see others and *our*selves as sharing common needs and a common fate. The task is one of developing and keeping in view our indelibly social condition. If we can do this, we can argue *with* Callahan on the merits of his proposals rather than deny that the problem exists, or restructure it to fit our preconceptions.

Many who have followed me thus far will likely respond that communitarian positions tend to assume consensus rather than argue toward it, and that individual liberalism persists as our best guide to resource-allocation problems. Many communitarians do seem to be possessed by a wistful nostalgia for an organic solidarity that is repressive of individual values. My position, however, is not an argument for any particular kind of community, but for the recognition of a social bond inherent in all expressions of liberal individualism. Liberal ideals are the flower of a communitarian rootage I have tried to designate by the term 'sociality'. I select this term precisely to steer clear of the current neoconservative notions of community, just as Etzioni uses the term "open community" to denote a synthesis which eschews the customary divisions between conservative and liberal philosophies. Liberal philosophers who attempt to reconstruct the foundations of social life in moral atomism have simply substituted a grandiose and fictional way of thinking for the more humble and accurate one.

Recognizing social roots does not, of course, give us a consensus on how to allocate scarce medical resources. But it does provide a different way to think, a different place to stand to see the problem. It helps us to see health care as a series of interrelated institutions, services, and needs, and not merely as the aggregate sum of individual choices and enlightened, self-interested actions. It also should go a long way to highlight things that we have in common and to de-emphasize principles of allocation based on things that distinguish and separate us—meritorious health behaviors, social worth, religious beliefs, race, the ability to pay for care, political influence, good looks, place of residence, age, the dread factor in one's disease, and so on.

Things which we have in common are a need for services; vulnerability to disease, disability, and death; a human condition of finitude; and an inability to accurately predict the time or extent of our health-care needs. While a consensus about how to allocate is not a given, the orientation point is. It need not be invented or chosen, but is provided in our common human finitude. Sociality is simply a term to help make that orientation point more visible.

NOTES

1. I have argued against these and other denials, dodges, and "solutions" in *Rationing Health Care in America: Perceptions and Principles of Justice* (Notre Dame, IN: University of Notre Dame Press, 1987), pp. 5–19.

2. Jeffrey Stout, *Ethics After Babel: The Languages of Morals and Their Discontents* (Boston: Beacon Press, 1988), pp. 243 ff.

3. Amitai Etzioni, "The Responsive Community (I and We)," *American Sociologist* 18 (Summer 1987): 146.

4. Cf. *Rationing Health Care in America: Perceptions and Principles of Justice*, pp. 43–58.

5. Charles Taylor, *Philosophical Papers*, Vol. 1, "Introduction" (Cambridge: Cambridge University Press, 1985), pp. 5–8.

6. René Descartes, *The Philosophical Works of Descartes*, Vol. 1, trans. Elizabeth S. Haldane and G. R. T. Ross (Cambridge: Cambridge University Press, 1970), p. 101.

7. Maurice Merleau-Ponty, *Phenomenology of Perception*, trans. Colin Smith (London: Routledge & Kegan Paul, 1962), p. 362.

8. Ibid.

THE LIMITS OF MEDICINE

....

STANLEY HAUERWAS

STANLEY HAUERWAS is Professor of Christian Ethics, the Divinity School, Duke University.

DEATH IN A LIBERAL SOCIETY

When I speak before lay audiences—that is, before people who are not directly involved with medicine—I ask them how they want to die. I do so because I think no question better illumines how our attitudes shape the form of medical care we receive. The presumption of many, a presumption I might add made by many in medicine, since it underwrites their own self-interest, is that medicine is basically a scientifically neutral set of skills at which all well-trained physicians are equally adept. Medicine is seen as a set of means, admittedly a very powerful set of means, that are in themselves value-neutral. The only moral questions occur concerning the use or misuse of those skills. Moral questions about medicine are about what ends these skills should serve.

When we consider how we want to die, we begin to appreciate how this view of medicine and the moral questions surrounding medicine are far too simple. Medicine reflects who we are, what we want, and what we fear. For example,

120

without fail when I ask people how they want to die, I am always told, "painlessly," "quickly," "in my sleep," and "without causing great trouble to those close to me." Such desires seem straightforward and rational. They are what any of us would want if we were to think about it—namely, we rightly want to die without knowing what is happening to us, without enduring great pain, and without being a "burden" to others.

Nonetheless, this understanding of death at other times and places would have been considered irrational if not immoral. For example, the medieval people most feared a sudden death, a death which did not allow them to prepare properly. Elaine Tierney notes that in the thirteenth century

> popular preaching instructed parishioners to remember death. Gottfried writes that "preachers advised people to go to sleep every night as if it was their last and as if their beds were their tombs." Thomas à Kempis wrote of death: "He who is dead to the world, is not in the world, but in God, into whom he lives, comfortable, and your life is hid with Christ in God." The preparation for death was important. To die without having confessed one's sins would submit one to eternal damnation. So the emphasis was upon death and from this developed the concept of dying well and the guides that described the "art of dying."[1]

The medieval world preferred those illnesses that gave one a lingering death or at least time to prepare for one's death. It is interesting to speculate whether cancer would have posed the same threat to that world that it does to ours, for our desire to "cure" cancer cannot be accounted for solely on grounds of the numbers that actually get cancer, but because cancer challenges our very conceptions of how we would like to die. Our understanding of violent death reflects similar attitudes. The medieval person could look forward to dying in war, since there was time prior to battle to prepare for

121

their potential death. We prefer to die in unanticipated automobile accidents.

Our medicine, moreover, reflects our way of death. There are few things as a society on which we agree, but almost everyone agrees that death is a very unfortunate aspect of the human condition which we avoid at all costs. We have no common sense of a good death; death threatens us, since it represents our absolute loneliness. Michael Ignatieff observes

> as secular people we may claim that ultimate questions about the ends of human life are unanswerable in principle and therefore are no business of ours, but each one of us has our hour of need. However blind life on the spiral may be, there is one hour when it all stops. What then will we say? What then will we need? . . . We no longer share a vision of the good death. Most other cultures, including many primitive ones whom we have subjugated to our reason and our technology, enfold their members in an art of dying as in an art of living. But we have left these awesome tasks of culture to private choice. Some of us face our deaths with a rosary, some with a curse, some in company, some alone. Some die bravely, to give courage to the living, while others die with no other audience than their lonely selves. Some of us need a cosmology in which we can see the spark that is our life, and some of us go to our deaths needing nothing more than the gaze of another to console us in the hour of our departing.[2]

According to Ignatieff, we share with other people and tribes the idea that certain forms of knowledge are important to our health, "but we are the only tribe which believes that such necessary knowledge can be private knowledge—the science of the individual. We have created a new need, the need to live the examined life; we pursue its satisfaction in the full babble of conflicting opinions about what life is for, and we pursue it in a collectively held silence about the meaning of death."[3] A project since the Enlightenment has been to show that a secular market society can provide competitive individuals with sufficient reasons for cooperating and for living. What can sustain such cooperation is our willingness to enter into a compact with one another through which we agree not to raise issues about what our lives ought to be about other than our mutual desire to avoid death and, in particular, the knowledge that we will have to die. We thus conspire to hide our deaths from one another and ourselves, calling our conspiracy "respect for the individual."

LIMITS OF MEDICINE: CALLAHAN'S CASE

Medicine cannot help but become part of this conspiracy, as now the task of medicine must be to keep us alive as long as possible, so that when we must die, we do not have to deal with the knowledge that we are in fact dying. Because cure, not care, becomes medicine's purpose, the physician becomes a warrior engaged in combat with the ultimate adversary— death.[4] Of course since this is a war that cannot be won, it puts physicians in a peculiar double bind. They must do everything they can to keep us alive, as if living were an end in itself, but then we blame them when, as they must, they fail. Almost as perplexing as this is the fact that although doctors are obligated to keep us alive using every possible medical technology in order to insure that we will die "only when everything possible has been done," we complain that doctors keep us alive beyond all reason.

Our attitude toward death and the corresponding conception of medicine has created the problem of how we can ever set limits to medical care. In our society of strangers who are held together only by the presumption that any need is legitimate as long as it does not unduly inconvenience others from pursuing the satisfaction of their needs, there seems to be no limit to the needs that medicine can be asked to serve.

In such a context medicine is in danger of being used as a means to eliminate all those "evils" that we believe are arbitrary because we presume that it is our task as humans to make our existence safe from outrageous fortune.[5] What, it seems, we cannot do is set limits on this project, since any such limits themselves seem arbitrary and thus unfair.

The dilemma has, of course, been caused by medicine's redefinition of aging and death. Whereas concepts such as "old," "aging," and "premature death" were determined by social roles correlative to the goods of society, now these concepts are a "function of the state-of-the-art of medicine at any given moment" (*SL*, 56). Once this transition has taken place, it is hard to determine what relationship health demands and what expectations the elderly should have.

I have no doubt of the accuracy of Callahan's account of the change in the perspective we have about illness and health which modern medicine at once reflects and underwrites. Moreover, like him I am sure most of us remain profoundly ambivalent about that change because as we sense that we are reaching limits, of which the elderly are but the most graphic example, we do not want to sacrifice the genuine gains that have been made. Yet it is unclear how we can change our understanding of the ends we want medicine to serve without some loss. In a way modern medicine exemplifies the predicament of the Enlightenment project which hopes to make society a collection of individuals free from the bonds of necessity other than those we choose. In many ways that project has been accomplished, only we have discovered that now the very freedom we sought has become, ironically, our fate. Put in the language of theodicy, we now suffer from the means we tried to use to eliminate suffering.

I am also convinced that Callahan is right to think we need to recover a more limited and modest conception of medicine. In order to do that, however, we need a better understanding of the illnesses and other maladies that we think justify medical intervention. Without that we cannot help but allow medicine, whose rationale and form must always be in terms of service, to become an end in itself rather than a service. If medicine is to serve our needs rather than determine our needs, then we must recover a sense of how even our illnesses fit within an ongoing narrative. The crucial question concerns what such a narrative is to be so that we can learn to live with our illnesses without giving them false meaning.

Such a narrative construal of life is what I think Callahan is attempting to provide by suggesting we need to recover a sense of "a natural span of life" and/or a sense of a "tolerable death." His definition of the latter is when "(a) one's life possibilities have on the whole been accomplished; (b) one's moral obligations to those for whom one has had responsibility have been discharged; and (c) one's death will not seem to others an offense to sense or sensibility, or tempt others to despair and rage at the finitude of human existence" (*SL*, 66). His account of a tolerable death seems not only reasonable but humane.

The problem with Callahan's recommendation for a recovery of "a natural span of life" and/or a sense of "tolerable death" is such concepts remain far too formal. What does it mean to have "one's life possibilities" accomplished? I should like to live long enough to have read all of Trollope's novels at least twice—but even if I accomplished that, I suspect I would want a try at three times. Moreover, when are our responsibilities to others ever fully discharged? The elderly can never cease to carry the wisdom of their culture and lives as a benefit to the young. Finally, the crucial issue is not whether our death seems to others offensive, but what expectations others ought to have about their own and others' deaths that make death, perhaps even untimely death, an event to be accepted with sorrow but still accepted.

One has the sense that Callahan is putting forth proposals for "a natural span of life" and "tolerable death" in the hope of beginning a conversation necessary to fill in their content.

But as his own analysis suggests, there is little reason to believe this possible in a society like our own, for our individualism tends to undermine the kind of commitments so necessary for a society to comprehend our deaths within an ongoing narrative.

My use of the language of narrative is not simply another conceptual alternative to Callahan's "natural span of life," but rather an attempt to elicit a different set of social and political presumptions. In particular it is an attempt to remind us that there is no "solution" to the problem of "setting limits" to medicine as long as the primary assumptions of liberalism are accepted—assumptions that Callahan, I think, continues to accept—for appeals to "natural span of life" or "tolerable death" underwrite the liberal political presumptions that our lives are ours to do with what we will within our "natural" limits. In contrast, the recognition that our lives are narratively determined is a reminder that insofar as we live well we more nearly discover than create our lives.

Of course, little hangs on whether "narrative," "natural span of life," or "tolerable death" as concepts best help us comprehend our deaths as part of our lives. What is crucial is the content of the narrative is such that the social practices are sustained necessary for us to be able to make our deaths part of our life projects. The appeal to narrative at least has the advantage of reminding us that our lives, and our deaths, are not occasional bits of unconnected behavior, but a pattern that gives purpose to our lives. When such a pattern is thought missing, death and illness cannot help but seem pointless and thus have no meaning. As a result, illness and death can be seen only as something to deny.

STORIES OF SICKNESS AND DEATH

In his recent book, *Stories of Sickness*, Howard Brody has begun to explore the relationship between sickness and narrative.[6] Brody notes that "suffering is produced, and alleviated by the meaning one attaches to one's experience. The primary human mechanism for attaching meaning to particular experiences is to tell stories about them. Stories serve to relate individual experiences to the explanatory constructs of the society and culture and also to place the experiences within the context of a particular individual's history" (Brody, 5). To be able to label an experience, for example an act of cowardice, is to place the experience within a set of practices as well as to see how the experience fits in the character of the upbringing and ongoing life of the one having the experience.

Brody argues that medicine is constantly engaged in this kind of placement of an experience by providing the patient with descriptions that turn the illness experience into a positive direction—thus the ubiquitous placebo effect in medicine. Brody distinguishes three closely related components of the placebo effect:

> The illness experience must be given an explanation of the sort that will be viewed as acceptable, given the patient's existing belief system and worldview. Second, the patient must perceive that he or she is surrounded by and may rely on a group of caring individuals. Third, the patient must achieve a sense of mastery or control over the illness experience, either by feeling personally powerful enough to affect the course of events for the better or by feeling that his or her individual powerlessness can be compensated for by the power of some member or members of the caring group (such as the physican).
> [Brody, 6]

Brody notes that these factors can have a negative as well as a positive side—for instance, when an individual's death is predicted in a fashion that leads to the withdrawal of family and close friends and the subsequent death.

In contrast, the reassuring story that is commonly told by the physician to account for the illness experience ("It looks like you've picked up that virus that is running around town—you're the sixth person I've seen today with exactly the same symptoms"), coupled with the caring and solicitous attitude of physicians and the reassuring rituals that promise control of events ("Take two aspirin four times a day, gargle with warm salt water every hour, and stay in bed till the fever goes away"), may well effect a speedier recovery than could be accounted for either by the usual spontaneous remission rate of the illness or by the purely pharmacological efficacy of the remedies administered. [Brody, 7]

Brody is reminding us that, as Paul Ramsey emphasized years ago, the subject of the physician's art is the patient.[7] The physician's task is not to cure disease in the abstract, as there are no diseases in the abstract, but to cure only Mr. Jones with this gall bladder and Mrs. Smith with this cancer of the jaw. As Ramsey put it, "Men's capacity to become joint adventurers in a common cause makes possible a consent to enter the relation of patient to physician or of subject to investigator. This means that *partnership* is a better term than *contract* in conceptualizing the relation between patient and physician or between subject and investigator" (Ramsey, 6). Thus we can understand Ramsey's insistence that medicine is morally formed by the physician's commitment to the overriding good of each patient in a manner in which that good can never be qualified by goods for society and/or future generations exactly because such "a" good is the good of us all.

Ramsey was well aware, of course, that to say this is but to begin the process, particularly in matters dealing with death and dying. For example, Ramsey asked

if in the case of terminal patients the quality of life they can expect enters into the determination of whether even ordinary or customary measures would be beneficial and should or should not be used, cannot the same be said of infants? It is not obvious that an anencephalic baby should be respirated while a grown man in prolonged coma should no longer be helped to breathe. In the first of life, a human being may be seized by his own unique dying. Indeed far from taking the death of the aged and the enormous death rate of zygotes and miscarriages to be part of the problem of evil, a religious man is likely to take this as a sign that the Lord of life has beset us behind and before in this dying life we are called to live and celebrate. There is an acceptable death of the life of all flesh no less in the first than in the last of it. An ethical man may always gird himself to oppose his enemy, but not the religious ethical man. [Ramsey, 132]

Ramsey notes further that when we are confronted by the death of a loved one, we find ourselves guilty of many a sin of commission as well as omission. Out of guilt members of the family require everything possible be done for he or she who is hopelessly ill or dying. At the same time, guilt-ridden people, in their grief, may be unable to bear the burden of the decision to discontinue useless treatment. In such situations Ramsey suggests "the physician must exercise the authority he has acquired as a physician and as a man in relation to the relatives and take the lead in suggesting what should be done. In doing this, the doctor acts more as a man than as a medical expert, acknowledging the preeminence of the human relations in which he with these and all other men stand. For this reason, the medical imperative and the moral imperative or permission are, while distinguishable, not separable in the person or in the vocation of the man who is a physician" (Ramsey, 143).

There is no doubt that Ramsey's emphasis on the "patient as person" as the central moral presumption of medicine is right. However, we need to know more about what constitutes our "personhood" if we are to understand the nature of medicine as well as how medicine is to be of service to patients, for in Ramsey's account of the matter there is a hint that medicine itself is a battery of technological "fixes" that are to be applied relative to individual patient's good. Such an account, an account I might say that is a good deal more nuanced in Ramsey's actual analysis of cases, betrays the complexities of the process of clinical medicine and judgment noted by Brody.

For example, Brody contrasts science with medicine by noting that science aims

> at the discovery of truth, and it succeeds precisely when it discovers a truth, regardless of whether that truth aids any other practical human endeavor outside of science itself. . . . Medicine, in contrast, seeks jointly the expansion of knowledge and the use of that knowledge to cure individual patients; but the first aim is in the service of the second, and it is only with actual cure that medicine considers itself to have accomplished its criteria for success. [Brody, 32]

Therefore the person that is the patient in interaction with the physician is not some generalized "person" but one that comes with a narrative which makes the patient aware that the very generalized knowledge the physician commands may, if applied, hurt her. "Indeed, modern medical practice, by focusing so exclusively on bodily pain and ignoring multiple aspects of personhood and personal meaning, may inadvertently increase suffering while seeking to relieve it" (Brody, 30). Yet I think our situation is more complex than Brody's account suggests.

THE PRACTICE OF MEDICINE AND THE LOSS OF NARRATIVE

In his article "Narrative Unity and Clinical Judgment," Thomas Long seems to offer an account very similar to Brody's.[8] Yet he comes to quite a different conclusion. Drawing on Alasdair MacIntyre's account of practice—that is, a cooperative activity that has standards of excellence in the pursuit of which "goods internal" to the practice are realized and human powers to achieve excellence are extended—he suggests that medicine might be considered such a practice concerned with a patient's well-being. Yet he goes on to argue that the goal of medicine cannot be "well-being" in the same way that the goal of painting can be a good painting. To understand why this is the case will also help us understand why we have so much difficulty finding the appropriate limits for medical care.

For MacIntyre, Long notes, our lives are not mere chronicity—that is, we are not the kind of beings to which just one damn thing after another happens and for whom there is no unity that can be discovered between those happenings. In contrast, our lives, according to MacIntyre, have narrative unity that can be embodied in a single life. "To ask What is good for me? is to ask how best I might live out that unity and bring it to completion. . . . Elsewhere he (MacIntyre) characterizes the unitary life as 'a life that can be conceived and evaluated as a whole'; he speaks of 'the unity of a narrative which links birth to life to death as a narrative beginning to middle to end.' " (Long, 79).

Interestingly, a life experienced as a narrative unit is one where the events of one's life are not experienced or remembered as foreign. A kind of fatalism in which one's life is seen as fundamentally out of control, in which we are victims of time, is rendered impotent by a narrative construal, since one is able to integrate one's misfortunes into an ongoing framework.

The terminal disease, the loss of a loved one, a financial loss—all such events, while coming from outside *qua events,* are given significance from within a framework of meaning already

131

in place. . . . To seek a patient's well-being . . . is to presuppose some framework of meaning already in place. Lowering an elderly patient's temperature or controlling his urinary tract infection is not necessarily a contribution to his well-being. The patient may feel better physically, yet be even more unhappy than before his hospital admission. The clinician who seeks the patient's well-being is necessarily constrained by the narrative unity into which he or she has entered. When physicians fail to perceive such unity in their patients' lives (assuming it is present), then clinical medicine, however scientifically well-founded its judgments may be, can enhance patient well-being, only by accident. [Long, 80]

Long notes that for MacIntyre, it is exactly the notion of life as a narrative unity that modernity undercuts and in the process renders the very notion of "sound clinical judgment" problematic, for we are unable to answer the question, "What would be better (or worse) for this patient?" because any answer to that question "presupposes an ability to identify a real narrative unity constitutive of the patient's life" (Long, 82). In order to have a sense of narrative unity a special kind of unity is required. Thus MacIntyre notes,

How we treat the aging and the dying and how we ourselves behave as we age and then die will depend in crucial part on what framework of beliefs we possess which enables us to identify aging and dying as particular kinds of social or cosmic events, possessing particular kinds of significance or insignificance. Spinoza's "The free man thinks nothing less than of dying" cannot be understood except in terms of the whole argument of the *Ethics:* the Catholic Christian who places a skull on his mantelpiece presupposes a quite different set of metaphysical beliefs; and the lady with the blue rinse in Florida who behaves as if she were twenty, but who knows all too well that she is seventy-five, is as frenetic as she is because she does not know what kind of experience she is undergoing.[9]

Long suggests (following MacIntyre) that in our society we are all a bit like the little old lady with blue hair.

> Just as these hapless creatures "do" things which are unintelligible to them, so this woman "has" experiences which make no sense to her. She has lost a framework, a feeling for a unity in her life, if she ever had it. Her behavior, dress, and physical appearance all shout self-deception. She is a casualty of 'modernity'. For a person like this there can be no sound clinical medicine, though scientific medicine may be able to make correct judgments about the proper treatment of any disease she develops. But this latter type of judgment is directed to the disease as simply an instance of a kind, not to the disease as present in *this person*. Only when the process of clinical judgment is personalized, that is, when well-being is the issue, will the process itself be complete. In the case of the woman in Florida this process inevitably will be aborted at the purely technical stage. This means that even if medicine succeeds in curing her disease, this will be simply another event in a life so disordered that she is unable to accept the past as past. . . .
> [Long, 83]

Of course, it may be objected that the suggestion that this woman is a typical representative of our society is quite unfair. Yet her representative character can be felt if we juxtapose her position with another quote from MacIntyre about our death. He says,

> If I have work to do in the world, the time will come when it is done; and when that time comes it is right to die. . . . Each of us is permitted to occupy a certain space in time, a certain role in history; without that particular place and role our lives would be without significance. To recognize that it is our particularity and finitude that gives our lives significance can save us from being consumed by that terrible destructive desire to remain young that preys on so many Americans. [Long, 84]

133

As Long points out, this passage has important implications not only for patients but also for those who practice medicine. Physicians, just like women with blue hair or elderly men who wear girdles, have their way of denying death. Aggressive medicine can result from familial pressures, but it can also be the result of our society's inability to place death in a morally intelligible narrative. In a society such as ours, however, the dangers of practicing such aggressive medicine go beyond the normal fear of finitude. Now the very inertia medicine has initiated through its technology cannot help but reinforce our society's presumption that our lives are fundamentally constituted by chronicity rather than narrative. In such a world our medical technologies have outrun the spiritual resources of a society that lacks all sense of an ending. That is, of course, exactly the problem that Callahan has rightly diagnosed. His solution, however, may be an attempt to cure the disease by the very disease itself.[10]

Long, however, seems to side with Callahan in this respect, for Long thinks MacIntyre's little lady with blue hair and her implications for our society is exaggerated. Such people certainly exist, but they are not typical of our society. In fact, gerontologists have found that the older people become, the less fearful they are of dying. In fact, some gerontologists see the aging process as one when people attempt to develop a view of their life that makes a type of sense which allows them to attain some control over their dying, if not death itself. Such a history is not a *discovered* narrative in MacIntyre's sense, but what Long calls a "fictionalized history"— that is, a narrative that is the result of "selective attention, emphasis, dim remembrance, and possibly even forgetting. The person makes choices about the importance of persons and events, decides on their meanings, though there may be only a minimal awareness of the resulting order as a partially created one. . . . The finished product is the 'fictionalized' history of a life, neither a lie nor 'the truth,' but instead a work of imagination, evaluation, and memory" (Long, 87).

Long fears, however, that even when people achieve such a narrative unity in our society—that is, when we sense our life has been properly completed so our death would not be untimely—we cannot avoid coming into conflict with clinical medicine. Patient and physician become strangers to one another when the latter will not accept death even though the former sees it as the completion of his story. Long suggests we should not be surprised by this conflict, since the heavy stress in clinical medicine on combating disease leaves physicians uncomprehending of a narrative approach to life. Physicians have been taught, after all, to delay endings, not to help patients to integrate their illnesses into an ongoing way of life.

Yet Long thinks it too much to ask that medicine aid our development as agents, for as MacIntyre has argued, our ability to have our lives achieve a narrative unity is dependent on our ability to comprehend our death. This usually occurs in our society, if at all, only very late in life. If the patient has not begun to think in a narrative fashion, we can hardly demand that physicians give us "plots."

Therefore, according to Long, medicine should stick to what it does best—namely, ridding us or alleviating those ills which respond to biochemical or mechanical manipulation. The aim of medicine cannot be the well-being of patients when such well-being presupposes a sense of the narrative unity that neither the patient nor the physician may have. Ironically, medical treatment, since it must be restricted to the mechanical, may undermine a patient's ability to maintain the narrative sense of life exactly because we drive him to distraction by procedures that only prolong his dying. Physicians cannot supply what is lacking if a patient does not know who she is. The physician may be able to help patients cope with their pain, but if the patient lacks a substantive narrative, the physician cannot provide a meaning for uncontrollable pain. We thus begin to understand why, given the absence of a shared narrative, we are condemned to live out only narratives we believe to be fiction because we know we are their arbitrary authors. As a result, we have no way to set limits to the care we would give one another through medicine.

A gloomy conclusion. But I believe our situation is still more difficult when we consider the death of children. For Brody and Long, who rightly remind us of how illness fits into our ongoing narratives, still think, with Nietzsche, that such narratives are our own creations. As a result, since young children have not had the opportunity to "create" such a narrative, we abandon them to the institutional means we have of giving them to gain time to acquire a narrative—i.e., medicine. There is no alternative as long as we do not believe that we are all, adults and children alike, born into a narrative not of our own making. I take it that such a narrative is what Christians in the past have claimed to discover about their lives and why attention to that narrative may at least help us understand our current inability to deal with issues raised by Callahan.

NOTES

1. Elaine Tierney, "Death and Dying in the Renaissance: An Analysis of Northern European Hospital Paintings," unpublished paper presented at the 1987 meeting of the Society for Religion and Medicine in New Orleans.

2. Michael Ignatieff, *The Needs of Strangers* (New York: Viking Penguin, 1985), pp. 76–77.

3. Ibid., pp. 78–79.

4. For an illuminating analysis of the limits as well as the possibilities of this image of the physician, see William May, *The*

Physician's Covenant: Images of the Healer in Medical Ethics (Philadelphia: Westminster Press, 1983), pp. 63–86.

5. For a further development of this point see my article "God, Medicine, and the Problems of Evil," *Reformed Journal* 38 (April 1988): 16–22.

6. Howard Brody, *Stories of Sickness* (New Haven: Yale University Press, 1987). All further references will appear in the text. For a similar perspective see Arthur Kleinman, *The Illness Narratives: Suffering, Healing, and the Human Condition* (New York: Basic Books, 1988). Kleinman notes "one of the core tasks in the effective clinical care of the chronically ill—one whose value it is all too easy to underrate—is to affirm the patient's experience of illness as constituted by lay explanatory models and to negotiate, using the specific terms of those models, an acceptable therapeutic approach. Another core clinical task is the empathetic interpretation of a life story that makes over the illness into the subject matter of biography. Here the clinician listens to the sick individual's personal myth, a story that gives shape to an illness so as to distance an otherwise fearsome reality" (p. 49). Kleinman's perspective is in many ways extremely sensitive and no doubt he is right about the therapeutic process. However, his argument is not philosophically rigorous, as he seems to think the physician's understanding of "disease" can be distinguished from the patient's understanding of his or her "illness." The latter is narrative dependent in a way the former is not. Yet that clearly cannot be the case. For an argument that the typological characterization of diseases is equally narrative dependent, see Per Sundstrom, *Icons of Disease: A Philosophical Inquiry into the Semantics, Phenomenology and Ontology of the Clinical Conceptions of Disease* (Linkoping University: Department of Health and Society, 1987). Sundstrom observes, "In clinical medicine at least our mode of oral production of works of discourse is very much alive, namely, the narration of patient-disease histories. All material differences between patients' narratives notwithstanding, there are common formal genre rules that are more or less diligently adhered to. There is always a

story, a succession of events which gain their real significance only as inserted in the whole of the story; the story typically proceeds up till now, till the present encounter with the physician, which marks a new phase in the story; this up-till-now character is there irrespective of whether the story is an exciting one, or just gloomy, or seemingly trivial, etc. The oral 'historical' work plays a considerable role in generation of the integral clinical conceptions of disease, and not only in their generations but in their very constitution. Narratives are inscribed in textbooks, though not in the unaltered genre form of oral history narratives. The didactic forms, the integration of relevant information from the laboratory sciences, the interest in somehow managing the patient professionally, etc., all these features emanating from the exigencies of the clinical encounter make for a transformation of the genre rules of patient narratives. Some features of patients' narratives are highlighted while others may be more or less ignored because considerations other than 'history' are deemed of greater significance for the managment of the patient" (p. 178).

7. Paul Ramsey, *The Patient as Person: Explorations in Medical Ethics* (New Haven: Yale University Press, 1970). All references in text.

8. Thomas A. Long, "Narrative Unity and Clinical Judgment," *Theoretical Medicine* 7 (February 1986): 75–92. All references in text.

9. Alasdair MacIntyre, "Patients as Agents," in *Philosophical Medical Ethics: Its Nature and Significance,* ed. Stuart F. Spicker and H. Tristram Engelhardt, Jr. (Boston: D. Reidel Publishing Company, 1977), p. 210.

10. For a fascinating account of the relation between our society's attitudes toward death and the presuppositions of liberal political theory, see Alfred J. Killilea, *The Politics of Being Mortal* (Lexington: University of Kentucky Press, 1988). It may be unfair to ask Callahan to deal with issues in political theory in a book about medicine, but it is the burden of my case to show how the fear of death is at the heart of the liberal democratic project. From Hobbes to the present, liberalism has

been that theory of society that has presupposed that the only thing people have in common is their fear of death even though they share no common understanding of death. Liberalism is based on the presumption that we must each die alone. That fear is the only thing we have in common and thus the only basis for cooperation. Medicine cannot help but become subject to the fear as we try to use medicine to prevent our single deaths. That project results in medicine becoming an end in itself rather than serving more determinative ways of life. For an extremely thoughtful essay that deals with these matters, see Harmon Smith, "Dying with Style," *Anglican Theological Review* 70 (1989): 327–45. As Smith observes, "If an important aspect of dying well means dying remembered, then there is a diminished chance for dying well when one's dying is insulated and privatized." (p. 343).

HEALTH-CARE ENTITLEMENTS AND THE ELDERLY: A LIBERAL CRITIQUE OF *SETTING LIMITS*

....

DAN W. BROCK

DAN W. BROCK is Professor of Philosophy, Brown University, Providence, Rhode Island.

THE NEED to control relentlessly escalating health-care costs has been a dominant theme in both public and policy-making discussions of health care in recent years. One widely perceived and hotly debated issue in these discussions has been the economic impact of the "graying" of America—recent and anticipated increases in life expectancy and in the proportion of the population over age sixty-five, and especially the even more rapid increase in the "old-old" population (those over eighty-five). The debate over health-care and other social-support programs serving the elderly is forcing a rethinking of questions of intergenerational justice and the claims of the elderly on social resources.

Daniel Callahan's *Setting Limits* addresses these issues. His argument appeals to a communitarian political philosophy and concludes that some direct appeals to age in determining these claims can be ethically unobjectionable. I shall argue that his communitarian argument fails and that individualist liberalism remains our best guide to the age-group problem.

Nevertheless, I will argue that what is most interesting and plausible in his view is compatible with liberalism and that remembering this part of his central thesis will yield a richer and deeper public debate about health care for the elderly than liberalism alone provides us.

WEAK VERSUS STRONG AGE-RATIONING

Probably the most controversial issue of health policy for Callahan's view is life-sustaining treatment. His notion of a "tolerable death" and his view of the place of aging in a complete life could be used as part of an argument to show why what I will call *weak age-rationing*—giving greater weight to the claims on social resources for treatment needed to sustain life up to, as opposed to beyond, the normal life span—need not always be unjust. We plan our lives and what will fill them based on expectations of what is roughly a normal life span in our society. Because we commonly try to give our lives continuity and coherence, as biographical lives lived by us from the "inside," the loss of life years needed to reach a normal life span and "complete the biography" is commonly a significantly greater loss than the loss of a comparable number of life years needed to live beyond the normal life span. Certainly, one ethically relevant consideration, even if not the only one, in distributing scarce life-sustaining health-care resources is to produce the most good possible with those limited resources. And if we simply look to the good we can do for persons whose lives are extended by life-sustaining medical care or by other health policies, we can often do substantially more good by preventing deaths before instead of after the normal life span has been reached.[1]

While Callahan might support weak age-rationing in this

141

way, in fact he does not. Instead, he defends a much more controversial position, which I shall call *strong age-rationing*—the elderly should have *no* entitlement to social resources for the provision of life-extending care once they have reached a normal life span, that is, the late seventies or early eighties. (Callahan explicitly does not support what can be called *very strong age-rationing,* which would prohibit persons even from using their own resources to purchase such care. He explicitly allows for private markets in this care, but notes the moral and political difficulties facing such a two-class system.)

Callahan's support of strong age-rationing is a part of what he takes to follow for health policy from his transformed view of aging and old age. In the broadest terms, he argues that the suitable goal for medicine is to assist all to achieve a natural life span and beyond that only the relief of suffering. Government would have no obligation to help people extend their lives medically beyond the natural life span. At the same time, Callahan argues for substantial expansion in the provision of long-term care and support services for the elderly. Thus, it is a mistake to view this change in perspective as merely a thin guise for cutting spending on the elderly—while it would support cuts in some areas, it would require major new commitments of resources in other areas.

Callahan in fact displays considerable ambivalence about the relation of scarcity, and an increased awareness of scarcity, to his proposal. On the one hand, he notes the familiar data on the expanding numbers and proportion of the elderly in society, as well as their disproportionate and rapidly growing use of health-care resources, and comments more than once that we cannot continue to pour resources into extending life and postponing death (*SL,* 21, 137; Appendix). On the other hand, he also repeatedly notes that his motivation is *not* simply to reduce health-care expenditures, but instead to

142

provide a revised view of aging and old age that will be a benefit to and improve the lives of the elderly as much as the young (*SL*, 53, 116).[2] Callahan spells out how this revised view of aging and old age can guide the establishment of priorities in public policy toward the elderly. Moreover, he explicitly adds that it would be unjust to restrict provision of care to the elderly merely in order to save money and in the absence of this change in view of aging and the elderly (*SL*, 153).

Much of the reorientation is well-taken, but most controversial is Callahan's support of strong age-rationing, which would leave the elderly with no entitlement to social resources for the provision of life-extending care once they have reached a normal life span. Precisely how is this strong age-rationing of life-extending treatment beyond the normal life span to be justified? I believe Callahan's answer rests with his dissatisfaction with pluralistic liberalism. Against that liberalism he insists that it is necessary to reach a *social* consensus on the meaning and ends of aging and old age, a consensus on a *single* view of their meaning and ends (*SL*, 220). He insists on this because he believes that we require a social policy concerning health care for the elderly, and that such a policy to be legitimate must be based on and express a social consensus. If a "consensus" is understood strictly as meaning that essentially *all* members of society share the view, and these members arrive at and accept the consensus freely, it would then not be necessary to impose the policy of not providing life-extending care to persons beyond the normal life span on anyone who does not accept that policy, even if weakness of will may lead some to seek such care when they come to need it. If all freely and knowingly accept the policy, then it is unnecessary or superfluous to provide any further argument that justice requires it. But is there any reason to expect such a strong consensus to come about in this country? I think the answer must clearly be no.

People now find meaning in their later years in many different ways and pursue a host of different ends in those years. Moreover, that seems inevitable in a large and diverse country that celebrates pluralism and gives such high value to individual liberty. Since a strong consensus on the meaning and ends of aging and old age would likely require deep and pervasive social transformations, including deep restrictions on highly valued liberties and on individual self-determination in shaping one's own conception of the good, we have good reason to resist steps for achieving such a consensus in the United States. Yet, lacking this consensus, we need a justification for denying social entitlements to life-extending care beyond the natural life span for those who reject the consensus and want that care. Since Callahan's only justification seems to suppose this missing consensus, does that mean we must systematically reject his position? I think not.

In this debate about health care and the elderly, Callahan's book forces a confrontation with the extremely important questions that *individuals* must face about how they will find meaning in old age and what ends will guide that stage of their lives. Many will no doubt reject the answers that he offers to these questions. But many others will find, as to a considerable extent I do, his criticisms of the modernizing view important and the alternative ideal of aging and old age that he offers deeply attractive. That his answers to these questions will achieve no full consensus does not detract from the importance of the questions or the answers. In fact, I believe it is here that his book's greatest strength and importance lies. Nevertheless, the absence of any strong social consensus along these lines undermines Callahan's appeals to a communitarian basis for at least the restrictive aspects of his policy proposals. In seeking a basis for public policy in a

144

pluralistic society like ours that lacks, and will continue to lack, any strong social consensus on the proper meaning and ends of aging and old age, I believe we must turn to the liberalism which Callahan rejects. Specifically, it is to liberalism that we must turn in thinking about just distributions of resources between different age groups.

A FIRST LIBERAL ARGUMENT—FAIR EQUALITY OF OPPORTUNITY

I want to note two possible lines of argument available to traditional liberal political philosophy for addressing the age-group problem—what ethical claims the elderly, as opposed to other age groups, have on social resources for the provision of health care—though neither can be explored in any detail here. Common to most versions of liberal political philosophy, and specifically to liberal theories of justice, is some principle of what Rawls has called fair equality of opportunity.[3] The distinction between a premature and what Callahan calls a "tolerable death" suggests that an argument based on a moral principle of fair equality of opportunity could directly support assuring the life years necessary to live out a normal life, at least where doing so is technologically and socially possible. This opportunity-based moral claim would not be absolute, in the sense of being unlimited no matter what the cost of meeting it, since equality of opportunity is only one moral principle or consideration among others in liberal theories of justice. Just as liberals accept that there are limits on what we should spend on education of the severely disadvantaged to try to equalize their opportunity, so there are limits on what we should spend on life-extending health care to try to ensure that people live out a normal life span. Norman Daniels has used the notion of fair equality of opportunity to develop a general theory of just health care.[4] My suggestion is that it can also be used to differentiate morally the claims to life-extending health care up to, as opposed to beyond, the normal life span. Such an argument, if more fully developed by detailing the notion of fair equality of opportunity to which it appeals, could support weak age-rationing, but would not support the strong age-rationing that Callahan defends.

A SECOND LIBERAL ARGUMENT— PRUDENTIAL LIFE SPAN REASONING

Norman Daniels has extended his earlier theory of just health care to the age-group problem.[5] His argument exploits the central fact that in the course of our lives we can expect to pass through each stage or age period of a normal life span. As a result, the much-discussed competition for resources between young and old is misleading in suggesting a conflict between different groups of persons. Instead, it is possible to frame the question of distribution of resources between different age groups as a problem of prudential reasoning for a single individual about how to distribute resources over the different stages of his or her own life. Daniels calls this the prudential life span account. Institutions such as social security and health-care insurance plans take more resources from workers in their middle, productive years than are returned to them then in benefits, but in turn provide more in benefits during retirement years than are then taken in taxes or premiums. Instead of thinking of these as interpersonal group transfers, they can be regarded as *intra*personal savings plans for persons as they pass through these institutions over the course of a lifetime.[6] At any particular stage of life all persons will be treated the same, though different birth cohorts will reach a particular stage of life at different times.

The prudential life span treatment of the age-group problem presupposes that we have both a general theory of distributive justice and a theory of just health care, which together de-

146

termine what is a fair lifetime share of health care for members of a particular society at a particular time. Prudential planning for health-care needs will then require an individual to choose a particular set of institutions that will distribute health care to her as she lives her life and passes through these institutions. Prudence requires neutrality toward all the stages of one's life, and not biasing the choice of institutions to favor one's present stage. Daniels argues that we can obtain the neutrality that prudence requires toward our different life stages by seeking to provide ourselves with a roughly equal opportunity at each life stage to revise and carry out our plans of life, whatever they turn out to be. Prudential planners can achieve this end by securing for themselves a bundle of Rawlsian primary goods that will provide them with a fair share of the normal opportunity range for their society at each stage of life.[7] In then planning for health care at different life stages, it will be rational for them to take account of the general prevalence of different diseases at different stages of life, of the effects of those diseases on the range of normal opportunity at particular stages of life, and of the possibilities and costs of treating those diseases.

Given these differences, prudential planners will provide for significantly different kinds and amounts of health care at different stages of life. Because their lifetime fair share of health care will not provide all possible beneficial care for all their health-care needs, without regard to cost, all of these age-related differences will affect how they allocate between different life stages in these conditions of moderate scarcity. It is important to be clear that the prudential life span argument and reasoning just sketched is meant to be an *argument* that can guide policy, not a process of reasoning that each member of society must actually carry out. If it were the latter, the position would be unworkable in practice, but as the former it could be explained in a simplified and comprehensible form to citizens generally. Thus, both the equal-opportunity argument and the prudential life span argument can be employed to support, in some circumstances, weak but not strong age-rationing.

Daniels's prudential life span treatment of the age-group problem is squarely within broadly individualist and pluralist liberalism. Rawls and other recent defenders of liberalism, in general, emphasize that a central feature of liberalism is that it appeals to no substantive, full account of the good life. Instead, liberals view justice as establishing the terms of social cooperation within which individuals are left free to choose and pursue their own inevitably differing plans of life. Thus, liberalism makes no appeal to any consensus on the meaning and ends of aging and old age, the consensus whose absence, I have suggested, undermines Callahan's treatment of the age-group problem. However, just because liberalism appeals to no full account of the good life, it is largely silent on issues of the meaning and ends of aging. In this respect liberalism is compatible with Callahan's proposals concerning the meaning and ends of old age. His proposals offer what many persons living within social, political, and economic institutions whose age-group distributions establish fair equality of opportunity across the life span and/or meet the requirements of the prudential life span account would find an attractive and appealing view of the meaning and ends of old age for themselves and their own lives.

For carrying out this view that they have freely adopted for their old age, such persons might employ advance directives such as Living Wills and Durable Power of Attorney for Health Care should they later be unable to make medical decisions for themselves. Some of Callahan's other policy recommendations and priorities, such as better enabling the old to serve the young, might be revised so as to affect only those who have freely adopted his view of the meaning and ends of old age, though I shall not explore that possibility further here. But this is not to say that these restrictions on social entitlements to life-extending care should be imposed as a matter of public policy on persons who have not freely adopted this view of old age. For determining just age-group distributions, individualist liberal theories of justice are the more reliable guides.

BEYOND THE NORMAL LIFE SPAN

I want to say a bit more about the specific policy issue of life-extending care beyond the normal life span. This issue has understandably been the focus of a great deal of attention, though other of Callahan's proposals, like improving long-term care and home-care services for the elderly, would probably have a greater overall impact on the well-being of the elderly. Can we use prudential life span reasoning to illuminate what is wrong with Callahan's proposal to deny *any* social entitlements to life-extending care for patients beyond the normal life span? A prudential planner deciding whether to make provision or insure for life-extending care beyond the normal life span would consider at least the following: What is the relative frequency of various life-threatening conditions in persons beyond the normal life span? What is the cost of various life-extending treatments for such conditions, and what other goods would have to be generally forgone if those costs are to be borne? What is the expected length and quality of life extension from such treatments, and what is the relative importance of the typical plans and projects that could be pursued or completed during that period of life extension?

It is obvious that a complete analysis would require a great deal of information, much of which we lack in any reliable form. But it is not hard to see that a prudential planner would provide for many possible (and actual) cases of life-extending care under today's conditions of moderate scarcity. To take an extreme example, consider a very healthy and vigorous eighty-two-year-old writer who continues to be actively engaged in several writing projects, has a full and satisfying family life, pursues a number of important community activities for the benefit of others, and greatly enjoys periodic travels. She develops pneumonia that is life-threatening without treatment, but that can be relatively simple and inexpensively treated with a short hospitalization and course of antibiotics. There is every reason to believe that with prompt treatment there will be no significant long-term impact on her health and that she will be able to return quickly and without any significant deficit or disability to her previous mode of life. Given her otherwise excellent state of health, with treatment she can expect to live another decade.[8]

Can there be any doubt that a prudential planner would devote the limited resources necessary to secure care in circumstances such as these? If not, then it follows that no *general* denial of social entitlements to life-extending care for persons beyond the normal life span can be derived from liberal theories of justice that employ the prudential life span account of just age-group distribution. And while this case is admittedly extreme in the very substantial benefits promised by treatment at a minimal cost, I believe the prudential planner would provide for treatment in many more common cases with the promise of sufficient benefits at an acceptable cost.[9] Each of the factors that would determine choice varies along a broad continuum, but the closer they get to the area in which a prudent planner would likely judge the benefits of life-extending care not worth the resources it requires, the closer one also is to the cases in which actual persons able to decide about treatment or to give advance directives about their wishes would not want the treatment for themselves regardless of whether resources were available to pay for it.

Thus, at current levels of overall resource scarcity in this country, it is not clear that prudent planners with a lifetime fair share of health-care resources would exclude coverage of substantial amounts of life-extending health care beyond the normal life span. Nor does Callahan's communitarian argument for denying all life-extending health care beyond the normal life span succeed. Instead, public attention would better focus, first, on developing and utilizing means of enabling patients to maintain control over what life-sustaining treatment they receive, especially should they become unable to make decisions about their treatment, and second, on programs that improve the quality of lives of the elderly. However, while I am skeptical about cost-containment measures narrowly focused on life-sustaining treatment for the elderly, nothing in this essay should be taken to indicate opposition to other differently focused cost-containment measures. These must be evaluated on their own terms, and I believe many are ethically justified. But the shameful inadequacies in many of our social welfare programs, including those designed to ensure that all citizens have basic goods such as food and shelter, as well as health care, are results of failures of political will, not of our failure to adopt strong age-rationing of life-sustaining health care.[10]

NOTES

1. It may be objected that this claim is class biased, and true only for persons whose work is satisfying and rewarding, but not for the many whose work is largely drudgery and who may look forward to relief from it in retirement. Two points largely, though not completely, undercut the force of this objection. First, a normal life span of at least seventy-five to eighty years already includes a significant number of these retirement "golden years," including those most likely to be free of disability. Second, even for many whose work may be largely drudgery, other central and satisfying projects of their lives, such as raising their children, are completed within the normal life span.

2. In this respect, it is worth noting that Callahan was defending

the main features of his view before the current obsession with cost containment. See his "On Defining a 'Natural Death,' " *Hastings Center Report* 7 (June 1977): 32–37.

3. John Rawls, *A Theory of Justice* (Cambridge: Harvard University Press, 1971), pp. 83–89.

4. Norman Daniels, *Just Health Care* (Cambridge: Cambridge University Press, 1985).

5. Norman Daniels, *Am I My Parents' Keeper? An Essay on Justice Between the Young and the Old* (New York: Oxford University Press, 1988).

6. Ibid., pp. 42–47.

7. Ibid., p. 69. Daniels defines the general notion of "the normal opportunity range for a given society [as] the array of life plans reasonable persons in it are likely to construct for themselves." The prudential planners disaggregate this notion and employ an *age-relative* opportunity range for different life stages.

8. Callahan makes an exception to his proposal for strong age-rationing of life-extending treatment for just such a case as this—what he calls the "physically vigorous elderly person" (p. 184). But he offers no principled basis for this exception to his general view, noting only that he does "not think anyone would find it tolerable to allow the healthy person to be denied lifesaving care" (p. 184).

9. It is unclear why very high-benefit/low-cost health care is substantially different from other high-benefit/low-cost necessities of life for a healthy person, such as food. It is therefore unclear why Callahan's reasoning in support of denying to persons beyond the normal life span all entitlements to social resources for life-extending *health* care would not apply to the use of social resources for other life-extension needs, such as food, as well, though he certainly would not welcome this implication.

10. This essay originated in a discussion of both Callahan's *Setting Limits* and Daniels's *Am I My Parents' Keeper?* for a sym-

posium at the American Philosophical Association Pacific Division meetings in 1988. A revised version of that discussion appeared as a review essay of those two books in *Philosophy & Public Affairs* 18 (Summer 1989). I am grateful to Callahan, Daniels, and the editors of *Philosophy & Public Affairs* for helpful comments.

PART VI

THE MEANING OF OLD AGE: IS THERE A "NATURAL LIFE SPAN"?

Perspectives on the meaning of old age and a "natural life span" engage the next three writers.

Nancy S. Jecker's liberal critique of the "natural life span" and her unwillingness to subordinate individual rights to the community good lead her to reject any form of age-based rationing of health care. She insists that although death may be tolerable after living a "natural life span," it is not necessarily tolerable. Jecker develops a liberty-based argument centering on quality-of-life criteria and the individual's need to maintain self-esteem, which enforced limits would seriously undermine.

Peter Singer underscores the difficulties with the term "natural." He argues that our sense of completeness is dependent on our circumstances in life. Following an analysis of the question, "For whom ought our public policies be designed?" Singer concludes that we ought to take into account the interests of future generations as well as those of presently existing individuals.

In his reflections about old age and its meaning,

Charles J. Fahey takes issue with assumptions that we ought to desire a consensus about old age and the "natural life span." Fahey believes that the process of evolving a new view of old age should celebrate individual differences and the primacy of conscience while it calls upon elders to be fully participating members of their communities. To guide this evolution, he introduces the paradigm of the Third Age and argues that its uniqueness offers individuals the time to be creative, to develop their individuality and their capacity to be moral agents. In the end, he believes that self-restraint would limit requests for life-extending therapies.

The "age-group problem," a serious philosophical concern about the nature and extent of intergenerational obligations, becomes the fiercely divisive "intergenerational equity debate" when situated in today's political environment. Policy analysts will greet a carefully argued ethical explication of the age-group problem skeptically when that focus renders invisible more powerful inequities based on gender, race, and class, and when the political system erects innumerable barriers to an explicit and thoughtful transfer of resources from one generation to another. Likewise, philosophers correctly insist that policymakers must provide ethical justifications for their policy choices and clearly articulated standards by which to evaluate policies. Although the differences between these two approaches should not be overdrawn, they may help to explain why the task Callahan sets out to accomplish—to bridge these two ways of looking at the world—has been both praised as a significant contribution to today's most intractable debates and vilified as a dangerous work inimical to elders' and society's well-being.

DISENFRANCHISING THE ELDERLY FROM LIFE-EXTENDING MEDICAL CARE

NANCY S. JECKER

NANCY S. JECKER is Professor of Medical Ethics, Department of Medical History and Ethics, University of Washington School of Medicine, Seattle.

WHAT SERVES to distinguish Callahan's views from the views of others, such as Norman Daniels and Margaret Battin who also call for a policy of age rationing medical care,[1] is that Callahan attempts to support age rationing independent of social justice arguments that appeal to the fact that rationed goods are scarce. In other words, Callahan intends to persuade us that we should accept [age rationing] even on the (contrary to fact) assumption that we possess an abundant supply of life-extending medical technology and other social goods. This is no mean feat. Crucial to Callahan's argument is that a death which comes at the end of a full life should be accepted; that although death is typically an occasion for sadness, limits to life must be set. Should Callahan's argument succeed, we could then make considerable headway in debates about the design of a just health care system: agreeing upon

Nancy S. Jecker's "Disenfranchising the Elderly from Life-Extending Medical Care" excerpted from *Public Affairs Quarterly* 2(3) (July 1988). Reprinted by permission of the author and *Public Affairs Quarterly*.

a theory of distributive justice would not be a prerequisite to progress. . . .

I want to present a number of reasons for doubting the soundness of Callahan's advice. An example will help to focus my objections. Suppose X is a widow who enjoys good physical health and is mentally alert. Let us imagine that X takes tremendous pleasure in a painting hobby, in visits from great-grandchildren, and in watching afternoon television shows. Suppose further that X is eighty-two and that she depends upon Medicare and Medicaid to cover her health expenses. Now if Callahan's proposal for age rationing is implemented and if X suffers a cardiac arrest, then the fact that X has had a long life history will militate against government financing of rescue measures designed to extend X's life—e.g., cardio-pulmonary resuscitation, coronary by-pass surgery to replace clogged arteries, and various medications. It is useful to imagine as vividly as possible what abiding by Callahan's proposal would involve. Suppose X's attack begins while she is at home. X calls an ambulance because she thinks her chest pains may be warning signs of a heart attack. After arriving at a hospital emergency room, X completes forms asking about her medical history, her age, and her insurance carrier. Shortly afterwards, she experiences shortness of breath and sharp pains in her chest; she murmurs, "Don't let me die!" and then passes out. The attending physician immediately picks up her chart, sees that she is eighty-two and Medicare dependent, and decides to conform with federal policy prohibiting life-extending treatment for indigent patients who are no longer eligible for Medicare reimbursement—having lived beyond, say, age seventy-five.

Is the reasoning supporting this policy sound? I do not think it is. X is entitled to receive government-financed life-extending medical care notwithstanding the fact that she is eighty-two. A number of considerations inform this judgment: (1) X's life is good, (2) people inevitably disagree about when an individual should be allowed to die or be kept alive, and (3) X prefers to live. Let us review each of these considerations in turn.

How might Callahan try to convince us that the physician can legitimately disregard the fact that X enjoys life and could continue to do so? I take it he would begin by reminding us of the factors he deems important in geriatric health policy. To the objection that X's life at eighty-two is still good, Callahan's reply would be that what determined whether or not death is tolerable "is not that life will . . . necessarily cease to offer us opportunities to continue experiencing its earlier benefits," but instead that "we have accomplished by old age . . . the having of the opportunities themselves." In other words, "for the painter, there will be an infinite number of further possibilities, as there will be for one who enjoys investing in the stock market, understanding nature, watching scientific and other knowledge being discovered, growing a garden, observing the sunset, enjoying music, and taking walks," but "in that sense . . . death at *any* time, at age 90, or 100, or 110 will frustrate . . . further possibilities." Death following a natural life span is tolerable, because "even if we will lose such possibilities by death in old age, we will *on the whole* already have had ample time to know the pleasures of such things. That is what is most important" (*SL*, 67).

Callahan's reply misses the mark. The quality of life objection to Callahan's proposal is that whenever the lives of elderly persons are enjoyable this is a reason to make life-extending treatment available to them. This objection allows that if someone has lived a natural life span then that person's death *may* be tolerable, but it is not *necessarily* tolerable. Whether a person's death is tolerable also depends upon what quality of life that person can in the future lead. In the case of X, even though a natural life span has been reached, allowing X's death by refusing to pay for the treatment X needs is intolerable, in part because X is not decrepit or mentally

159

incompetent; her life has not lost its dignity or pleasure. Arguably, it is permissible for government to refrain from Medicare support for life-extending treatment when quality of life falls below a certain minimal level. However, a large portion of the elderly population enjoys relatively good health and experiences a relatively high quality of life. A large scale policy of denying these people Medicare support for life-extending medical treatment is intolerable if it is predicated on the idea that reaching old age signifies that people are no longer entitled to have their lives extended.

I next want to call into question an assumption that is apparent in the writing of Callahan. The assumption is that it is possible to regain something like the cultural consensus regarding ideal old age and death that existed in our predecessor cultures. I want to motivate a sober skepticism about this suggestion. One reason for doubting that a cultural agreement about ideal old age and death is realizable is that what makes death and old age good or tolerable may be inherently individual. The philosopher and geriatrician Christine Cassel has argued persuasively for such a position. Cassel maintains that there is no such thing as "the elderly patient" because "[t]he individual differences between human beings . . . grow more particular with age."[2] While this point may be overstated, it is well taken. It cautions against forming generalizations about what is good medical care for old people. It raises doubts about the possibility of reaching a consensus about what we want from geriatric medicine: "One person wants comfort and help in confronting pain and frailty and another is more interested in pride and independence than in treatment for swollen ankles." Likewise, for some elderly dying, "the fight to continue living has intrinsic meaning in itself, and should continue as long as there is breath; these people believe doctors should be helpers in that fight"; but others do not want ambulances, doctors, or hospitals to be part of the final scene.[3]

160

Even if conceptions of old age and death are not inherently individual, surely there is an enormous diversity of conceptions in contemporary American culture. Thus, even if it was possible to reach a consensus in the small city-states of ancient Greece, it may not be possible to do so in our time and place. Observations of individual differences in contemporary society lead Cassel to conclude that if the goals of medicine are, as they should be, to promote the patient's interests, then we should turn to the patient to make the decision about treatment rather than use a global criterion based on age.[4]

Callahan is apprised of the perspective Cassel urges. He distinguishes, however, between the meaning of old age and the significance of old age and judges that the latter, not the former, should be the basis of public policy. "The meaning of old age" is "the interior perception, backed up by some specifiable traditions, beliefs, concepts or ideas, that one's life is purposive and coherent in its way of relating the inner self and the outer world—and that even in the face of aging and death, it is a life which makes sense to oneself; that is, one can give a plausible, relatively satisfying account of oneself to oneself in aging and death." "The significance of old age" refers to "the social attribution of value to old age, that it has a sturdy and cherished place in the structure of society and politics, and provides a coherence among the generations that is understood to be important if not indispensable" (SL, 33). Callahan does not deny that individuals hold diverse views concerning the meaning of old age and dying. What he denies is that these differences foreclose the possibility of a social attribution of value to old age.

For the kinds of reasons Cassel notes, I remain unconvinced that there ever has been or can be a consensus about ideal old age and ideal geriatric health care. But we might put aside the question of whether it is *possible* to achieve consensus, and ask instead whether it would be *desirable* to base public policy on a consensus. The answer to *this* question puts a finger on what is most troubling about the advice of Callahan. What is most troubling is not the recommendation to *forge* a consensus, but instead the recommendation to *enforce* a consensus. It is a bad idea to restrict access to life-extending medical care and thereby deny individuals latitude in making their own health care decisions.

This brings us to a third objection, namely, the liberty objection, which stresses the importance of respecting the wishes of an autonomous agent. In the case of *X,* death is intolerable in part because *X* wants to live. Even if *X*'s preference to extend her life is somehow wrong or at odds with a cultural conception of the significance of old age and death, it would be wrong to deny *X* the right to be wrong. Assuming that *X*'s statement, "Don't let me die," reflects her true preferences, it takes a certain kind of hubristic conceit for the medical vanguard, here represented by the emergency room physician, to take matters into their own hands. Callahan does not regard the doctor's decision to thwart *X*'s wishes as hubris, so long as the doctor is acting in accordance with a social consensus about old age and dying. According to Callahan, "the needs of the aged [should be] . . . based on a general and *socially* established ideal of old age and not exclusively, as at present, on *individual* desires—even the widespread desire to live a longer life" (*SL,* 135, emphasis added).

The obvious analogue of the position to which Callahan subscribes is the position that decisions to receive or forego life-extending medical treatment should be left to individuals. Callahan dubs this alternative viewpoint "the thin theory of aging and health care." The thin theory of aging and health care holds that medicine should "serve the diversity"—i.e., encourage people to design their own conceptions of ideal old age and, where doing so does not harm others, allow them to make autonomous health care decisions in old age. But Callahan maintains that the modern tradition of liberal individualism is inferior to its predecessors. He thinks that "individualism should . . . give way to a community-based and affirmed notion of the value of the aged in society . . . [and this] requires a thick, not a thin, theory of the good" (SL, 60).

How does the liberty objection I mentioned earlier lend credence to the view that we should stick with a thin theory of old age and health care? The liberty objection holds that there are certain genuinely laudable values that only a thin theory serves or serves well. These values include among others personal integrity, self-confidence, self-respect, self-understanding, and self-esteem. That these values are related to liberty is shown by the fact that all of them presuppose that individuals possess a significant degree of freedom, both in the sense of having certain opportunities available to them and in the sense of not being prevented from acting on these opportunities. A thick theory does not serve these values well because it restricts the range of medical care options available to people and thus makes achieving certain preferences impossible.

Why, more specifically, would a thick theory of aging and health care fail to serve these values adequately? Take self-respect; self-respect includes, first, "a person's sense of his own value, his secure conviction that his conception of his good, his plan of life, is worth carrying out. And second, self-respect implies a confidence in one's ability, so far as it is within one's power, to fulfill one's intentions."[5] Self-respect in old age involves the belief that life in old age is valuable and one's plan for old age is worth carrying out, together with the conviction that one is able to execute one's plan for old age. Restricting access to life-extending treatment by incorporating age rationing into public assistance programs (such as Medicare or Medicaid) would make development or maintenance of self-respect difficult for a number of reasons. One reason is that age rationing would [result in the inability of many individuals to execute their plans for old age simply] because they will not live long enough to do so. Another reason is that many people's plans for old age include a desire to maintain autonomy and independence. But autonomy and independence are undercut by a policy that dictates what course health care will take. The general point is that age rationing would impede, rather than facilitate, the implementation of individuals' plans for old age and it would inhibit, rather than elicit, self-confidence in one's ability to carry out these plans.

The importance of having a system of geriatric medical care for the elderly poor that sustains and nourishes self-respect is that without self-respect, "nothing may seem worth doing, or if some things have value for us, we lack the will to strive for them." Persons whose self-respect is diminished "sink into apathy" and lose hope for the future.[6] If age rationing would imperil self-respect, as well as other values that presuppose liberty, this suggests rather strongly that it would not be good for old people. Regardless of whether age rationing is just or unjust, it does not promote the well-being of old people.

How might Callahan respond to the above objection?[7] One response he might give is to point out that the values associated with liberty are given shape by social norms. On this view, although liberty requires having a reasonable range of opportunities from which to choose, what constitutes a "reasonable range" is not determined in a vacuum. It is conventionally determined. Presumably, if the consensus Callahan recommends were to take hold, old people would rarely request life-extending medical treatment. When they did, their request would not be viewed as reasonable. For example, a seventy- or eighty-year-old who demands that government finance life-extending medical treatment would be regarded in the same way that we now regard a spoiled adolescent who demands that his parents buy him an extravagant automobile. Parents' refusal to do so does not qualify as an unreasonable restriction on their child's liberty. A child who thinks otherwise and complains that he is unable to carry out his plan for adolescence without a car of his own does not evoke much sympathy. The proper response to this demand is not to meet it, but to recommend to this person that he either think of ways to achieve his present plan without a car or else revise his plan so that executing it does not necessitate owning one. Similarly, an old person who expects more from government-financed medical care than most people do and so develops overly ambitious plans for her last days may need to revise her goals. If age rationing medical care puts a minority of old people in a situation of having plans they cannot execute, the answer may not be to grant them what they want but rather to encourage them to develop less ambitious plans.

This reply to the liberty objection initially appears quite compelling. Upon further consideration it is much less compelling. Granted, a thick theory of aging could *on the whole* sustain the liberty-related values mentioned above. Nonetheless, mavericks will, in no small number, persist in dissenting from any cultural consensus and so persist in the design of alternative plans. To suppose otherwise is to suppose implausibly that as a society we could persuade everyone of the cogency of a particular view, i.e., reach not only a *general* agreement but a *unanimous* agreement concerning old age and health care. Surely not even the most sanguine communitarian theorist supposes this. This suggests, then, that even if enforcing a thick theory would not interfere with the plans of a majority of old people, it would still interfere with the plans of a considerable number of old people. A thick theory would do a disservice to the self-respect, personal integrity, self-confidence, and self-esteem of a minority group. That remains a serious matter. It may be that the *scarcity* of medical and other resources necessitates injuring people in this way. But this is an altogether different argument. The reason Callahan adduces in support of age rationing is predicated upon collective *wisdom*. His argument is that we should deny old people the means to extend their life, because old people's request for more life is *unwise*. This is different from arguing that a certain allocation of goods would be more fair on the supposition that there aren't enough of the goods in question to go around.

The alternative to requiring that dissenters conform to a prevailing view need not be that government agree to satisfy the wishes of each individual. A more plausible alternative is for government to support a number of health care options that represent the more common kinds of preferences dissenters hold. In other words, the alternative to enforcing the views of a dominant group is to support a plurality of groups. Advocates of a thin theory of health care need not oppose the establishment of communities of shared values; what their position rules out is hegemony. What truly pits liberal individualists against communitarian theorists is not that communitarians embrace community and individualists oppose it, but rather that communitarians favor having a dominant community and liberals insist upon fidelity to a diversity of groups.

In closing I want to say something to reinforce the elevated role that a theory of distributive justice occupies in current debates about allocating medical resources. Factors such as the accessibility, extravagance, cost, and abundance of life-extending medical goods do and should enter into our perceptions about the tolerability of withholding these goods from old people. In order to highlight the significance of these considerations, it is useful to consider one further example. Suppose Y is diagnosed with breast cancer at age seventy-three and wants a partial mastectomy because without it she has two or three years to live, but with it she has a good chance of living much longer. Or suppose there are inexpensive pills around that cure cancer but have unpleasant side effects and Y wants to try them. It seems clearly wrong to

166

deny Y either of these treatments on the ground that she has lived a natural life span [and that once a natural life span has been reached government should pay only for care devoted to relieving pain and suffering]. It would be unthinkable to say to her: we will not pay for pills to cure your disease because they cause painful side effects. But we will pay for pills to cure the pain and alleviate the suffering you may experience as cancer spreads throughout your body.

What makes this kind of policy perverse is not that Y is entitled to receive from government whatever she needs to sustain her life. It is rather that government has a duty to underwrite a decent minimum of health care. A decent minimum [includes both life-extending and palliative care. It] is to some extent relative to the level of health care available to society at large. This means Y is entitled to receive government support for a routine mastectomy or for some of those (hypothetical) pills to cure her cancer, but Y is not entitled to receive government support for the most advanced [rehabilitative services] or the services of the most famous oncologist. Analogously, something has gone awry if a person can use food stamps to buy caviar or fine port wine but cannot use them to buy bread. Like caviar and port, the latest [rehabilitative] treatment or the services of a famous oncologist are expensive and extravagant, but bread is a cheap and basic staple. The imagination strains at attempting to picture a Medicare or Medicaid system that covers such things as expensive or rare pain-cure medication or computer-assisted rehabilitative treatment but does not cover cheap drugs or routine surgeries. This is because the cost and supply of medical goods inform to some degree all of our deliberations about medical care. They determine in part the kinds of care we can and should offer people. Because we frame discussions in this way, we understand that in an aging society there simply may not be enough medical care or enough public funds to purchase medical care for everyone who needs it. We already accept the task to design and live with a fair method for distributing scarce medical goods.

As individuals who age and die, we should each try to envision what old age and death will be like for *us* and we should try to form ideas about how we would like our old age and death to be. This process can be facilitated by a public *debate,* although a public *consensus* would hamper it. It can also be fostered and encouraged by a health care system that empowers people to carry out their plans in old age and restricts people only to the extent justice demands.

In this paper I have argued that (1) living a natural life span is but one consideration among many that are relevant to assessing the tolerability or intolerability of letting people die; (2) a consensus on ideal old age is probably not realizable in contemporary society; and (3) a thin theory of old age and health care best serves the interests of old people. If my reasoning about these matters is sound, it does not necessarily follow that age rationing medical care is unfair. There may *be* overriding reasons to support such a policy. What my arguments show is that we should not disenfranchise old people from life-extending medical care on the grounds that they have achieved a natural life span. We should not limit access to health care in order to enforce a consensus about what life and death in old age should be like. Doing so violates both the rights and the welfare of old people. It is contrary both to justice and to charity.[8]

NOTES

1. Norman Daniels's most extensive defense of age rationing to date is *Just Health Care* (New York: Cambridge University Press, 1985), especially Chapter 5. See also *Am I My Parents' Keeper? An Essay on Justice Between the Young and the Old* (New York: Oxford University Press, 1988). Margaret Battin's

most recent defense of age rationing is "Age Rationing and the Just Distribution of Health Care: Is There a Duty to Die?" *Ethics* 97 (January 1987): 317–40.

2. Christine Cassel, "The Meaning of Health Care in Old Age" in *What Does It Mean to Grow Old? Reflections from the Humanities,* ed. Thomas Cole and Sally Gadow (Durham, NC: Duke University Press, 1986), p. 184.

3. Ibid., pp. 184–85.

4. Ibid., p. 185.

5. John Rawls, *A Theory of Justice* (Cambridge: Harvard University Press, 1971), p. 440.

6. Ibid.

7. This way of responding to the liberty objection was pointed out to me by Robert Fullinwider.

8. This paper was written at the Center for Philosophy and Public Policy during the summer and fall of 1987. I am grateful to the Rockefeller Foundation for a grant which supported my research and to the associates and staff at the center for their helpful feedback. The following individuals read and commented on an earlier draft of the paper: Daniel Callahan, Robert Fullinwider, Judith Lichtenberg, David Luban, Douglas MacLean, Claudi Mills, Mark Sagoff, Jerome Segal, and Robert Wachbroit.

SETTING LIMITS:
FOR WHOSE BENEFIT?

PETER SINGER

PETER SINGER is Professor and Director, Centre for Human Bioethics, Monash University, Victoria, Australia.

A NATURAL LIFE SPAN

In using the idea of a natural life span Callahan is careful to avoid the well-known pitfalls of deducing values from "nature." Instead he specifies that his use of the term will already involve a judgment, in fact "a persistent pattern of judgment in our culture" of what it means to live out a whole and relatively complete life. This is a conservative strategy, drawing support from the supposed collective wisdom of past generations. To the degree that our situation is unprecedented, the value of that legacy is lessened. Why should we accept the judgments of our culture on when a life is complete, if those judgments were made in the expectation that physical and mental degeneration was inevitable, and usually severe, after the age of eighty, and these conditions have subsequently changed? Dylan Thomas urged a different attitude:

Peter Singer's "Setting Limits: For Whose Benefit?" excerpted from *Bioethics* 2(2) (1988). Reprinted by permission of the author and Basil Blackwell, Oxford, U.K.

Do not go gentle into that good night.
Rage, rage against the dying of the light.[1]

What better way of raging, than to strive to keep the light
burning steadily when nature's storms are threatening to ex-
tinguish it?

Perhaps, though, the grounds on which people have made
these persistent judgments about the completeness of a life
area more universal and less vulnerable to changing circumstances than one might think. Ultimately our acceptance of
the central thesis of *Setting Limits* will hang on our opinion
of the strength of that section of its third chapter in which
Callahan presents his case for believing that death at the end
of a reasonably complete life is tolerable and it is therefore
not the proper role of medicine to resist it. Callahan sets out
three conditions for a "tolerable death": (a) one's life possibilities have on the whole been accomplished; (b) one's
moral obligations to those for whom one has had responsibility have been discharged; and (c) one's death will not seem
to others an offense or a cause of despair or rage at human
finitude. A "natural life span" is then defined as one after
which death can be seen as tolerable, for the reasons given.

Since the satisfaction of the first two of these conditions
would seem the best possible basis for claiming that the third
has also been satisfied, we can focus on the first two alone;
and since the second is more tangible than the first, we shall
begin there. Callahan's point is that most parents have their
children in their twenties, thirties, or at the latest forties, and
so their children reach adulthood as they themselves move
into their fifties and sixties. Though close bonds may remain,
death after this time will not leave unfulfilled responsibilities.
The point is a sound one, and does suggest that there is one
less reason to battle against death beyond a certain age. But
what if aging itself could be slowed? Here we are immediately
confronted with the sharp difference between reduction in

171

aging, and a prolongation of life. If we aged more slowly, our reproductive systems might remain, at fifty or sixty, in the conditions that they now are at thirty and forty. Alternatively, by freezing our sperm and ova, and making use of *in vitro* fertilization combined with surrogacy or ectogenesis, we could have our children at any age, irrespective of whether we remained naturally fertile. If (though speaking now as a parent, I voice the thought with trepidation) we slowed the rate of aging even in childhood, our responsibilities for our children might last another forty years!

Seriously, while the grounds for prolonging childhood are hard to see, the reasons for delaying the period at which we have our children are more readily apparent, especially for those eager to establish themselves professionally before embarking on parenthood. Hence the age at which we are likely to be free of parental responsibilities is not fixed for all time.

The more difficult criterion is the accomplishment of one's life possibilities. The idea is that life affords us opportunities for work, love, raising a family, pursuing ideals, experiencing beauty, gaining knowledge, and so on. Death in old age is therefore more tolerable, because by then we have had as much opportunity for these goods as we are likely to get. The problem with this reason for accepting death is that what we consider to be our life's possibilities is, precisely, dependent upon our expectation of how long we shall live in health and vitality. Callahan mentions the case of his own mother, who took up painting in her early seventies, by eighty was selling her pictures, and continued to do so until she died at eighty-six. He then dismisses such cases: "They are the exceptions." Would the author's mother be exceptional, however, in a society in which everyone expected to live in health and vigor into their nineties? Surely then many people would take up new directions later in life. If you had always had a yen to try your hand at painting, but were too busy with your career or family to give it a try, you might, at age seventy in a society with an average life span of only seventy-three, think that you had missed the bus; but with, say, the prospect of twenty years ahead, a host of new possibilities beckon.

The extent to which our sense of completeness is relative to our circumstances poses a major problem for Callahan's account of a tolerable death and a natural life span. It is not difficult to imagine future generations pitying us because so few of us have had the opportunity for multiple careers. "What a tragedy," they may say, "that Einstein had such a short life, and so had to devote it so narrowly to physics with just a bit of dabbling in philosophy and a few other interests." It might come to be seen as a possibility open to everyone (perhaps in the United States it will be regarded as a right) to spend thirty years mastering one profession, trade or area of knowledge, and then to start again on something completely different, and perhaps after thirty years at that, to take up a third field of specialization. Could one argue against such expectations on the ground that such a life exceeds a "natural life span"? Only if one uses "natural" in the sense in which it refers to biological processes immune from human intervention—and this is the very sense which Callahan has explicitly disavowed.

A more plausible counter-argument, especially if we limit our sights to what medicine can now achieve, is that by the time Einstein died, at the age of seventy-six, his capacity for important original work in physics or any other subject had diminished. Bertrand Russell is a clear example: if we can judge from the last five years of his life, he could not have accomplished anything else of significance even if he had lived another twenty years. But this does not allow us to conclude as much as Callahan wants. The correct conclusion to draw from such cases is that without certain mental qualities, the preservation of the life of the body is of little value. This sets limits to what medicine should seek to achieve, however, only if we take it as given that the requisite mental qualities cannot be retained. It does not provide a reason for holding that it is beyond the proper role of the medical sciences to seek such a longer tenure of our intellectual faculties, and, consequent upon the success of this venture, of our body as well.

FOR WHOSE BENEFIT?

I could find only one argument in *Setting Limits* which holds up in the face of possible future developments in our control of aging. This is in a passage from Hans Jonas, which is worth quoting here:

> ... the wisdom [of] the harsh dispensation of our mortality [is] that it grants us the eternally renewed promise of the freshness, immediacy, and eagerness of youth. ... There is no substitute for this in the greater accumulation of prolonged experience: it can never recapture the unique privilege of seeing the world for the first time and with new eyes. ... This ever renewed beginning, which is only to be had at the price of ever repeated ending, may well be mankind's hope, its safeguard against lapsing into boredom and routine, its chance of retaining the spontaneity of life. ... Perhaps a nonnegotiable limit to our expected time is necessary for each of us as the incentive to number our days and make them count.[2]

In a footnote Callahan links this passage with Bernard Williams' well-known essay "The Makropulos Case: Reflections on the Tedium of Immortality,"[3] Williams argues that immortality would not be desirable, because a limit to our days saves us from the fate of an unrelieved boredom resulting from having experienced everything there is to experience. It is, however, only in the final sentence of the quoted passage that Jonas is concerned with the effect of immortality on the immortal individual. In the context of what is medically possible now or in the foreseeable future, this "argument from the tedium of immortality" is the least significant of the points

Jonas makes, for it can be met by the reply that increasing the number of our days by fifty or a hundred percent would be far from tedious, and preferable to our present modest allocation.

The more significant point Jonas makes is that there would be a loss to our species—or to put it differently, the outcome would, taken as a whole, be worse—if we were to achieve any major prolongation of our lives. A longer life may indeed be in the interests of individuals who will gain extra years; but this gain must be set against two different kinds of loss: the loss to our species of spontaneity which comes from the renewal built into the cycle of generations; and the loss to the possible future generations who will not come into existence—or not in the same numbers—if the present generation continues indefinitely. (This last point assumes, plausibly, that our planet is approaching the limit of the number of people it can support, and if there are fewer deaths, there will have to be fewer births.) This possible loss to future generations is not made up, if Jonas is right, by the gain to the present generation, because the "freshness, immediacy and eagerness of youth" is of greater value than "the greater accumulation of prolonged experience."

It might be doubted whether youth really is all that better, or more enjoyable, than experience. One of my colleagues remarked, on reading this claim, that he escaped youth with a sense of relief! But let us grant, for the sake of the argument, that the freshness of youth really does make that period of our lives better than old age, both for ourselves and for its leavening effect on society as a whole. I, at least, do not find the picture Jonas presents unpersuasive; but for Callahan to rely on it would cut against other elements within his position. Callahan seeks to defend the view that indefinitely extending the life of the elderly is "neither a wise social goal *nor one that the aged themselves want . . .*" (my emphasis). Youth may be fresh and eager, even more joyful than maturity, and the youthful perspective may bring all kinds of benefits to society as a whole; but unless the aged are unusually altruistic, the benefit of their demise to future generations will be insufficient to induce more than a few of them to stop looking for ways of postponing the moment at which that event takes place. . . .

We must consider one more philosophical problem, perhaps the deepest of all those raised by Callahan's book, which is inherent in the view taken by Jonas. Should our policies in this area be designed to further the interests not only of presently existing individuals, but also of yet-to-be conceived future generations? Or should our concern be only for those individuals who exist now? Or should it be neither of these, but instead the species as a whole? Once it is conceded that these three do not run in harmony, the question must be faced; but each answer has its own difficulties. Let us take them in reverse order.

Suppose we answer that our policies should be designed to further the interests of the human species as a whole. This answer implies that the species has interests which are distinct from those of the individuals—past, present and future—who make up the species; and that these interests override the interests of individuals. We may doubt, however, whether a species is the kind of entity that can have interests at all. A species cannot feel joy or misery. It cannot make plans, or reason. It has no central organization, or point of control. It is, roughly speaking, a collection of individuals who can interbreed. Admittedly, we would generally regard the deaths of the last twenty California condors as a greater loss than the deaths of twenty of the similar but more common Andean condors; but holding this view does not require us to regard species as entities that can have interests. Each species has a part to play in an ecological system; the extinction of one reduces the complexity of the system, which may have unforeseen harmful ramifications. Species extinction may also be opposed on aesthetic grounds; as an act of vandalism, driving the blue whale into extinction could be compared with burning down the Louvre. To regard this as a great evil is not to say that the species of blue whales has interest above and beyond the interests of the individual blue whales, any more than it is to say that the Louvre, or the pictures in it, have interests.

If we abandon the idea that it is the interests of the species as a whole which should direct our actions, we may be tempted to reach for something more tangible, such as the interests of those individuals who are already in existence. An ethics based on the notion of social contract inclines one toward such a position, because we can make no contract with posterity—"what did posterity ever do for me?" as the oft-quoted quip puts it. A social contract theorist can appeal to the desires of the present generation for the welfare of future generations, but if such desires may be absent, or overriden, the interests of future generations, in themselves, will count for nothing. To adopt this stance would exclude the use of arguments like those of Jonas against prolonging life. That is not in itself a reason against adopting it; but its implications may be. It implies, for example, that if we do not care about the interests of those living a century hence, we are free to put the radioactive waste from nuclear power stations into containers which will last just that period of time, and then dump the containers in any convenient river. On this view, while it would be a terrible thing to inflict radiation poisoning on thousands of people who exist now, it doesn't matter at all if we bring about similar illness and death a century hence. Yet people living in 2087 will, presumably, feel the same when they are poisoned as we would feel now. Whatever difference the time of one's existence may make, it surely does not make this kind of difference to the ethics of how one is treated. If there are going to be future generations of beings like us, their interests should count as ours count.

So we come to the third possible answer: that we should count the interests of future generations as well as those of presently existing individuals. In the light of the deficiencies of the previous answers, this may appear obviously correct; and so, indeed, I believe, it is. But the issue is more complex than it may yet appear.

Here is a scenario which shows the complexities. Let us assume that the world cannot support, in the long-run, a population any larger than it is at present. Now imagine that we discover a simple and inexpensive drug which does not affect our aging until we reach middle age, but then slows the onset of old age. The effect is to double the average life span in a way that preserves much, but not all, of the health and vitality that we have in middle age. In other words, we can expect our health over the additional seventy-five years to be not quite as good as the average over a normal life span today, but still not so poor that we would regard those extra years as not worth living, or even come close to making such a judgment. Suppose that it is in our power to decide if this drug will be made available or not. If we allow the drug to be used, we shall have to take stringent measures to cut the number of births—otherwise, since people are living twice as long, there will soon be more people than the world can support. We shall suppose that we achieve this by persuading people to have children only when they reach about fifty, rather than when they reach about twenty-five, as they do now (fortunately the drug will make this possible). If we do not allow the drug to be used, we can allow people to be born when the parents are around twenty-five; the total number of people existing at any one time will be roughly the same, but of course over a century or two, many more people will have lived if we do not allow the drug.

In favour of allowing the drug to be used, it can be said that it will benefit people who exist now, since their lives will be prolonged and the extra time they have will, as far as anyone can predict, be well worthwhile. As for future generations, they too will be able to use the drug, and so will have better lives than they would have had if the drug had not been used. So judging on the basis of what benefits both present and future generations, the drug should be released.

So what can there be against allowing the use of the drug? For a start, that the average quality of life, at any given time, will be lower if we allow the drug to be used than if we prohibit it. The reason for this lower average may be that proposed by Jonas: that the accumulation of experience does not make up for the loss of the freshness of youth. This may well be true, even though if we allow the drug to be used, every present and future individual will be better off than if we do not allow it. The apparent contradiction disappears once we recognize that the expression "future generations" does not refer to a fixed number of people, but rather expands or contracts to accommodate different numbers—and indeed, different people—depending on whether we allow the drug to be used. If we do not have the drug, we will have new generations every (say) twenty-five years, with each generation living about seventy-five years, generally at a high quality of life because for a comparatively large proportion of this time they will enjoy the freshness of youth. If we allow the drug, we will have new generations every fifty years, with each generation living about one hundred and fifty years, generally at a quality of life which is good, but not so high as if we did not allow the drug, because they will enjoy the freshness of youth for a comparatively small portion of that time. Thus as well as saying that banning the drug leads to a higher *average* quality of life at any given time, we can also say that it leads to *more* people living worthwhile lives, and to a greater *total* amount of happiness over a period of time.

179

The choice is baffling. It has been discussed by philosophers, most notably by Derek Parfit, but it has certainly not been solved by them.[4] Even those who consider themselves utilitarians differ among themselves about whether to maximize the total happiness, or to consider only those who will exist independently of our actions, thus denying that the creation of happy people is on a par with making existing people happy. Intuitively, most non-philosophers take the view that it is better to make an existing person happy than to bring into existence an additional person who will be happy. Those who never exist, they will say, should not be thought of as somehow waiting in limbo sadly missing out on the benefit of existence. One cannot harm a non-existent being, so allowing the drug benefits some and harms none.

Unfortunately the situation is not so simple. Over a longer-time scale there may be *no* future people who exist independently of our policies. In the situation we are considering, for instance, while the present generation can straightforwardly claim to be worse off if we prohibit the drug it cannot be said of any subsequent generation that *those people* will be harmed if we do not allow the drug to be taken—unless not coming into existence is a harm. For if we do not allow the drug to be taken, reproduction will take place at different times than if we do allow the drug to be taken. They will develop from different gametes, and quite possibly even from different partners, and so they will not be the same people who would have existed under the alternative policy. Hence the people who would be born subsequently if the drug is permitted will simply not exist at all if the drug is not taken. Should we then ignore all future generations, and consider only the benefits to the present generation? But if we would not do this in the case of radioactive waste disposal mentioned earlier, does it become acceptable to think only of ourselves whenever the identity of the future individuals is dependent on what we decide to do?

With considerable hesitation, I have come to the view that we should maximize the total happiness; but I can easily understand why someone else might take the view that only the interests of those who exist, or will exist independently of our choice, should be considered. As we can see from the example I have used, different policies for prolonging life will be justifiable according to which of these two positions we choose. The one I support comes down in favour of setting limits, as Callahan would wish; but those who take the opposite view have grounds for opposing this position when there is a conflict between the interests of existing people and future generations who may not exist under a different policy. Callahan himself does nothing to show that they are wrong; he seems oblivious to the differences between the two views, and to the way in which coming down on one side or the other materially affects the strength of his case for setting limits to the prolongation of life.

NOTES

1. "Do not go gentle into that good night," Dylan Thomas, *Miscellany One* (London: J.M. Dent & Sons, 1963), p. 31.

2. Hans Jonas, *The Imperative of Responsibility: In Search of an Ethics for the Technological Age* (Chicago: University of Chicago Press, 1984), p. 19.

3. Bernard Williams, *Problems of the Self* (New York: Cambridge University Press, 1973), Chapter 6.

4. Derek Parfit, *Reasons and Persons* (Oxford: Oxford University Press, 1984), Part IV.

Toward a Public Dialogue on the Meaning of Aging and the Aged

....

MONSIGNOR CHARLES J. FAHEY

CHARLES J. FAHEY is Director, Third Age Center, Fordham University, at Lincoln Center, New York.

THIS ESSAY will explore the elements that inhibit or enhance a dialogue about the meaning of old age, aging and the aged in contemporary American society, and offer a paradigm that may serve to initiate public dialogue. Finally, based on this paradigm, the paradigm of the Third Age, I will comment on and challenge the need for age-based rationing of health care.

Let me say at the outset that I applaud a call for public dialogue. It is essential for society and for individuals. It can contribute to a personal quest for meaning and offer a moral guide for public and social policy. However, this concurrence does not mean that we could or would want to develop a vision so compelling that everyone would assent to it. Our nation has not yet experienced a generation living to such advanced old age. There is still need for creativity and individuality as we sort through what this will mean. Hence, I think broad social agreement is neither likely in the short haul nor useful in the long term, particularly if it were to produce policies that have life and death implications. As a practical matter, in the few areas in national community life where social consensus exists, it rarely leads to agreement about public policy. We probably all perceive equal opportunity as a critical social value, but we are anything but in agreement about quotas in public policy. The poor should have what is necessary for life, but the extent of actual welfare benefits, even for the "deserving poor," is a matter of dispute. Moreover, in terms of relevant public policy, we have only begun discussion about what constitutes a meaningful and significant old age. Challenges to standard theories about old age force us to set forth and examine our general assumptions about aging and old age in America. Only by such explicit analysis can we develop fruitful public dialogue about aging.

In response to Callahan's challenge I want to articulate what I consider to be the basic premises about aging in our society. First, it is important simply to note that it is only in our time that we have large numbers of the very old, many of whom are frail and dependent for a significant period of time, even without heroic medical measures.

Second, today's older cohorts are in many ways different from one another. Even individuals who are of the same cohort age differently, making chronological age alone a poor predictor of capacity and behavior. While we may generalize to the degree that most young old (sixty-five to seventy-five) are likely to be healthy, and many old old (over eighty-five) are likely to have physical and/or mental conditions which compromise activities of daily living, older persons still remain quite heterogeneous.

Older people's lives assume complex patterns because of the embedment in multiple relationships and in the greater society. War and peace, affluence and poverty, opportunity and discrimination, education and ignorance, and positive and negative social strictures affect the complexity and contribute to the richness of individuals. Over their lifetimes, elderly individuals face many physical, social, economic, psychological, and spiritual changes. While the general course of these changes is common to virtually all, the actual pace of each individual's life is different. Thus, with a significant range of individual variation, elderly individuals can expect: an inevitable physiological decline accompanied by increasingly frequent bouts of acute illness, with the likelihood of chronic disease and the need for assistance from others before the ultimacy of death; the capacity for continued growth of the interior life, in other words, for reflection, analysis, self-integration, and self-awareness; the need for new and continuing relationships as well as adjustment to the loss of former ones; and a period of unemployment and fewer formal social roles.

When considering the elderly as a group we must recognize several important trends. The most rapid rate of population growth is in the oldest of the old. In addition, persons who have been poor are likely to continue to be poor in old age; some, particularly women, will become poor in old age. Women will live longer than men and are more likely to live alone than are men; the older the age group, the higher the ratio of women to men.

The population structure is likely to have distinct characteristics and implications. The growth in the numbers of older persons, both absolutely and relatively, will be modest and steady until approximately 2010; the growth after 2010 will be dramatic. At the same time, the dependency ratio, that is, the number of retirees to workers, will rise dramatically if current fertility, mortality, and immigration rates remain constant. We can also expect that older persons will continue to be perceived as a powerful political force, but governmental programs for them will continue to be subject to close scrutiny. This will likely lead to intergenerational tensions in the social order.

This complex of factors indicates that public dialogue on the meaning of aging will be carried on in the midst of diverse individual, group, and population pressures. Some of these pressures will, of course, inhibit dialogue and work against our efforts to give personal and social meaning to the extended life-style. From the very start it is crucial to examine these countervailing forces, since only by understanding them can we hope to overcome them.

Several powerful elements confound public conversations about the meaning of aging. Many persons are hesitant to face their own aging. The admission that losses, limitations, and vulnerabilities are inherent in aging is often written off as ageism. Moreover, there seems to be a general reluctance to deal with personal, value issues in the public forum. In our celebration of individual freedom we are not clear when and where it is appropriate to apply (and enforce through public policy) culturally sanctioned norms. Recognition of the value of the separation of church and state makes us wary about public religion, yet religious insights are paramount in many individuals' understanding of aging, losses, suffering, and death. Finally, few of us are conversant with the diction of ethics. We have systematically excluded the study of ethics from the elementary and high school levels and allowed it to languish in higher education as well. So the very nature of our society constrains Callahan's call for public dialogue.

PARADIGM FOR DIALOGUE: MORAL AGENCY AND THE THIRD AGE

I have already suggested that extended aging as a broad societal phenomenon is in its infancy, that we are just beginning to evolve a conception of what it ought to be. Additionally, I have set forth some assumptions about the "facts" of that old age and noted why the potential for dialogue is so limited. I would now like to offer the paradigm of the Third Age and its potential for moral agency as a way to initiate and structure that dialogue. In the end, I believe that a morally examined Third Age will make Callahan's policy prescriptions needless.

THE FIRST AND SECOND AGE

The First Age extends from conception through the period of emancipation. It is the time of physical, emotional, intellectual, and spiritual growth. The person lives within a socially accepted set of expectations, roles, events, and values. Although the First Age is evolutionary in development, it is important for society to have culturally sanctioned norms for it. Society, first through parents and the family, helps the child to develop its "heart, head, and hands." Intermediate structures and government share in providing the means for the young person to mature. There is general agreement in society about the meaning of this period of life. Culture, social structures, public policy, and individuals work together to assure that a child has the opportunity to mature. Formally and informally, we require those in the First Age to "learn to be adults," to develop so as to be able to move into the new roles that are needed both for personal fulfillment and the common good.

The transition into the Second Age occurs as the individual leaves home to begin the cycle anew. Now the individual begins to make choices about work, living arrangements, new friends, and for most, spouse and children. While persons in the Second Age are heterogeneous, there is a culturally sanctioned place for them in the life course. They carry on the species through reproductive and parenting functions and/or contributing to the common good through their work. Culturally supported expectancies move those in the Second Age to seek advancement in their jobs, to care for their children, to participate in the neighborhood, to improve their life-styles by acquiring better housing and opportunities for leisure activities.

However, for many, the multiple demands of this period, coupled with general cultural and social expectations, combine to slow the development of moral agency. Family and work relationships create set patterns of choice and behavior. Individuals make important choices but all too commonly live their lives in an unexamined, uncritical manner.

THE THIRD AGE

The three-age concept of the life cycle, based as it is on multiple internal and external factors, recognizes a gradual evolution as persons lose old roles and acquire new ones, assimilate changes in status, become conscious of new challenges, experience different psychological reactions to life, and find themselves freer to be themselves and exercise greater moral agency. They are evermore capable of developing convictions and values, of being held accountable for their behavior, and of reflecting on and altering both values and personal actions. Persons continue to exercise moral agency, not only in regard to themselves, but also in interactions with others and with social structures.

Typically, the Third Age is a period in which "developed" societies lower their expectatons for individuals. There are few socially sanctioned roles besides the pursuit of personal goals and interests. This period of life tends to be centered on retirement and family life. As important as these may be, neither alone nor taken together are they likely to be adequate to fulfill the need for personal meaning and significance, nor do they particularly contribute to society. Unlike the First and Second Ages, the Third Age provides no series of distinct life events and activities—other than disability, loss, and death—in which persons of this age are expected to engage.

Although there are a number of events that mark passage into the Third Age—children leaving home, a changing relationship to one's spouse, and often the loss of a work role—

they are less clear than those marking the passage from the First to the Second Age. Progress into the Third Age happens gradually and often unnoticed. Inertia, distraction, and denial can further blunt the moral agency of later life.

TOWARD A PHILOSOPHY
OF THE THIRD AGE

A philosophy of the Third Age attempts to overcome these impediments. From both personal and societal perspectives it urges older persons to pursue their lives with increased moral agency. The Third Age is a time to strive for personal authenticity (to use an Ericksonian concept) and to contribute to societal authenticity as well. While there may be physiological decline, lowered social expectancies and greater freedom from the need to conform, these changes permit a new moral freedom.

Such freedom and authenticity involve "intentionality," an examination of one's values and behaviors and a conscious questioning of life. What indeed has made me whole? What has brought satisfaction? What are the structures which have enabled me to be? Conversely, what has served me or society poorly? Given the "capital" of a period of reasonable health and freedom from other responsibilities, how do I engage in the life that I am likely to have with all of its challenges, its opportunities, its diminishments and losses, including, finally, the loss of life itself?

Increased moral agency involves a heightened awareness of the responsibility I have to myself and others. Part of the Third Age's moral imperative is to shape a life, energized and directed by memory, conscience, and the acute awareness of suffering and deprivation. The older person is free at least in the realm of conscience. Our most fundamental obligation is to seek the truth and follow where it leads. For older persons it means a continued development of their interior lives, that is, the use of their memories and the faculties of judgment, imagination, awareness, and will.

Unfortunately, there is little expectancy that older persons will continue to grow intellectually or emotionally, even though they face personal and societal challenges which are staggering. For example, we associate friendship and living with passion with the teenage years and young adulthood. But these are vitally important continuations in the Third Age. Married couples must develop a new sense of the meaning of their relation with one another and with others. Many older persons are without a spouse. Many lose friends; yet, they have the capacity and need to love. While the ability to propagate and nurture children may be over in the Third Age, the needs of the human family—for a decent and just social order—continue to call out to the elderly. The Third Age should be a time of community within and beyond the boundaries of families. Older persons in the United States have been the beneficiaries of unprecedented opportunities. They have a collective experience and memory of great importance to the body politic. They have power. And the power of the old, like that of scientific and technological advances, is undifferentiated. It can be used for good or evil, selfishly wielded or given over to generosity of spirit. It can be focused on the immediate, economic wants of the old or on the needs of all and the claims of the future. It can split the generations, geographic sections, ethnic groups, and classes, or it can contribute to the solidarity of people, regions, and generations.

As in the first two ages, there is a continuing tension between personal interest and common good. The Third Age should be a time of personal resolution of this conflict. It seems inherent in our very nature that we make sense out of our personal lives even as we recognize obligations to the society that has enabled us to be. Individuality makes sense only in the context of society. For persons to achieve old age their personal efforts and wise choices must find fortunate contexts. The old are the beneficiaries of others, of generations who have preceded them, of their peers and those who are the current producers of goods, services, and financial support. Persons achieve old age because of human accomplishments that ward off disease and sustain life. Culture, freedom, access to services, and wealth generated over time by many persons have enriched the life of the old. It would seem that there is a positive moral obligation on the part of the old to contribute to the human journey prior to withdrawing from it. Whether it be with one's family or neighborhood or in the world of ideas or politics, the old are needed, and can contribute and find significance.

SETTING LIMITS IN THE THIRD AGE:
AN EPILOGUE

Setting Limits poses both a theoretical and practical challenge to all interested in aging, their own and that of society. Reaction to the book gives evidence of the timeliness of the questions it raises. It is timely that there be a societal discussion, and I offer the paradigm of the Third Age as a way to engage that discussion. It is essential that we make personal sense of our aging and that society as a whole infuse with significance this basically new phenomenon of a longer and more certain life span. However, it would seem that there is more to the Third Age than merely moving gracefully aside and allowing for ensuing generations to move to the fore. As I have suggested, the Third Age has its own special and productive place in the cycle of aging.

To return, in closing, to the policy prescription of *Setting Limits:* Should high tech, costly medical services be rationed by age? The question is fair, but I feel that for the foreseeable future the answer should be no—precisely because such rationing is not needed. It is my conviction that few if any elderly wish to prolong their lives in a mindless fashion. If there is a problem today, it stems not from the desires of the old but from the zealousness of providers and others with an understandable but mistaken commitment to life at any cost.

In the interaction of policy and culture it would seem better to wait for the wisdom of the old to determine the question of limits. We will best modify unnecessary public expenditures in health not by statute but by older persons asking that their lives not be unduly prolonged by measures esoteric at any age and relatively inappropriate at theirs. This process has already started through the use of living wills and durable powers of attorney for health care. Although some in the medical profession, the health-care system, and the right-to-life movement encourage relentless treatment, senior groups and elder empowerment, I believe, will serve as countervailing forces. Further, new relationships with physicians encourage greater openness. Out of these changes self-limits will emerge—less unsettling than limits derived from an adversarial relationship. Moreover, tough cases make poor laws. The aberrant ninety-year-old who wants a heart transplant should not shape legislation.

Although it is morally irresponsible to hold fiercely and endlessly to life, the "natural life span" is simply not objectifiable. Furthermore, it is both futile and counterproductive to try to limit the inquiries of science. This is particularly true when the investigation is of phenomena associated with the latter part of life—whether in its biological, physiological, social, psychological, or spiritual dimensions. These investigations nearly always reveal messages about the whole of the life span and each of the processes therein.

While the notion of a normative consensus may strike one as frightening, a shared, thoughtful series of reflections is essential as we—a gifted people—struggle together through the great mystery of life and death.

PART VII

Drawing a Fine Line: Medicine, Research, and Economic Justice

The next group of authors reflect specific disciplinary and analytical frameworks.

A number of physicians, like Christine K. Cassel, are disturbed by Callahan's sharp and clear distinction between curing and caring, between interventions that prolong life and those that relieve suffering, and particularly by Callahan's explicit policy of denying life-extending treatment. To Cassel, an age standard does irremediable harm to patients and allows physicians too easy an escape from directly confronting death and their own relationship to the dying patient, thus relieving physicians of the responsibility for making difficult treatment decisions. She insists that physicians have a "duty to struggle" with patients and their families to determine the best action in any given circumstance. Cassel defends the importance of individual differences in desires, expectations, and prognoses, and calls for medicine to reaffirm its commitment to honor the heterogeneity of individual patients.

A criticism of vanguard scientific research, with its high price tag, powerful claim on available funds, and unintended and often unexamined consequences, is the center of Robert Morris's analysis. Morris reiterates Callahan's criticism of the misuse of technology in the unrelenting pursuit of prolonging life but argues that the proposal for age-based rationing, which he opposes, detracts from more serious concerns. Morris argues for better balance in funding between the life sciences and the social sciences to enable us to make advances and at the same time to cope with present long-term care needs.

Meredith Minkler broadens the critique by refuting the intergenerational equity framework on which Callahan relies. She argues that posing the question as a search for fairness between the old and the young is necessarily a limited and a flawed approach either to understand or to remedy the policy problems he confronts. Class, gender, race, and ethnicity, rather than overexpenditures on the elderly, are far more powerful explanations of basic inequalities. Minkler introduces a new policy framework and policy recommendations that emphasize interdependence between generations and calls upon more affluent elders to play a substantial intragenerational and intergenerational supportive role.

Elizabeth A. Binney and Carroll L. Estes offer a comprehensive critique of health care, economy, and society. They challenge the "natural life span" argument on the grounds that it ignores the differences in life histories that class, gender, and race so powerfully influence. While praising Callahan for integrating a number of issues often viewed separately, they fault what they believe is his narrow perspective and uncritical acceptance of the roots of the predicament that so alarms him. Hence, he misreads the causes of health-care inflation,

194

focuses on *structurally induced scarcity, and solves the wrong problem. In the end, they believe his policy prescriptions will harm elders and exacerbate inequality while failing to redress the runaway costs of health care. Before considering the last resort of Callahan's Draconian measures, we must, they argue, implement a number of other justice-driven solutions, especially a plan for universal health insurance.*

THE LIMITS
OF *SETTING LIMITS*

....

CHRISTINE K. CASSEL

CHRISTINE K. CASSEL is Chief, Section of General Internal Medicine, University of Chicago, Pritzker School of Medicine.

Setting Limits calls for and seeks to defend a new realism about the limits of medical technology, an integral sense of the life span and the ends of medicine appropriate to each part of that life span, a communitarian view of the resources of society, and a principle of fairness in allocation of healthcare resources especially concerning the needs of different generations. I find this book to be misleading and even dangerous, but not because of the above-mentioned goals. Rather, the policy approaches Callahan maps out to achieve those goals are narrow and incomplete. In addition, some of the premises he accepts are highly questionable—in some cases because of inadequacies in the facts at his disposal, in others because of faulty interpretation of certain data, and most fundamentally because of an antimodernist ideology that does not allow a full appreciation of the radical demographic, scientific, and cultural changes possible in the society of the future.

Daniel Callahan says explicitly he intends *Setting Limits* to be provocative. This it certainly is. But it is harder to tell just where the author ceases his genuine scholarly appraisal of the problem of limiting medical-care costs of the elderly and begins to play the role of agent provocateur.

Callahan wants to set an age limit for the use of expensive and extensive life-sustaining medical treatment. He urges us to consider death a natural part of life, not to be resisted after a "natural life span." The "natural life span" is defined "biographically" by Callahan to include the range of things one can expect in life in terms of family, work, and personal experiences. The concept of a "natural life span" then becomes the basis for an ostensibly "fair" approach to rationing medical care: He proposes "setting limits" of age (seventy? eighty?) above which no life-prolonging medical care would be provided by public programs.

A longing for community and a sense of fairness between generations in this book strikes part of its antimodernistic tone; Callahan views these undeniably positive goals as achievable only in a world where people don't live so long— a world of the past. Assuring this "fairness" requires across-the-board limits to physicians' freedom to care for their patients. It requires physicians to transfer their primary responsibility from the patient to the community, as represented by some kind of government regulatory function. It gives over to the state the basic function of medical decision-making for an entire group of patients. While I have not before viewed myself as one of the strongest champions of physician autonomy, I find this shift of the object of the physician's responsibility from the patient to the state to be extremely troubling. Indeed, although the "slippery slope" risk is sometimes overstated, we must not forget that medicine working as the arm of the state has always led to major ethical disasters in wartime or in the service of ideologies such as national socialism or Stalinism.

For the individual, to counsel acceptance of death may be sage advice. But such counsel is dangerously misplaced when it is translated into public policy, for the foundation of the American legal system is acceptance and—indeed—protection of diversity and pluralism. The courts, with support from ethicists, have firmly asserted that decisions about life and death, and life-sustaining medical care, must rest on respect for the right of self-determination.

One major premise that must come under question, which prompts and indeed justifies the major conclusion of *Setting Limits,* is that we as a society will not be able to afford to support either unlimited individual choice or unlimited health care as people grow older. This language of crisis, when applied to health-care spending, is widely accepted but rarely examined in detail and outside of any specific rhetorical agenda.

It is not that I view health-care resources as infinite. Nor do I think that we as a society can or should continue to use life-sustaining technology, or any technology for that matter, without a moral context in which its use makes sense, is cost effective, and is in the interest of the community as well as the individual. This is the correct definition of "appropriate"—a term whose complexity must not be underestimated! But looking to an arbitrary age cutoff as a way to achieve these standards is not only politically unrealistic but also ethically flawed.

The first mistake is to assume that at age eighty or eighty-five so little potential benefit can be gained from medical care that few months or years of remaining life would be lost by an arbitrary cutoff of life-sustaining or -extending medical treatment at that point. Callahan chooses the wrong number—somewhere in the seventies or eighties is not the appropriate limit. This is a completely inaccurate interpretation of modern demographic forecasts. While life expectancy has risen to seventy-four for men and seventy-eight for women, this is a statistical projection based on average age at death. Since there are still "premature" deaths, depending on definition—caused by car accidents, hip-fracture complications, suicide, preventable illness such as heart and lung disease—the real limit to natural life of the human species is longer, probably around ninety or ninety-five years.[1] This "biological" natural life expectancy allows for a much greater opportunity range than that defined by Callahan's "biographical" limit. Which shall we use as a standard for letting human beings die—the average life expectancy or the optimal life span? Current demographic studies suggest in fact that not only is life expectancy increasing but life span itself may be increasing.[2] Even if biological life span is limited to ninety-five to one hundred years, there will easily be twenty million people over age eighty by the year 2020. Most of them will be healthy, active people who could contribute to society if our society would allow them to do so. Treatment of a life-threatening illness in an eighty-five-year-old could save ten or fifteen years of life.

A second major and arguable point of Callahan's analysis is his conclusion that arbitrary cutoffs are fairer and thus have a more positive moral and intergenerational effect on society than will our present course. Five million people currently over eighty would be subject to this rule; under current estimates of life expectancy, in thirty years this number will be twenty million, and if life expectancy continues to increase, that number could be millions more. I suggest that our society will not be able to tolerate such a Draconian policy, resulting precipitously in five million deaths. No advanced society could easily accept an across-the-board denial of medical care (which might improve the quality of life as well as extend its duration) to such substantial numbers. The potential for a very negative impact on our society's moral fiber, respect for age, and, indeed, respect for people overall, and on the future facing young people growing up in such a society is profound.

This categorical cutoff is neither the most practical nor the most morally acceptable way to begin cutting health-care costs and rationing health-care spending. There are other ways that lead to a third critique of Callahan's choice of how our nation might save health-care dollars. It has become a truism to point to the amount of waste and excess profit in our health-care system.[3] By combining administrative overhead of $50–$60 billion a year with profits from the range of health-care technologies, an extraordinary savings could then be applied to other worthy purposes such as education, housing, transportation—even long-term care. Furthermore, the clinical influence that these profits and the people who derive benefits from them have on the policy process is as pernicious, if not more so, than the dramatic waste of resources. Because of financial incentives to create and use more technologies, Medicare and other payers continue preferentially to favor high technology interventions over lower technology quality-of-life care or long-term care. Reducing profits to be made would reduce the inappropriate use of such technology and still allow individual decisions.

Two billion dollars per year is spent on renal dialysis; a similar amount on coronary artery bypass grafts. One is clearly a lifesaving treatment; the other is lifesaving only in a minority of cases. Is this too much to spend in either case, in a country that spends $3 billion annually on potato chips?[4] Do we know that dollars spent on dialysis would not be better spent for flu shots in nursing homes? Outcomes of patients with gastrointestinal bleeding are equivalent regardless of whether the patient has endoscopy to determine the source of bleeding, and yet we continue to prescribe and Medicare continues to reimburse endoscopy for that purpose.[5] Physicians are encouraged to request subspecialty consultation at greater cost because of financial incentives established by hospital policies. Geographic variations in rates of surgical procedures—ranging from tonsillectomy and hysterectomy to prostatectomy and lens extraction—suggest surgeons are considering their target incomes rather than demographic needs.[6]

There are a number of additional examples of medical situations where efficacy, not age, should be the discriminating factor in utilization decisions.

Change, however, requires political action. Are we so helpless in the face of our own political structure that we are unable to identify more obvious solutions to rising healthcare costs than one as extreme and morally treacherous as arbitrary age cutoffs?

Although economists have found that people in the last year of life consume a major part of the Medicare budget, it is not obvious that this is money wasted.[7] All medical care in critical illness is a gamble. People who die may have spent the previous year struggling with illness when death was not predictable. Certainly there are instances of overuse of medical technology at the end of life that prolong dying rather than prolong life. Physicians must learn to deal more directly, reasonably, and compassionately with dying patients.[8] All of us—health professionals, families, and potential patients— must learn to accept the uncertainty inherent in decisions about the use of high technology. I would prefer to work for social change than accept social engineering—the former seems so much more hopeful and humanistic, the latter so pessimistic and mechanistic. Any arbitrary limit on treatment that excludes the professionals from the agony of uncertainty gives up on the human being as the measure of moral reality.

A fourth problem has to do with "life-prolonging treatments." Medical technologies must be understood in their context. How are we to distinguish between life-extending care and life-improving technologies? For example, a ninety-nine-year-old patient who develops syncope (fainting spells) is admitted to the hospital and found to have periodic interruption of the heart rhythms during which time she passes out. She lives alone, has very severe arthritis, but no other serious illnesses. The treatment of choice for her heart disease (conduction system disorder) is a pacemaker. Without the

201

pacemaker, we will send her home to continue fainting and falling. Either she will fall, break a hip, and lie there until she dies of dehydration, or she will be admitted to the orthopedic service, where at great cost and very poor likely outcome, the broken hip will be tended. The alternative is to give her a pacemaker, which will not only improve the quality of her life by preventing these things from happening but will also extend her life. How are we to make such a decision according to Callahan's proposed scheme?

Manifold other technologies offer the same conundrum to the practicing clinician. Moreover, chronic illness is so complex that any treatment which aims to improve the quality of a person's life may in fact extend that life. Those without terminal illness no doubt will live longer if given meticulous nursing care, good attention to their diabetes, and everything from human interaction to podiatric care. Because these things extend life, should we not use them? The only way to treat the discomfort that would arise would be wholesale anesthesia through morphine or widespread physician-assisted euthanasia. These scenarios would be morally detrimental to our society, no matter how much money they may save or however logically consistent they may be with an abstract idea of a "natural life span."

As life expectancy increases in our society, the variability of health status in old age increases also. A time when many eighty-year-olds can expect to live in good health for fifteen more years is not the time to propose an arbitrary age limit in health-care delivery. "The elderly" are the most diverse, least generalizable group in our society. Physicians need to make more individually tailored decisions, not more arbitrary ones. Urgently needed is better training in geriatric medicine for physicians and a stronger scientific and moral capability to make appropriate decisions on an individual basis.[9] Physicians as a group have been woefully inadequate at assessing individual patients and allowing death to come when that is appropriate. If they understood more about the process of aging—biologically, as well as socially—they would make better decisions. They could better judge the chances of a reasonable outcome of diagnostic or treatment plans if they were more familiar with physiological and clinical studies in aging, and had the clinical skills to differentiate treatable from untreatable disorders. Unfortunate tendencies to generalize about the elderly lead to both overly aggressive and overly nihilistic approaches. Ethics would have a better-defined context with better training in medicine, but better training in ethics is equally important. Callahan is clearly skeptical that physicians will ever be able to claim the moral authority to make appropriate decisions to limit their use of technology and to respect the life span and the time when death comes. I think he gives up too soon. It is only within the last fifteen or twenty years that the explosion of technology has both seduced the profession of medicine and now in a backlash has begun to force us to learn to confront death.[10] The profession has a long way to go, but must be assigned major responsibility for the moral and social challenges that medical technology poses. An approach to rationing health-care resources which demands that the system treat people as individuals, that efficacy be the major goal of medical treatment, and that the professions and the industry see themselves as serving the public rather than as profit centers would contribute a great deal more to the quality of our culture, to our society's moral fiber, the beneficence of its intergenerational networks, and its respect for age itself than would an arbitrary age-based cutoff. Better training in how to make these medical and moral judgments needs to be bolstered by better social support for physicians who are able to confront and deal with these shifting grounds. Protection from unjustified liability litigation would go a long way toward improving this decision-making process and making it more individual and more humane, as well as more morally correct.

Setting Limits may have come at exactly the wrong time. Recent studies indicate that, in fact, older and sicker people are now being given less high-technology, life-sustaining treatment, and that what costs money is chronic, long-term care. If we rush too quickly to set limits on aggressive medical treatment, such as treatment of pneumonia, we could play right into an unholy alliance, cutting costs not for any reasoned communitarian motive, but in response to government-directed spending priorities.[11]

If we withhold life-sustaining treatment on an arbitrary basis, we come too near the slippery slope of discrimination or even genocide based on social characteristics which are "undesirable," such as disability, race, religion, class, or sex. This is certainly not Callahan's intention, but the risk is still starkly visible with the hindsight of historical perspective so vivid in the accounts of physician complicity with Nazi anti-Semitism or with psychiatric oppression of dissidents in the Soviet Union, and thus warrants our concern. It is one thing to let people die because their lives have become an inconvenience to them; it is quite another to let them die because their lives have become an inconvenience to us. Some of these people will suffer from chronic illness, which causes them to be dependent and need a great deal of care. Many of those people with chronic illness will want to forgo life-sustaining therapy, and we are obliged to create an ethical system that respects their wishes. But that system will never be created in a society in which a large number of people are fearful that they will not receive appropriate treatment simply because of their age.

In addition, the whole society will suffer. The current aging of society is an unprecedented event, a success of civilization, and we have both an opportunity and a responsibility to shape a society that can appropriately and positively embrace this measure of success.[12] It is the challenge of our success that we create employment, educational and economic structures, and medical care that give all of us as we grow older a positive attitude about the future and about the people with whom we share our society. Callahan's proposal does not allow for medical progress. New treatments for the scourges of old age—Alzheimer's disease, stroke, arthritis—may significantly enhance the quality of life for years before death occurs at the end of a "natural life span," biologically longer than ever before anticipated.[13]

Physicians have indeed been overly strenuous in applying medical technology to some people at the end of life, sometimes even against the patient's expressed wishes. *Setting Limits* is an attempt to take physicians "off the hook," to give them a formulaic approach to these morally and emotionally difficult choices. The attempt fails—it doesn't fix what is broken. We do not need an arbitrary age at which to define someone as socially finished and thus dispensable. Instead, we need a structure for an age-irrelevant society where medical decisions are made on an individual basis. In this latter context, physicians cannot escape their responsibility to understand the biomedical issues of aging and, equally important, to deal sensitively and responsibly with the ethical issues.

NOTES

1. S. Jay Olshansky, "On Forecasting Mortality," *Milbank Memorial Fund Quarterly* 66 (1988): 482–530.

2. Kenneth G. Manton, "Past and Future Life Expectancy Increases at Later Ages: Their Implications for the Linkage of Chronic Morbidity, Disability and Mortality," *Journal of Gerontology* 5 (September 1986): 672–81.

3. David U. Himmelstein, Steffie Woolhandler, and the Writing Committee of the Working Group on Program Design, "A National Health Program for the United States: A Physicians' Proposal," *New England Journal of Medicine* 320 (January 12, 1989): 102–8.

4. Nancy B. Cummings, "Social, Ethical and Legal Issues Involved in Chronic Maintenance Dialysis," in *Replacement of Renal Function by Dialysis,* ed. John F. Mayer (Boston: Kluwer Academic Publishers, 1988).

5. John M. Eisenberg, *Doctors' Decisions and the Cost of Medical Care* (Ann Arbor: Health Administration Press Perspectives, 1986), pp. 5–27.

6. Uwe E. Reinhardt, "Resource Allocation in Health Care: The Allocation of Lifestyles to Providers," *Milbank Memorial Fund Quarterly* 65 (1987): 153–76.

7. Louise B. Russell, "An Aging Population and the Use of Medical Care," *Medical Care* 19 (June 1981): 633–43.

8. Sidney H. Wanzer et al., "The Physician's Responsibility Toward Hopelessly Ill Patients: A Second Look," *New England Journal of Medicine* 320 (March 30, 1989): 844–49.

9. Robert N. Butler, "The Triumph of Age: Science, Gerontology and Ageism," *Bulletin of the New York Academy of Medicine* 58 (May 1982): 347–61.

10. Christine K. Cassel, "Decisions to Forego Life-Sustaining Therapy: The Limits of Ethics," *Social Service Review,* 1987, pp. 552–64.

11. Christine K. Cassel, "Doctors and Allocation Decisions: A New Role in the New Medicare," *Journal of Health Politics, Policy and Law* 10 (Fall 1985): 549–64.

12. Jacob A. Brody, "The Best of Times/The Worst of Times: Aging and Dependency in the 21st Century," in *Ethical Dimensions of Geriatric Care: Value Conflicts for the 21st Century,* ed. Stuart F. Spicker, Stanley R. Ingman, and Ian R. Lawson (Boston: D. Reidel Publishing Company, 1987): pp. 3–21.

13. Jacob A. Brody, "Prospects for an Ageing Population," *Nature* 315 (June 6–12, 1985): 463–66.

BALANCING OUR CAPACITY TO HOPE WITH OUR NEED TO COPE: THE ROLE OF SCIENCE IN CREATING HEALTH-COST DILEMMAS

....

ROBERT MORRIS

ROBERT MORRIS is Cardinal Medeiros Lecturer, Gerontology Institute, University of Massachusetts, Boston.

Setting Limits has generated controversies, for the most part, about the use of age as a criterion for disentitling people to certain kinds of publicly funded health care as one remedy for the fiscal crisis in the American health-care system. This focus has deflected attention from more serious and complex concerns that Callahan raises, concerns which I strongly share. In particular, concentrating on the growing numbers of aged and their use of health services tends to obscure another basic cause of our current crisis discussed in *Setting Limits:* the direct and indirect role of vanguard scientific inquiry in cost escalation. In this speculative essay, I want to look beyond the gains and benefits of recent scientific advances to consider their ill consequences—their social and economic costs. I want to ask whether unanticipated consequences and failures follow the short-term successes. Finally, I want to suggest alternative, more acceptable ways than age-based rationing to balance the costs and benefits of science and medicine.

It is risky to challenge conventional faith that future achievements of vanguard scientific inquiry will solve most contemporary problems, since scientific advances have strikingly improved the material living standards of millions, relieved their physical pain and disability, extended the very span of their lives. But revolutions in physics, biology, and chemistry have also nurtured the radical view that we can not only dominate our environment but even remake ourselves, at least our physical bodies. Thus, enormous public confidence fuels the scientific quest; the extension of life justifies the costs.

But those concerned about *both* economic and ethical consequences should pause to evaluate the impact of this cultural mind-set. Our widespread confidence in science and technology, I believe, confers on its institutions the power to dominate the course of social arrangements, the nature of relationships between individuals, and the policies adopted for the well-being of society. In the health field in particular, scientific advance shapes the functioning of health professions, medical institutions, drug and insurance industries, welfare organizations, and government budgets. Public enthusiasm for medical advances supports scientific research but *not* basic inquiry into how we might adapt to the wide-ranging consequences of research. Thus, we generously fund those whose research seeks a new scientific future and we allocate meager resources to those who struggle with present economic and social problems. The mirror image of our high valuation of medical advance is our devaluation of programs such as home care and long-term care, which tend to conditions that are neither preventable nor effectively treatable; they are considered "burdens," not necessities.

IMBALANCED PRIORITIES

Scientific advances have left in their wake a fragmented approach to health care, especially in terms of the comparative attention that short-term curative procedures and long-term maintenance for persisting disabilities receive. Citizens of all ages live with illness and associated severe disability affecting more than one activity of daily living. Among the elderly, over six million are disabled, half of them severely.[1] There are millions of infants, youths, and adults with severe lifelong neurological damage and disability.[2] They require access to intermittent medical care, plus continuous nonmedical or sustained social care. The costs of caring and providing for this large group of chronically ill falls to families and to public programs with severely limited budgets. Meanwhile, government investment in research that could improve *current* care in nursing homes or private homes goes instead to research on possible *future* solutions to chronic conditions. The mind frame seems to be: If we invest more in technology and research now, then sometime in the future the prevalence and nature of long-term chronic health problems will drop. We will fund technological solutions to social and personal problems of chronic illness but devote only marginal intellectual and scientific attention to improving the long-term social-support systems that are an integral part of health care.

The resulting imbalance between priorities is dramatically evident in research funding for aging. In 1976 the National Institute on Aging allocated about 26 percent of its research budget for social science research; the balance went to biological and clinical study, where much technology research takes place. In 1986 the social science share dropped to 22 percent. The Administration on Aging, mainly concerned with social care, has a most modest budget for both research and demonstration, totaling in 1986 $21 million. In 1976 standard dollars, this sum had shrunk to $5 million.[3] The costly Catastrophic Health Insurance Act of 1988 will benefit an estimated 15 percent of long-stay hospital patients not already protected,[4] while the marginal expansion of home-care benefits is sharply limited. The act addresses the narrow, hospital-based, high-technology corner of the problem and does nothing for the larger nonhospitalized population. In general, the current system encourages costly hospitalization but fails to address the out-of-hospital needs for regular primary care and aftercare alternatives. One careful study found that 52 percent of a sample population discharged from hospitals were frequently readmitted for the same condition.[5] Such high-cost readmissions accounted for 46 to 79 percent of all hospital charges in the study hospitals. Arguably, the bias toward hospital care rather than aftercare explains the costly result. The Diagnosis–Related Groups (DRG) system of reimbursement has altered hospital functioning and has been criticized for causing the transfer of patients out of hospitals to home care and long-term care settings without financial provision. Despite this trend, hospital costs have continued to escalate.

A more reasonable set of priorities, adopted in most other industrial nations, would call for delivering basic necessities to the majority of people first—primary medical care, support services, related social care, and reliable after-treatment care for the long-term disabled. When such priorities are met, remaining resources could be allocated for frontier research on less widespread problems. In the United States, the opposite seems now to be the case. We invest in probing the frontier and ration our response to basic needs.

THE DESTABILIZING EFFECTS OF RAPID SCIENTIFIC CHANGE

In addition to controlling the priorities of resource allocation, technological change can destabilize patterns of thinking, and of social and political organization. Thus, biologists challenge the millennial belief that human beings have a relatively fixed life span, suggesting that a life span of 120 years is not unreasonable. Others seek an indefinite extension of life through use of transplants. Since these prospects still seem a long way off, there is little inclination to think immediately about the effects of such life extension on population growth and consumption of nonrenewable resources, or the probability that longer life may simply result in newer and more intractable disabilities. Recent history has already offered some lessons that can guide our thinking. The discovery of antibiotics has almost wiped out the death by pneumonia that was nature's way of ending a "normal" life span. But the defeat of pneumonia has allowed the emergence of longer-term chronic disabilities for which there are no cures and for which care has become a major social and familial obligation. Other examples include the retarded, who now live long lives but once died before reaching adolescence. The same is true for the 600,000 persons with spinal cord injuries who can now live many years, but who, until 1940, died within a year or two of paralysis.[6]

The destabilizing effects of scientific change also affect the health professions. The rapid flow of new technologies and instrumentation is a contributing cause of the transformed structure and financing of hospitals—more specialized and costly equipment, more staff, more space, and more borrowing for capital improvements. The cost spiral, increasing at three times the rate of resource growth,[7] has triggered the introduction of costly fiscal-control structures in hospitals, insurance, and government. Because of the sweeping nature of these changes, many physicians and agencies believe that clerks in distant offices, using protocol checklists for determining how much of what kind of medical care shall be given, control their mission of treating patients.

Simultaneously, the tempo of technological innovation produces a proliferation of medical specialization which has flourished as new knowledge floods in and exceeds the capacity of one professional to absorb it all. This results in increasing the number of professional and support personnel engaged in treating any one patient. When well executed, the results benefit the individual, but that is not always the case. Good and bad consequences flood the institutions within which medical care is delivered; administrative costs climb, as do the costs of treatment and support staffs. Complexity in coordinating the work of large teams increases in conjunction with uncertainty about whether the quality of care can be monitored and maintained. The danger of treatment errors increases, too, accompanied by higher malpractice costs. And, in the end, patient care is impersonalized.

Finally, technological changes are transforming hospitals so that more and more patients are discharged earlier or are treated on an ambulatory basis. This change means that care once given in hospitals to patients treated by advanced technology is now pushed out into the community and borne either by family members (most likely to be working women), by social agencies, or by new types of home-health services which have not yet been tested such as home-delivered inhalation and intravenous therapies.[8] The posthospital pressures of care are shifted to an amalgam of nonhospital services lacking in professional training and skills, financial supports, and public understanding.

THE UNSCIENTIFIC BASES FOR MEDICAL INNOVATION: MOVING FROM LABORATORY TO PRACTICE

Unsettling evidence counters a prevailing belief that technical advance can be transferred safely to practice by means of adequate laboratory tests, safe field trials, and responsible use by physicians. These transfers are less controlled than we would like to believe. In 1981 McKinlay offered a conceptual outline of the process by which medical innovation is introduced and adopted.[9] According to this paradigm, either the scientist in the laboratory or a physician identifies a treatment that seems to work for a given condition first on animals, then on human subjects, then in field trials. From there pacesetters in medicine—institutions and physicians willing to try new and promising treatments—move innovation toward acceptance. They publish accounts of their successful research. It becomes quickly available to a wider circle of physicians and patients. Hospitals, accrediting bodies, review boards, insurance companies, and third-party payers accept the innovation, and the scientific advance becomes standard.

The weakness in all of this is twofold. Very few of these medical innovations are subjected to longitudinal controlled testing (except for drug testing to secure FDA approval). Therefore, it is difficult to be certain that benefits claimed are really the result of the new treatment. Later study often finds that the control population does as well as the experimental group. In fact, most control studies seem to be undertaken long after a procedure has become embedded in institutional conventional wisdom. These later studies sometimes determine that the innovation was ineffective, that it might even have been more harmful than useful. Thus, recent studies indicate that 20 to 30 percent of major surgical and diagnostic procedures are inappropriate;[10] that for some heart problems, intensive care is less effective than more conservative treatment; that cesarean sections are often unnecessary; and that angioplasty adds little to conservative drug treatment of cardiac risk.[11]

A further weakness lies in the absence of long-term followup studies on patients who have undergone major intervention against severe illness. If patients improve, they go home and, as often as not, receive no follow-up. They may go to another doctor or disappear from view in nursing homes. A

213

longitudinal record of hospital readmissions is seldom assembled for one patient, and no such record is aggregated for a class of conditions or patients.[12] Records are episodic, but the episodes are seldom compiled to give a comprehensive picture of how the health system works. A common example is drug therapy that has been a blessing in the short term; but for older patients and for the mentally ill, the absence of any continuity in care means that we do not know the long-term effects of drug use. Available evidence suggests that drugs are often an iatrogenic cause of illness. The point is not that science is harmful in its origins, only that in its applications we are less successful than we would like to think.

THE FAILURES OF SCIENTIFIC SUCCESS

Some of the great successes of modern medicine have generated serious problems, which, to adapt an old Chinese proverb, may only mean that every success creates two new problems. The mixed consequences of antibiotics have already been mentioned. But this maxim applies to other areas as well. Our ability to keep alive the developmentally disabled means that a whole host of care- and cost-management issues arise. Medical advances since World War II have had dramatic results for people paralyzed with spinal cord injuries, yet we ill attend to their complex medical and social needs. Medication succeeded in stabilizing the bizarre behavior of many mentally ill people, enabling them to be discharged from institutions. However, medicine took little note of the consequences (except by routine referral to clinics), and as a result we seem to have enlarged the problem of homelessness, as the mentally ill often end up on the streets without stabilizing community environments of social support. Some years ago success with renal dialysis led an optimistic nation to adopt a most generous policy of dialysis for all. Today dialysis has given many patients longer life and funded many profit-making centers, but it has also added several billion dollars a year to the tax bill. Such costs can be justified, but they also challenge those struggling to keep the costs of medical care down.

Some of these consequences could have been anticipated. We need to acknowledge that the high costs of chronic and long-term illness and disability arise from prior medical success, not from overconsumption by the surviving long-term ill or enfeebled.

QUALITY FLAWS IN THE NUMBERS GAME

As research has extended medical frontiers, it has become commonplace to talk of the increasing number of individuals who survive a new procedure to live long enough to go home. Such a homecoming suggests that great breakthroughs have occurred, but in many cases the average survival after "cure" may be a few months or a year. For some organ transplants, the figures, discouraging though they are, have been justified by experimenters as steps on the way to conquering disease. But do we have to accept that as a worthy promise—that someday humans can be kept alive forever by organ transplants? Even if they could, are we ready for the ethical and economic costs of organ "farming" and "marketing" when the number of patients vastly exceeds the number of organ donors?

Apart from organ transplantation, life-sustaining measures can mean a few brief months spent "tethered" to support machines with pain, continual adjustment in medical treatment, and constant dependence on social supports for the basic activities of living, or with activity reduced to the minimum of basic survival. Many will choose this, with hope for respite, but the successes of such survival are hardly measured by the quality of life that results. The medicalization of survival has meant that limited attention is given to the social sequelae that require as much attention and investment in social technology as does the initial medical technology. Quality of life, and how to measure it, in this highly medicalized system has hardly been explored but already begs for sustained inquiry.

SUMMING UP THE CASE FOR BALANCE AND CAUTION IN MEDICAL RESEARCH AND DEVELOPMENT

My argument should not be interpreted as an attack on technological or scientific innovation. Rather, I want to suggest that we reexamine the bias toward dramatic high-technology investment that governs public choice, and that we consider options other than age-based rationing to address the linked crises of scientific change, values, population change, and financial cost in the health field.

I find some support for my critique in recent work that conceptualizes chaos in terms that are much more subtle, and not as negative, as the popular vision of a world run amok. Complex relationships in the physical world (weather systems, behavior of molecules, etc.) seem to support the idea that very small change in initial conditions can give rise to a pattern that leads later on to very large and upsetting changes, to conditions that appear to be chaotic. In short, an ordered structure, affected with infinitesimal but critical change, destabilizes into a dramatically different structure. The new structure arrives as chaos.

This can be closely traced in the laboratory. But in the health field, I submit, the elemental pattern consists of less clear conditions and less well-understood relationships—between medical technology, professional practices, social institutions like hospitals and social agencies, patient life or death, and the national economy represented by allocations

216

from the public purse. We have done very little to examine the consequences of change in these relationships within the health and economic system. If the logic of chaos in the molecular world as developed by science has any validity, it may have utility in our larger health world as we ask: How shall we handle the inflating costs of health care in an aging society and its destabilizing impact on the functioning of health-care institutions?

There is another reason the problems of cost should be approached at the root of scientific change and not simply as an age disentitlement issue. The culture of science and technology has created, whether intended or not, a widespread public belief that medical intervention can cure or prevent many or most ills. In old age, when the years remaining are few and increasingly valuable, the elderly feel most vulnerable. Hence, an older population will take full advantage of the hopes raised by medical advances. The utilization of health care in an aging society is driven more by the promises of medicine than by the population curve.

SOME POLICY ALTERNATIVES
TO AGE DISENTITLEMENT

If the foregoing analysis is at all near target, then the attempt to cap or limit access to certain benefits by age is a well-intended, readily understandable remedy, but one which is very likely to fail in its purposes. I suggest several alternative approaches. Although none of them promise quick change, they seem to be more equitable and to be more effective over time.

One approach would be to slow down, not repeal, scientific inquiry into the high technology of medical care, to broaden the range of sanctioned research, and to distribute research and development funds more evenly to include funds for an examination of the social and organizational consequences and costs of technological innovation in medical care. If our innovations result in people not only living longer but living with serious disabilities that produce dependencies, if such dependencies are a direct result of medical/science inquiry, and if these dependencies involve physical and social care as much as they require medical oversight, then human needs are best met by some integration of the two modes of intervention—curative and supportive. Their respective scientific foundations are the so-called life sciences and social sciences.

Our curative and support systems have evolved two parallel structures of organization that will not be easily joined. A more balanced allocation of research and development funding and activity between the physical and social sciences is needed to integrate them. The former has been relatively well financed, the latter has starved. Both involve the use of scientific methods, but these methods differ because of the difference in subject matter. The former is concerned with the complex organisms of the human body, the latter with the complex organizations that humans create. Increasing the proportion of appropriately directed research funds for the social sciences can provide for better management of the care and support of the disabled—better both in quality and in economy or efficiency—so that organization in health can catch up with the rapid changes made possible by biological and physical studies.

We might usefully develop stronger practical measures of quality of life linked to selected therapies whose consequences in terms of disability, pain, or limited life conditions can be established. If such criteria were developed and tested, it could provide guidance in several ways: to medical judgments in applying or recommending the use of certain interventions, to improving patient and family understanding of the probable consequences of some treatments, and to the priorities given to vanguard research alternatives.

Another, very unlikely approach would be to combine, in the public and private medical structure and budget, the full responsibility for acute medical treatment, primary care, and social sequelae of illness or therapy. This would greatly enhance the medical system's authority and raise its total budget substantially. But it would also place in one organizational system the responsibility for balancing and controlling the growth of various sectors of the full span of health care, the curative and the social. It would make clear the moral as well as the professional responsibility for the consequences of technological initiatives.

While medical systems in the past have found ways to circumvent their social-care responsibilities in favor of higher technology, new methods for assuring responsible attention to the full spectrum might be devised. The Social/Health Maintenance Organization experiment now under way in four cities may be an early test of the feasibility of such an approach.[13] Recent proposals to give family physicians the budget responsibility for purchasing hospital care, and thus accountability for costs, are another sign that such an approach may be further tested.

CONCLUSION

This by no means exhausts all the possibilities. But my aim has been to direct attention to the root causes of the crisis which *Setting Limits* rightly raises to public visibility. I have argued that the main cause is popular acceptance of the seductive view that individual self-realization (by scientist, researcher, citizen, patient) shall be the measure of all we do, and that the realities of our biological fates can be, if not ignored, at least hidden from view. The Nobel Prize-winning physician P. B. Medawar observes: "People look first to science and then away in disappointment . . . partly because they have grown so used to thinking of science and technology as a secular substitute for the miraculous; but most of the

219

problems that beset mankind call for political, moral, and administrative, rather than scientific solutions."[14]

What the citizenry will support and pay for will depend on how we attend to the consequences of medical advances as they filter through the social structures of health care.

We could decide that it is worth more than doubling our expenditures to take advantage of all that science can produce. Or we could decide that there are limits to what can be done to make human beings invulnerable. This decision would require that we turn more of our scientific resources and our thinking to how we will manage the persisting inevitabilities of dependency, decay, and death. In the end, the costs may not be that much different, but the burdens of being human may be more equitably shared and borne, by all of us, with less illusion, frustration, and disappointment.[15]

NOTES

1. Alice M. Rivlin and Joshua M. Wiener, *Caring for the Disabled Elderly: Who Will Pay?* (Washington, D.C.: The Brookings Institution, 1988).

2. Ernest M. Gruenberg, "The Failures of Success," *Milbank Memorial Fund Quarterly* 55 (Winter 1977), pp. 3–24.

3. Pamela Kerin et al., *Public Policy and the Future of Aging Education* (Washington, D.C.: Association for Gerontology and Higher Education, 1988).

4. *OMB Watch,* Washington, D.C., April 17, 1987, quoting the American Association of Retired Persons.

5. Christopher J. Zook, Sheila Flanigan Savickis, and Francis D. Moore, "Repeated Hospitalization for the Same Disease: A Multiplier of National Health Costs," *Milbank Memorial Fund Quarterly* 58 (Summer 1980), pp. 454–71.

6. Gruenberg, "The Failures of Success."

7. W. A. Manning et al., *Health Insurance and the Demand for Health Care* (Santa Monica, CA: Rand Corporation, 1988).

8. C. R. Neu and S. C. Harrison, *Post Hospital Care Before and After Medicare Prospective Payment System* (Santa Monica, CA: Rand Corporation, 1988).

9. John B. McKinlay, "From 'Promising Report' to 'Standard Procedure': Seven Stages in the Career of a Medical Innovation," *Milbank Memorial Fund Quarterly* 59 (Summer 1981), pp. 374–411.

10. Milt Freudenheim, "New Guidelines to Control Health Costs," *New York Times,* 4 April 1989, p. D2.

11. William A. Knaus, Elizabeth A. Draper, and Douglas P. Wagner, "The Use of Intensive Care: New Research Initiatives and Their Implications for National Health Policy," *Milbank Memorial Fund Quarterly* 61 (Fall 1983), pp. 561–83.

12. Zook, Savickis, and Moore, "Repeated Hospitalization for the Same Disease."

13. Walter Leutz et al., "Targeting Expanded Care to the Aged: Early SHMO Experience," *Gerontologist* 28 (February 1988), pp. 4–17.

14. P. B. and J. S. Medawar, *The Life Science: Current Ideas of Biology* (New York: Harper and Row, 1977), p. 172.

15. The editorial help of Paul Homer, Bartholomew Collopy, and Martha Holstein was important in crafting the final version of this essay and is gratefully acknowledged.

Generational Equity and the Public Policy Debate: Quagmire or Opportunity?

....

MEREDITH MINKLER

MEREDITH MINKLER is Professor and Chair, Department of Health Education, School of Public Health, University of California, Berkeley.

GENERATIONAL EQUITY or intergenerational justice is one of several philosophical underpinnings of Daniel Callahan's *Setting Limits,* and one particularly deserving of scrutiny. On the one hand, attempts by Callahan and others[1] to frame complex policy issues in terms of generational equity are problematic, since the concept itself is based on the questionable assumption that our policies for the old unfairly burden the young. On the other hand, calls by Callahan and others for a broader sense of community, with elders responding in particular to the needs of younger and future generations, are both timely and sound.

GENERATIONAL EQUITY: A FLAWED BASIS FOR PUBLIC POLICY

The concept of generational equity suggests that all age groups and generations have a right to fair treatment, and that, therefore, benefits for one group (e.g., the elderly) should

222

not be advanced without carefully considering the competing needs and rights of other groups.[2]

Implicit in this framework is the notion that America's younger generations are suffering in part as a consequence of an elderly population unprecedented in size (and affluence) and in the proportion of the federal budget it commands. The elderly, it is argued, represent about 12 percent of the population but consume some 30 percent of the national health-care budget; while poverty among elders had dropped to just 12–14 percent by the early 1980s, the incidence of poverty in children had climbed to 12.7 percent. Thus, although poverty in children was 56 percent greater than among the elderly, children were receiving only a sixth as much in federal expenditures as the elderly.

To his credit, Callahan does point to large discrepancies in income and well-being within the elderly population, noting, for example, that well over a third of elderly blacks live in poverty. Yet the bottom line in the generational equity framework—that the elderly are doing far better than younger Americans financially and yet receiving a disproportionate share of federal resources—must be viewed with caution.

Such caution is merited, first, simply on the grounds that our methods of measuring poverty in the elderly are seriously inadequate. Comparisons which stress the favorable economic status of the aged vis-à-vis younger cohorts, for example, fail to acknowledge the use of two separate poverty lines in the U.S.: one for those sixty-five and older and another for all other age groups. In 1985 the poverty line for a single elderly person was $5,156—fully 8.5 percent lower than the $5,593 poverty line used for single persons under age sixty-five. Had the same poverty cutoff been used for both groups, 15.4 percent of the elderly would have fallen below the line, giving the aged a higher poverty rate than any other age group except children.[3]

Even the higher poverty index is inadequate in failing to account accurately for inflation. By revised estimates, Molly Orshansky, the original developer of the poverty index, suggests the number of elderly persons living in or near poverty almost doubles.[4]

While it is true that the elderly have a lower poverty rate than children even when these revised calculations are taken into account, suggestions by Callahan and others that recent economic improvements among the old are somehow linked to growing poverty in the nation's youth are inaccurate at best. As Richard Easterlin has pointed out, "the divergent trends in poverty rates of children and the elderly chiefly reflect two different and largely independent causes."[5] The improved financial status of the elderly in large part is a consequence of favorable government policies, especially improvements in Social Security. A 20 percent increase in Social Security payments in 1972, for example, and linking these benefits to the Consumer Price Index to protect them from inflation, has dramatically decreased poverty rates among the elderly.

In contrast, the rise of poverty rates among children is primarily attributable to market forces, including dramatic declines in the absolute level of real wages of young males in the 1980s, adverse unemployment trends among the young, and, indirectly, the rise in female-headed households. As Easterlin notes, because it is shaped primarily by these market trends, the rise in poverty in children would have occurred even in the absence of programs improving the lot of the elderly.

Unlike some of his colleagues in the generational equity movement, Callahan does not suggest radically "reforming" Social Security as a means of saving government monies that could then be spent on youth. His proposed reformation of Medicare would, by his own admission, cost more money than it would save. Callahan thus would support a national health program covering long-term care as well as acute care needs and offering far more liberal home-care benefits. Yet in arguing that federal monies for life-extending technology be restricted to those who have not yet lived out a "natural life span," Callahan reverts in part to the same spurious "generational equity" arguments: Society must "set limits" on care for the elderly partly so that more of its resources can be used to benefit the young.

This notion that society must "set limits" on care for the elderly to preserve more of its resources for youth is open to immediate criticism. As a number of analysts have suggested, the current health-care crisis is fueled in large part not by too many elders requesting high tech medicine, but by escalating medical costs generally. Expenditures on hospital care, for example, grew from $14 billion in 1965 to $167 billion in 1985.[6] Even when inflation is controlled for, it still represents a threefold increase over this period.[7] With health-care costs inflating at a rate roughly double that of the Consumer Price Index, "generational equity" as such would seem less an issue than introducing some sort of reform into medical-care cost structures.

A current provocative attempt at the latter may be found in Oregon's controversial effort to rank Medicaid-funding priorities, with immunizations, prenatal care, inpatient psychiatric care, and the diagnosis and treatment of acute illnesses at the top of the list and organ transplants—regardless of the age of the recipient—at the bottom.[8] Wherever one stands on the ethics of such an approach, it does suggest that consideratons other than chronological age may provide a useful—and possibly more equitable—basis for health-care rationing.

On still another level, arguments that we must restrict government spending on medical research and life extension for the very old in order to redirect scarce resources toward children and youth assume a zero-sum game in which other possible options (such as raising taxes) are implicitly ignored.[9] Yet in reality, some of these options merit a close second look. Corporate taxes, for example, dropped from 4.2 percent of the GNP in the early 1960s to 1.6 percent in the early 1980s. And over the period 1980–1986 the money lost to the Treasury through tax loopholes grew from $40 billion to a whopping $120 billion.[10] Restoration of some of these lost revenues, while doubtlessly unpopular politically, would provide major new sources of funding for health and social service programs for young and old alike.

The nation's military budget has also tended to be overlooked in discussions of the costliness of medical care for the elderly. Indeed, as gerontologist Robert Binstock has noted, we are taught to think in terms of how many workers it takes to support a dependent old person, but not how many it takes to support an aircraft carrier. The classic political-economic trade-off "guns versus butter" has been reframed in his words as "guns versus canes."[11]

In addition to playing into a narrow, zero-sum-game mentality, the concept of generational equity has been criticized for deflecting attention from more basic inequities within American society. Indeed, as Kingson has noted, "explanations drawing on class, race, gender, and ethnicity are far more powerful [than those based on generational equity] because the inequality within all age groups (or within generations) is far greater than that existing between age groups."[12] In particular, Kingson suggests, justice between rich and poor must be considered, with a more equitable "distribution of burdens" on the basis of wealth regardless of chronological age.

Curiously, Callahan's partial "solution" to the problem of generational inequity—his call for restricting government monies for life prolongation in the very old—ignores the grave social justice questions raised by a plan that allows the rich to purchase life-extending technologies when the poor cannot. What he labels a move for "generational equity" in this sense houses within it the very inequities between rich and poor that have plagued American health-care policy from the beginning.

Still another problematic assumption underlying the concept of generational equity has to do with its notions of who benefits and who pays for policies and programs "for the old." In their narrow framing of these questions, early spokespersons for Americans for Generational Equity (AGE) went so far as to suggest that young Americans had become "indentured servants" as a consequence of our bloated entitlement programs for the old.[13]

Callahan, by contrast, has praised Social Security and Medicare as "a communal expression of solidarity between the generations" and has recognized some of their cross-generational benefits. Yet, he too falls prey to a tendency to view services and programs for the elderly far too narrowly. Callahan's proposal to redirect most medical-research funding away from conditions affecting mainly the elderly, for instance, is an example of a strategy in which shortsighted concern with "generational equity" misses the bigger cross-generational picture.

In the United States today families provide 80 to 90 percent of the care received by the elderly living in the community.[14] The word "families," of course, is largely a euphemism for women, for it is the adult daughters and daughters-in-law of the old who provide the bulk of this cross-generational care giving. Typically, these female caregivers are themselves older—their average age is about fifty-seven—and they are, in Elaine M. Brody's words, part of a "sandwich generation" of "women in the middle."[15] As such, they find themselves squeezed between the often competing needs of their elderly parents, their spouses, their jobs, and their children.

Many of these "women in the middle" are finding that their caregiving responsibilities necessitate regular and often significant cutbacks in their paid work. A recent survey by the Traveler's Insurance Company, for example, revealed that its employees were taking more time off work to care for frail elderly parents than to care for sick children.[16] Such caregiving may have serious economic consequences. A recent national long-term-care study by Robyn Stone and colleagues revealed that 9 percent of caregivers quit their jobs, 21 percent reduce their work hours, and 18.6 percent take time off work without pay in order to accommodate caregiving demands.[17] Minority women are far more likely than Caucasian women to continue to work full-time jobs while providing equally demanding care.

Of perhaps even greater concern, moreover, are the physical and mental health consequences of caregiving, which have been shown to result in high rates of clinical depression and a variety of other stress-related illnesses.[18] While Callahan does recognize the toll that certain conditions such as Alzheimer's disease and incontinence take on families as well as their elderly members, and acknowledges that a handful of these conditions therefore are deserving of research monies, his overall prescription—that research funds go principally to studying conditions prevalent in younger age groups—sadly ignores the salience of the whole caregiver issue.

While funding for research on AIDS, multiple sclerosis, and other conditions affecting primarily the young must certainly be given high priority, to argue against allocating research money for conditions affecting the old is to ignore the reality of extensive cross-generational caregiving for the elderly and hence the substantial cross-generational benefits of such research. Further, because women are far more likely to live into advanced age than men (there are 100 women aged eighty-five and over for every 41 men), and to have more associated disabilities,[19] suggestions that we cut back on research into health problems of the old imply de facto gender discrimination as well as discrimination based on age.

In sum, generational equity is a flawed basis on which to ground public policy decisions. In ignoring market forces and other structural causes of increased poverty in the young, it spuriously suggests that the costly elderly are somehow to blame. In portraying the elderly and their "relentless pursuit" of life-extending technology as responsible for skyrocketing federal medical-care expenditures, it overlooks continued escalation of health-care costs as a primary cause of the current crisis. By fostering a zero-sum-game mentality, the notion of generational equity discourages us from looking at options (such as tax increases or curtailed military spending) other than taking from the old to give to the young. Finally, by framing issues in terms of competition between groups for scarce resources, the concept ignores other, far more potent bases of inequity and further overlooks the tremendous cross-generational impacts of caring for the elderly.

GENERATIONAL EQUITY OR GENERATIONAL INTERDEPENDENCE?

Paul Berry once remarked that if we don't know we're a community, we can't know our losses. Generational equity is only one of the reasons that Callahan would have us "set limits" on care for the old. He appears to give equal weight, for example, to the notion that in setting limits, we in fact may add meaning to old age by affirming its uniqueness as a stage in the life cycle. He suggests that if the elderly don't see themselves as part of a larger, intergenerational whole, if they don't speak the language of community and mutual responsibility, not only are they as elders denied some of the meaning and richness of old age but society itself is the loser.

Ironically, the call for "generational equity," while resting on shaky and sometimes spurious assumptions, nevertheless has served to remind us of the critical stake elders and the whole of society has in policies aimed at children and other age groups. As Kingson and colleagues have noted, the generational equity issue thus may be seen as "an opportunity to develop a multi-generational advocacy agenda and strategy."[20] To exploit such an opportunity, however, we would be well advised to change our terminology from that of generational *equity*, stressing conflict and competition for scarce resources, to that of *interdependence of generations*.[21]

The moral and spiritual basis for such a broadening of focus is well captured in *Setting Limits*. Callahan argues for an Eriksonian view of old age as emphasizing "integrity," or the coherence or wholeness of life, through an active concern for younger and future generations. In part, of course, Callahan sees this role as requiring that elders accept their own aging and death. Yet, equally important, he prescribes an old age in which elders are oriented toward serving youth, not merely in their own individual families, but in the broader society as well.

It is unfortunate, I believe, that the outcry over Callahan's notion of setting age limits on medical treatment has all but obscured his vision of the aged's role in providing perspective and a world "hopeful for the young and worthy of bequest," for it is this latter message that may ultimately be among the book's most important legacies.

How might such a vision guide those of us concerned with an aging society and the role of elders within it? Kingson has set forth several key principles and directions for action that provide a useful starting point to reinforce a more communal vision in which the interdependence of generations is the primary focus.[22]

First, Kingson argues, an approach stressing the interdependence of generations would have us look broadly at the ways in which policies and programs aimed mainly at one group affect other age groups, over both the short and the long term. This approach would have us view such benefits as public education and Medicare as transfers across generations that meet different needs across the life course, ultimately to the advantage of all.

Second and relatedly, the interdependence approach would have us recognize and act on the fact that elders and their advocates have a tremendous stake in policies for children and other age groups. Such a perspective does not mean that elders and their advocates should fight for expanded child-care benefits because in the process they might create a wedge for increased support for adult day care or adult day health care. While such an outcome might well flow from improved family policy legislation that began with a focus on child care, elders and elder advocates should also view adequate child care as constituting *in and of itself* a vital national goal. The seven million children under age thirteen now without any care or supervision for a part of every day and the millions of others who suffer from grossly inadequate child-care provisions must not merely be viewed as problems of the poor or of young working parents but of the whole of society including, importantly, its oldest members. It is the well-being of these children that represents the older generation's gift to the future.

Third, an approach to policy stressing intergenerational dependence rather than intergenerational equity would create an awareness that interest group competition systematically disadvantages the least powerful members of the community. A concerted effort to move from interest group politics to what James Q. Wilson has termed "majoritarian" policy efforts would appear an important alternative to more competitive approaches implied in notions such as generational equity and intergenerational justice.[23] Such efforts occur around universalistic programs and policies such as Social Security and Medicare, which disperse costs and benefits widely throughout the population.

Kingson's fourth principle would have us work toward an "equitable distribution of burdens" and consider policy changes that would increase the tax burden on the wealthy elderly. While close to half of the elderly live within extremely modest means, many elders who are quite comfortable financially pay only a relatively small tax on their Social Security earnings. (Since 1984, single individuals with incomes of over $25,000 and married couples with incomes of over $30,000 have paid taxes on half of their Social Security benefits.) Taxation of all Social Security benefits for individuals with over an annual income of, for example, $30,000 would seem an important and overdue means of rectifying this situation. Further, it would strike yet another blow at what Binstock has termed "compassionate ageism"—the tendency to portray elders in general as poor, frail, and vulnerable as a means of garnering support for favorable old-age-based policies and entitlements.[24]

Kingson's fifth principle encompasses suggestions that have been widely supported by elders and their advocates for years: the ending of mandatory and "pressured" early retirement, the introduction of flex-hour work policies, job retraining, and improved opportunities for volunteer service among the old. Such approaches have in common an emphasis on the positive aspects of aging and on the tremendous and often untapped potential of elders for continued learning, growth, participation, and contribution.[25] As such, policies like these provide an important counter to our Western preoccupation with the problems of late life and our tendency to equate the latter with "a specter of decline," as Moody puts it.[26] As he has argued, the majority of our policies for the elderly make a fundamental error in addressing "the deficits of old age without attending to opportunities. . . . We offer old people help with their needs but do nothing to nurture the strengths" that would allow them to engage in more effective personal problem-solving and to contribute to the larger society. While carefully noting the continued need for supportive welfare policies, Moody suggests that these must be complemented by human development policies and programs that to date have been largely limited to children and younger segments of society. Retraining older workers and providing more flexible work-hour schedules and more creative volunteer opportunities are among the approaches critical to an expanded and more positive vision of later life.

Kingson would also have us recognize and act on our societal responsibilities in both childbearing and care giving across the generations, and this too is vital. The last two decades have seen the importance of self-help and mutual aid on the individual, family, and community levels translated into the rhetoric of individual and family responsibility and government "noninterference." This rhetoric in turn has been used to support the dismantling of major health and social service accomplishments of the last half century, and elders and their care givers have been among the losers.[27]

In the arena of caregiving across the generations, there is a vital need for more, rather than less, government and other extrafamilial support. In supporting the family (and hence women caregivers), we must see ourselves as doing no less than supporting the whole of society. And in failing to do so, we similarly must acknowledge that we have failed a critical test of our wisdom and our humanity as a nation.

Kingson's final principle for action involves creating coalitions to protect existing services and to extend them to all in need. Kingson appears to acknowledge that a move from age- to strictly need-based services often is neither wise nor politically astute. Medicare, for example, by serving all elders regardless of income, remains a politically popular program, while means-tested Medicaid unfortunately lacks an equal level of political or popular support. At the same time that we work to defend age-based programs like Medicare against further cuts, however, Kingson's final admonition would have us fight to enact a national health program benefiting all Americans regardless of age. It would recognize that access to health care is a particular problem for the 37 million Americans under sixty-five who are uninsured[28] and the millions of others who are underinsured.[29] Such a vision, moreover, would have us join forces with groups like the Children's Defense Fund, the National Health Program Coalition, and the Health Security Action Coalition in working to make health care a right for all rather than a privilege for a certain group or for those who can afford it.

Kingson's principles and policy guidelines, in short, help us translate part of the positive message of *Setting Limits* into practical directions for reflection and action.

Fortunately, there are already many positive examples of such principles in practice:

- The mayor of Miami recently gave the city's large population of elderly voters most of the credit for passage of a crucial school bond initiative that would affect mainly Hispanic youth.
- IBM, The Traveler's, and some other major corporations are taking steps to provide both child- and parent-care leave and day-care facilities for their workers.
- Fully one-third of America's elders are currently volunteers, and increasing numbers are active in intergenerational tutoring, etc.
- Organizations such as the Gray Panthers, the American Association of Retired Persons (AARP), the American

Society on Aging (ASA), and the Gerontological Society of America (GSA) have formed effective coalitions with groups such as the Children's Defense Fund and Health Security Action Coalition to protect and/or create programs and services essential to cross-age-group constituencies.

But much remains to be done. Overall, support among the elderly for public education is relatively poor. A nationwide survey by AARP plans to increase its efforts to convince members that the education of today's youth is vital to the elderly.[30]

Such "reeducation" is critical, yet perhaps more important than convincing elders that things like the education of youth is in the best interest *of the elderly* is the establishment of a new societal norm that goes such thinking one better. Such a norm would see the good society as, in Callahan's words, "inherently communal," rather than individual, in orientation. A more generalized commitment to the equitable distribution of burdens and to shared responsibility for maintaining community and social institutions would replace narrowly conceived, interest group politics.

A perspective like this assumes, of course, that it is *feasible* to work toward societal consensus on such fundamental issues as the nature of a good and just society. Such an assumption may be unduly optimistic in a nation where consensus seems rather to be around the desirability of individualism. The question becomes, then, can this preoccupation with individual rather than community be changed, and should it be?

An early visitor to the People's Republic of China reported that his last image on leaving was a huge red and white banner in the airport that read, "Serve the People." On reaching the United States, one of his first images was an airport Coke machine bearing the red and white slogan "Serve Yourself."

A critical and often overshadowed part of Callahan's message is that our culture, which "does not easily speak the language of community," must learn to do so. And the call for "generational equity," for all its faults as a policy framework, may be a blessing in disguise to the extent that it reawakens in us this broader, interdependent sense of who we are as a people.

NOTES

1. Philip Longman, *Born to Pay: The New Politics of Aging in America* (Boston: Houghton Mifflin Co., 1987); Samuel H. Preston, "Children and the Elderly in the U.S.," *Scientific American* 251 (December 1984): 44–49; Paul Taylor, "The Continuing Conflict as We Soak the Young to Enrich the Old," *San Francisco Chronicle,* 2 February 1986, pp. 6–16.

2. Harry R. Moody, *Abundance of Life: Human Development Policies for an Aging Society* (New York: Columbia University Press, 1988); Preston, "Children and the Elderly in the U.S."

3. Ronald F. Pollack, *On the Other Side of Easy Street* (Washington, D.C.: The Villers Foundation, 1987); Robert H. Binstock, "The Aged as Scapegoat," *Gerontologist* 23 (April 1983): 136–43.

4. Binstock, "The Aged as Scapegoat."

5. Richard A. Easterlin, "The New Age Structure of Poverty in America: Permanent or Transient?" *Population and Development Review* 13 (1987): 195–208.

6. Mark Schlesinger et al., "The Privatization of Health Care and Physicians' Perceptions of Access to Hospital Services," *Milbank Memorial Fund Quarterly* 65 (June 1987): 25–58.

7. Mark Schlesinger, personal communication, June 1988.

8. Senate Bill 27 of the 65th Oregon State Legislature Assembly, March 31, 1989. See also John D. Golenski and Stephen R. Blum, "The Oregon Medicaid Priority Setting Project," unpublished report, March 1989.

9. Eric R. Kingson, Barbara A. Hirshorn, and John Cornman, *Ties That Bind: The Interdependence of Generations in an Aging Society* (Cabin John, MD: Seven Locks Press, 1986). Passim.

10. Ronald F. Pollack, "Generational Equity: The Current Debate" (paper presented at 32nd Annual Meeting of the American Society on Aging, San Francisco, March 24, 1986).

11. Binstock, "The Aged as Scapegoat," p. 8.

12. Eric R. Kingson, "Generational Equity: An Unexpected Opportunity to Broaden the Politics of Aging," *The Gerontologist* 28 (December 1988): 765–72. For an expanded critique of the assumptions behind and strategies of generational equity, see Meredith Minkler, " 'Generational Equity' and the New Victim Blaming: An Emerging Public Policy Issue," *International Journal of Health Services* 16 (1986): 539–51.

13. Paul Hewitt, "A Broken Promise," Brochure of Americans for Generational Equity (Washington, D.C.: AGE, 1986); Meredith Minkler, "The Politics of Generational Equity," *Social Policy* 17 (Winter 1986): 48–52.

14. Kenneth G. Manton and Korbin Liu, "The Future of the Long-Term Care Population: Projections Based on the 1977 National Nursing Home Survey and the 1982 Long-Term Care Survey," (paper presented at the Hillhaven Third National Leadership Conference on Long-Term Care Issues, The Future World of Long-Term Care, Washington, D.C., March 7–9, 1984); Robyn Stone, G. Cafferata, and F. Sangl, "Caregivers of the Frail Elderly: A National Profile" (Washington, D.C.: Department of Health and Human Services, U.S. Public Health Service, 1986).

15. Elaine M. Brody, " 'Women in the Middle' and Family Help to Older People," *Gerontologist* 21 (October 1981): 471–80.

16. The Travelers Companies: The Travelers' Employee Caregiver Survey (Hartford, CT: unpublished manuscript, 1985).

17. Stone, Cafferata, and Sangl, "Caregivers of the Frail Elderly."

18. Dolores Gallagher et al., "Depression and Other Negative Effects in Family Caregiving," in *Alzheimer's Disease Treatment*

and Family Stress: Directions for Research, ed. Enid Light and Barry Leibowitz (Washington, D.C.: National Institute of Mental Health, Government Printing Office, 1989); Alfred P. Fengler and Nancy Goodrich, "Wives of Elderly Disabled Men: The Hidden Patients," *Gerontologist* 19 (April 1979): 175–83; Janice K. Kiecolt-Glaser et al., "Chronic Stress and Immunity in Family Caregivers of Alzheimer's Disease Victims," *Psychosomatic Medicine* 49 (September/October 1987): 523–35.

19. Jacob S. Siegel and Cynthia M. Taeuber, "Demographic Dimensions of an Aging Population," in *Our Aging Society,* ed. Alan Pifer and Lydia Bronte (New York: W. W. Norton & Co., 1986), pp. 79–110.

20. Kingson, Hirshorn, and Cornman, *Ties That Bind.*

21. Siegel and Taeuber, "Demographic Dimensions." See also "Uniting the Generations: Moving States Toward Family Policies Across the Age Spectrum" (Springfield, IL: Department of Aging, October 1987).

22. Kingson, "Generational Equity"; "Uniting the Generations."

23. James Q. Wilson, *The Politics of Regulation* (New York: Basic Books, 1984). See also Fernando Torres-Gil, "Long-Term Care Policy and Interest Group Struggles," *Gerontologist* 26 (October 1986): 488–95.

24. Robert H. Binstock, "The Oldest Old: A Fresh Perspective or Compassionate Ageism Revisited?" *Milbank Memorial Fund Quarterly* 63 (Spring 1985): 420–51.

25. Alan Pifer, "The Public Policy Response," in *Our Aging Society,* ed. Alan Pifer and Lydia Bronte (New York: W. W. Norton & Co., 1986), pp. 391–413.

26. Moody, *Abundance of Life.*

27. Marc Pilisuk and Meredith Minkler, "Social Support: Economic and Political Considerations," *Social Policy* 15 (Winter 1985): 6–11.

28. "Analysis of March 1987 Current Population Survey Data Tape," in E. Richard Brown, "Principles for a National Health

Program: A Framework for Analysis," *Milbank Memorial Fund Quarterly* (forthcoming).

29. Pamela J. Farley, "Who Are the Underinsured?" *Milbank Memorial Fund Quarterly* 63 (Summer 1985): 476–503.

30. "Yankelovich Survey Finds Conflict Among Generations Mostly Fiction," *National Retired Teachers Association News Bulletin* 28 (Washington, D.C., April 1987): 2.

SETTING THE WRONG LIMITS: CLASS BIASES AND THE BIOGRAPHICAL STANDARD

ELIZABETH A. BINNEY AND CARROLL L. ESTES

ELIZABETH A. BINNEY is Research Associate, Institute for Health and Aging, Department of Social and Behavioral Sciences, University of California, San Francisco; and CARROLL L. ESTES is Professor and Chair, Department of Social and Behavioral Sciences, and Director, Institute for Health and Aging, University of California, San Francisco.

In *Setting Limits: Medical Goals in an Aging Society,* Daniel Callahan asserts that our aging society faces a crisis of exceptional magnitude, fueled by an impending demographic revolution, skyrocketing health-care costs, and an increasing loss of meaning in old age. Callahan criticizes various interests—doctors, aging advocates, and those who promote individualism—for their role in the crisis and their lack of leadership in resolving it. He suggests that our survival and well-being as a society depends on a radical response. This essay will illuminate Callahan's most important unexamined assumptions and discuss their implications for his radical response—a proposal to use age as a basis for limiting access to life-extending technologies. The essay will then argue that the current health-care system contains inequities that Callahan's proposals would not remedy and might exacerbate.

240

UNEXAMINED ASSUMPTIONS

At the heart of *Setting Limits* is a criticism of a modernized view of aging that encourages activity, new work roles, and the possibilities of limitless and artificial (or unnatural) longevity. Callahan blames this view and its "politically motivated" advocates for preventing older people from disengaging and accepting decline and death.

Perhaps the most troubling part of this assumption is the notion that there are "reasonable" and "moral" standards of longevity, a "natural life span," and meaning. If only restraints could be placed on the actions of misguided aging advocates who have filled the elderly with ideas of immortality and selfishness, these standards would be clear. The idea that gerontologists and aging advocates are to blame for this problem is naive, that absolute standards exist is frightening.

Callahan's proposal to limit medical interventions on the basis of age implicitly assumes that the old have had an opportunity to achieve most of life's possibilities. Despite his acknowledgment of certain differences among the old, Callahan assumes that life chances are basically equitable for all people and experienced at a similar chronological age (for Callahan, around the late seventies). By assuming comparable life opportunities and historical biographies and imposing a hegemony of meaning through public policy, Callahan's view is invidiously class biased. Hegemony is a concept that describes how the values of the dominant class are exercised throughout society, regardless of the real interest of other groups.[1] This imperialism of "meaning," individualism for the rich and communal responsibility for the rest, is at the core of the class argument against Callahan.

A major portion of Callahan's argument assumes such a hegemonic process, that is, that the elderly will and should accept limits to the end of life *if* that end is made socially meaningful. This raises important social and ethical questions: What are these standards of meaning, for whom do they apply, and who should establish and administer them? *Setting Limits* ignores the question of how societal values about aging, dying, and the elderly will change to give the new and deeper meaning which Callahan recognizes as necessary to the viability of his proposal. It seems inconceivable to propose a serious policy to withhold life-extending treatment requiring major changes in deeply held individual and societal values while discarding as failures or as unrealistic, creative financing, provision, and technological development options.

Although Callahan makes an important point in suggesting that we must, as a society, reassess how we view aging and the elderly *and* how the elderly come to view their own lives and human experience, this reassessment is necessary not for cost containment, and not for intergenerational transfers. It is necessary to improve the quality of life for us as a society. The question remains, however, how we might accomplish this goal.

Callahan's exhortation that his proposals are necessary because of rampant and unreasonable costs assumes that his plan will save money and better allocate limited resources. This is a major unexamined assumption and one which, in all likelihood, is false. Data on the present U.S. health system indicate that cost savings primarily depend on decreasing the overall quantity of services offered. Changes in productivity and imputed prices (mostly wages) have contributed little to slowing health-care expenditures.[2] If there is no alteration in the supply of physicians, technological capital, and facilities and if uniform cost-containment mechanisms such as global hospital budgeting, physician assignment, and fee schedules are not imposed (and there is no indication, either from Callahan's proposal or from current policy, that they will be), medical costs will continue to escalate. The inherent logic of the current health-care financing and delivery system and the vested interests benefiting from the continuing growth in for-profit medical-care expenditures mean that costs saved by rationing will be shifted to other currently unidentified areas. How these areas will be determined is a crucial, yet unaddressed, issue in *Setting Limits*. There is certainly no guarantee that any saving will be transferred to the most needy, the poor, the uninsured, or the nation's children.

Disparity in health care currently exists. Despite public assumptions and political pronouncements, a policy of health rationing is presently in effect in the United States. American public policy treats health care as a market good; by definition that means it will be subject to rationing. Since 1980 a market ideology has strongly influenced health-care policy, justifying competition and rationing. This ideology has permeated the debate about aging issues with an unprecedented fervor. It has hastened the abandonment of policy goals of equity, access, and accountability (hallmarks from the mid-1950s), and promoted the idea that increasing competition in health care will result in the delivery of a more efficient mix of services, thereby reducing costs.

While rationing exists in many forms in the American health-care system, including rationing by price, central authority, disease, age, race, and merit,[3] a class-based rationing system (with elements of deservingness) dominates. In our system of primarily fee-for-service acute-care provision, there is essentially no entitlement to any health care until Medicare eligibility. In general, coverage is employer based. This system immediately creates a class bias based on occupational strata; those in higher strata are more likely to be covered, and more likely to have broader and more comprehensive coverage. Out-of-pocket payments constitute the second major source of health-care financing. It is clear how this is class based. The irony, of course, is that the regressiveness of out-of-pocket financing most deleteriously affects the working poor, who are least likely to have any coverage, and the elderly, whose coverage is often inadequate. And finally, there are entitlement and welfare programs, with their own class-based biases. For example, discrepancies in the fifty state policies which govern Medicaid, its often penurious eligibility requirements, its limited coverage, and its low payment levels have created a "second-tier" health system for the poor, the underinsured, and those without private insurance.

For the elderly, the prospective payment system of reimbursement based on DRGs (diagnosis-related groups), coupled with exorbitant premiums, fees, and copayments, has created an expensive, acute-care-biased system disproportionately available to those who can afford out-of-pocket expenses. For chronic and long-term-care services, elders must spend down their assets in order to be eligible for coverage by the federal-state Medicaid program. There is considerable evidence of the deleterious short-term effects of DRGs and other recent cost-containment policies, including earlier discharge from hospitals and increased use of post-hospital care (especially home health and nursing home services), and increased constraints on the community health and social service delivery system.[4] By increasing out-of-pocket costs and transferring millions of days of care from the paid labor force in the hospital to the largely unreimbursed community and informal care sectors, these policies further exacerbate class-based rationing.

CLASS AND THE "BIOGRAPHICAL STANDARD"

Callahan's proposed "age as a biographical standard" criterion will deepen the present class basis of rationing. The notion of a "natural life span," especially as determined by biographical standards, is very much a factor of life history and the events that one's social class heavily influences. Poverty and privilege, far from being inconsequential, shape one's life chances and follow an individual into old age, greatly influencing not only life expectancy but also the health, quality, and even meaning of a life.[5] To the extent that those with more advantageous life experience (including support in old age) have a greater chance of escaping the effects of Callahan's proposal for a longer period of time, another major class issue remains unattended.

Setting Limits only cursorily acknowledges an even more thorny issue of differences in the ability to buy or otherwise obtain the care that a policy mandate would deny to many on the basis of class. Callahan acknowledges this crucial issue which would allow the affluent to circumvent the general policy as troublesome, but certainly not "morally intolerable." Yet to prevent this inequity, if it can be done at all, would be to set a precedent heretofore unknown in our modern society. To fail to prevent it would clearly be to set a policy standard of death by class.

These class biases also reflect some important race and gender biases in America's current rationing schemes. Just as significant racial and ethnic differences are associated with occupational strata, we can assume that inherent racial/ethnic biases join class biases in the existing system. Even more significantly, the acute-care bias of health-care financing implicitly favors the white, middle-to-upper-class man, who is more likely to need these services. Although men use fewer total services than women, they use more acute care. In contrast, women, especially the poor and minorities, are the most likely to suffer from chronic illnesses. Yet they, who have the lowest incomes, must pay for a large share of their costs out-of-pocket or not receive treatment.[6] Further, since women are the principal informal caregivers in this nation's long-term-care system, they, who are more likely to live longer but enter old age disabled and poor, will also be without caregiving support.

The most tragic part of Callahan's effort to shift implied rationing standards to an explicit age-based standard is that there is no evidence to suggest that such a change will ameliorate the class bias inherent in the current system. The unstated assumption is that the money "saved" by a stringent system of aged-based rationing would automatically be shifted to more needy population groups, presumably the young, who Callahan claims are suffering most from the elders' overuse of resources. This assumption must be examined closely in light of current policies and values in order to see the likely effects of Callahan's policies. The evidence shows, contrary to the particular crisis mentality that conditions many of Callahan's proposals, the real crisis is not caused by an expanding welfare state, by inordinate public-sector spending on health care, or by the elderly. The attack on the U.S. welfare state during the last decade, particularly on its health and services sector, has been unprecedented in Western democracies, even as others (most notably Thatcher's Britain) have also mounted attacks on the welfare state. As such, it is important, in the context of Callahan's allegations of crisis, to examine the concept and origins of crisis, especially as they pertain to the health-care sector.

CRISIS AND HEALTH-CARE SPENDING

As we head into the final decade of the century, debate has intensified concerning the strength of the U.S. economy and its role in the larger capitalist world system. Since the early 1970s, Habermas,[7] O'Connor,[8] and others have examined "crisis tendencies" in the realms of economics, politics, culture, and personality. As government or the state addresses what are defined as economic crises, sacrifices are deemed necessary and social struggles inevitable. Further, U.S. state policy is pressed to protect and stimulate market investment opportunities for private business in areas that promise the likelihood of profitability. In health care such markets include hospital and home-health services, pharmaceutical and medical equipment manufacturers.

In the past decade state policy has promoted the private sector in many ways including: (1) the creation of productive opportunities for private investment in health care; (2) the restriction of state activities in health and social services to those that support and complement the market achieved by financing limited programs of health insurance, while also providing 40 percent of U.S. health-care spending through the expansion of a costly, but profitable, medical-industrial complex; (3) the engagement by the state in "market-replacing"[9] actions to stimulate economic growth; and (4) the reduction of state support for social and community-care services—services that, at present, tend to be less profitable avenues of private investment.[10]

As many attribute the difficulties and crises in the economy to the government and its welfare policies, the state has experienced a "credibility gap." The threats to Social Security and the attempts to replace it with private pension schemes in the mid-1980s exemplified what can happen to major federal programs in periods of crisis—for example, when the symbol of Social Security bankruptcy called into question the ability of government to manage such a program. The economic, political, and social crises of the 1980s have placed the legitimacy of the state in jeopardy; this shift has contributed to emerging state actions in favor of market norms and market solutions. Major issues concern the continued availability of legitimating beliefs supporting the two cornerstones of aging policy—Social Security and Medicare. The result is the social production of a crisis mentality in which the elderly become the scapegoats and pressures mount on the state for "solutions" to larger economic or political problems.

Actual data on the "crisis" of health-care spending present a different and far more complex picture. The overall rise in health-care spending in the United States has been inordinate, at an annual rate of three to five times the cost of living.The role of the public sector in this financing is important. In fact, the growth of public expenditures from 1960 to 1982 is a phenomenon common to all advanced capitalist countries. Some suggest that this transfer of funds from the private to the public is the major contributing factor to the economic crisis for which dismantling the welfare state, especially entitlement programs, is offered as the solution.[11]

In actuality, the United States has experienced considerably *less* growth in public expenditures as a percentage of the GNP than any other advanced capitalist country and in 1982 had a lower public expenditure (37.6 percent) than any country except Japan. Likewise, public outlays for education, social and health services, and Social Security were lower in the United States (20 percent of the GNP) than in any other advanced country. Further, between 1975 and 1981 U.S. expenditures on Social Security exhibited one of the lowest growth rates (3.7 percent) of sixteen advanced capitalist countries.[12]

More significantly, the United States ranks considerably behind almost every major industrialized country in terms of *public sector* health expenditures as a percentage of the GDP (gross domestic product)—4.4 percent—ahead of only Spain, Portugal, and Greece. The United States also ranks dead last among major industrialized countries in public health expenditure as a percentage of total health expenditure at 41.1 percent, with the mean percentage at 78.1 percent.[13] Nevertheless, the United States spends a higher total health expenditure (from combined public and private sources) as a percentage of the GDP (10.8 percent) than any of these same countries, suggesting that Callahan's argument as to the crisis in health-care costs needs to be reconceptualized.

Contrasted with comparable countries, a much higher percentage of our health-care spending comes from and returns to the private sector. While it may be argued that the percentage of GDP devoted to medical care is unacceptably high, it must also be noted that this expenditure is fueling a medical-industrial complex that is consuming more than $500 billion per year, and one that is highly profitable for a number of powerful interests.

Rather than blaming the elderly for this new phenomenon of skyrocketing costs, we need to look at historical trends in the spending of the U.S. health-care dollar. The reasons for these rising costs are well understood. They lie in the structural incentives built into pluralistic financing (no single uniform payer-control mechanism such as the state or state-imposed global budgeting), the regulatory and administrative costs of a complex and multi-layered system, fee-for-service payment for physicians and license to extra-bill, a retrospective cost-based system (until DRGs), and the added costs of marketing and profit making in a largely private medical-care delivery system.[14] Berk, Monheit, and Hagan investigated spending trends over the past fifty years and concluded that health-care spending on the top 5 percent and the top 30 percent of the U.S. population ranked by per capita medical-care expenditure has remained remarkably constant in this period, with an estimated 52 percent of health expenditures spent on the top 5 percent of the population in 1928 and 55 percent spent on an equivalent percent of the population in 1980.[15]

This concentrated but stable distribution over more than fifty years would suggest that the proportion of expenditures for high-cost techniques has not dramatically escalated in relation to overall health expenditures during this period, despite the introduction of Medicare and Medicaid and many new and expensive technologies. However, two important differences in the composition of the high-expenditure group have been identified. First, those sixty-five years and older are a growing proportion of those with the top 1 percent of per capita expenditures. However, among those with the top 5 percent of expenditures, the proportion of the elderly has remained constant, comprising 31 percent of that population. Second, the poor are disproportionately represented both among the top 1 percent and the top 5 percent of persons with highest per capita expenditures.[16] These findings are pertinent to Callahan's proposals to limit access by limiting current health expenses. The implementaton of such a proposal would surely affect those with the highest health-care expenditures—the elderly and the poor. One highly probable result would be the limitation of health-care benefits to those who need them most, and, accordingly, the discrimination against selected social classes (lower socio-economic groups).

These data do not support the conclusion that the elderly are primarily responsible for the rise in medical-care costs. A better argument may be that data that would blame the elderly are scant. Over the past decade the rise in health-care costs has been attributed to (in rank of importance): (1) price increases and inflation, (2) higher intensity of services/increased technology, and (3) population changes. The structural sources of the cost increases are in the aforementioned private and pluralistic organizational and financing system. More importantly, as costs have risen, access to health care has declined[17] and service utilization has not increased commensurately—there has been a decline in hospital admissions and lengths of stay, but only minimal increases in utilization of home-health and nursing-home care.

The reality is that elders are caught between the dual interests of government and business. Both are attempting to constrain and reduce their own respective costs and neither is particularly concerned about access to health care. At the same time, the elderly are caught in the tensions between government and industry, each wanting to reduce their respective medical costs versus those of the medical-industrial complex (including hospitals and physicians), which wants expansion of a profitable market in health guaranteed by government subsidy. A major result has been a more costly and deeply stratified health-care system for the elderly (and the young).

CONCLUSION: A CRISIS IN MEANING

Callahan's proposal offers a dramatic solution to a problem, but a solution with serious and far-reaching repercussions. The failure to examine important assumptions has led Callahan to ignore some of the most critical factors about the "crisis" of aging and health and, as a result, to construct a policy solution around a false conception of the problem. We suggest that the "problem" Callahan seeks to remedy is actually a symptom of a larger crisis—a crisis of both capitalism and meaning. The ultimate contradiction that Callahan does not acknowledge or address is that the breakdown of meaning, to which he attributes much of the crisis, has its origin in the overall crisis of capitalism. His inability to recognize the impact of this larger crisis on the rationing of health care renders his solutions naive at best, and dangerous at worst.

Holstein has observed that the lack of social significance accorded the old rests "less on our failure to ascribe value to the old . . . [than to] American capitalism with its denial of opportunities, superannuation, commodification of need and creation of dependencies."[18] But even this important observation neglects the more fundamental point that meaning in our culture is tied to capitalist society and its social, economic, and political order. They cannot be analytically separated from each other.

In his basic recommendations about the "ends of medicine," Callahan suggests that we reconsider and develop a consensus on the meaning and social significance of aging. In Callahan's view, individualism must give way to a commu-

251

nity-based and -affirmed notion of the value of the aged in society and an acceptance of limits to health care for the aged and medical research of benefit to them. These limits, he says, will not result in the abandonment of the old, because the new social consensus will provide older people with a deep sense of value in the community and also the guarantee that they will receive comfort, care, and relief from suffering.

In the earlier discussion of hegemony, the use and manipulation of meaning to further the interests of one class over others was cited as one of the most serious omissions in Callahan's argument because it left unaddressed the question of what standards of social meaning are applicable and who would be setting those standards. In addition to ignoring the role of capitalism in defining, setting, and enforcing those standards, he also ignores the fact that the standards currently operating have also been greatly influenced by capitalist class interests. The inherent contradiction between developing more appropriate or humane standards of social meaning and the interests of capitalism lies at the core of the problem. One of the primary requirements of capitalism is a culture oriented to individualism and consumption, and in health care this is expressed as the drive for capital and technological expansion of a profitable medical-industrial complex.

Thus it is fruitless to suggest the radical transformation of cultural meaning without recognizing the role that both capitalism and public policy play in shaping that meaning. Public policy formation represents one arena in which the dialectic between fulfilling the needs of capital and the creation of meaning operates. While not solely an instrument of capital, public policy is often used to enforce a certain consensus about issues and values. If public policy is used under current assumptions and structures to promote Callahan's suggested changes in the significance and entitlement of old age, class differences and other existing inequities will be exacerbated rather than eradicated.

In arguing that the loss of meaning is primary, Callahan confounds the meaning and cost issues and ignores the contradiction in his proposal. O'Connor suggests that at least three types of explanations may operate to produce crises of meaning in society: (1) unemployment and the growth of low-paid service jobs and the polarization of the income distribution with a decay of the patriarchal family structure; (2) the breakdown of traditional institutional ties and the incapacity of the bureaucratic state and impersonal corporation to produce new values and meaning; and (3) the rise of consumerism and the obsession with personal growth and the "cult of the self."[19] Habermas argues that crises of meaning in advanced capitalism result from the replacement of traditional values by the growing state and, we would add, the growing technology/profit motive embodied in the medical-industrial complex. The latter contributes substantially to capitalism and bolsters the theoretical framework that assures a distribution of health resources consistent with capitalism.[20]

The economic and political factors in these alternative explanations for the crisis of meaning are readily apparent, especially when considered in the context of meaning and the provision of health care. The commodification, consumerism, and the cult of self that fuel the medical-industrial complex each are integral to capitalism. Consistent with the tenets and orientation of capitalism, for-profit medicine and the interests of the medical-industrial complex are not likely to accommodate a shift that fundamentally threatens their investment. The implementation of Callahan's proposal fundamentally countervails an important source of capital investment and accumulation (the needed market from the old). Since the elderly, who comprise 11 percent of the population, account for more than 30 percent of medical-care expenses, the severe rationing of medical care to this population group would surely affect the fortunes of important elements in the medical-industrial complex. Indeed, a great deal of profit and

253

commodification potential would likely be lost if the elderly were deemed ineligible to receive benefits based on age.

There are clearly alternatives that would resolve some of the problems that most concern Callahan. The most obvious is the implementation of publicly funded national insurance without profit in a manner that would provide equitable access to care for young and old and with the efficiencies of a single-payer source (the national government). However, even this major step is not likely to change the meaning of age. To accomplish such a feat would require an even more radical step—the implementation of a serious agenda of economic democracy.

NOTES

1. Antonio Gramsci, *Selections From the Prison Notebooks,* trans. Quintin Hoare and Geoffrey N. Smith (New York: International Publishers, 1971).

2. Victor R. Fuchs, "The 'Competition Revolution' in Health Care," *Health Affairs* 7 (Summer 1988): 5–24.

3. Larry R. Churchill, *Rationing Health Care in America: Perceptions and Principles of Justice* (Notre Dame, IN: University of Notre Dame Press, 1987).

4. Carroll L. Estes, Juanita B. Wood, and Associates, *Organizational and Community Responses to Medicare Policy* (San Francisco, CA: Institute for Health & Aging, University of California, San Francisco, 1988). See also C. R. Neu and C. Harrison, *Posthospital Care Before and After the Medicare PPS* (Los Angeles, CA: Rand, UCLA Center for Health Care Financing Policy Research, March 1988).

5. Jane S. Zones, Carroll L. Estes, and Elizabeth A. Binney, "Gender, Public Policy and the Oldest Old," *Ageing and Society* 7 (September 1987): 275–302.

6. Villers Foundation staff, *On the Other Side of Easy Street: Myths & Facts About the Economics of Old Age* (Washington, DC: Villers Foundation, 1987).

7. Jurgen Habermas, *Legitimation Crisis,* trans. Thomas McCarthy (Boston: Beacon Press, 1975).

8. James O'Connor, *The Fiscal Crisis of the State* (New York: St. Martin's Press, 1973). See also James O'Connor, *The Meaning of Crisis: A Theoretical Introduction* (Oxford: Basil Blackwell Ltd., 1987).

9. Habermas, *Legitimation Crisis,* p. 53.

10. Carroll L. Estes and Elizabeth A. Binney, "The Biomedicalization of Aging: Dangers and Dilemmas," *Gerontologist* (forthcoming, 1990).

11. Vicente Navarro, "Federal Health Policies in the United States: An Alternative Explanation," *Milbank Memorial Fund Quarterly* 65 (1987): 81–111.

12. Vicente Navarro, "The Welfare State and Its Distributive Effects: Part of the Problem or Part of the Solution?" *International Journal of Health Services* 17 (1987): 543–66.

13. George J. Schieber and Jean-Pierre Poullier, "DataWatch: Recent Trends in International Health Care Spending," *Health Affairs* 6 (Fall 1987): 105–12.

14. Uwe E. Reinhardt, "The Battle Over Medical Costs Isn't Over," *Wall Street Journal,* 22 October 1988.

15. Marc L. Berk, Alan C. Monheit, and Michael M. Hagan, "How the U.S. Spent Its Health Care Dollar: 1929–1980," *Health Affairs* 7 (Fall 1988): 46–60.

16. Ibid.

17. Howard E. Freeman et al., "Americans Report on Their Access to Health Care," *Health Affairs* 6 (Spring 1987): 6–18.

18. Martha Holstein, "Discussion on *The Limits to Life*" (California State University, Hayward, unpublished manuscript, 1989).

19. O'Connor, *The Meaning of Crisis,* pp. 44–48.

20. Habermas, *Legitimation Crisis,* p. 53.

PART VIII

PRACTICAL DECISION-MAKING: LAW, POLITICS, AND PUBLIC POLICY

The last three writers are not sanguine about the political or legal feasibility of setting limits. Attorney Marshall B. Kapp speculates on whether age-based rationing violates the Fifth and the Fourteenth Amendments, and constitutional guarantees of due process and protection from arbitrary and capricious exercise of governmental authority. Kapp also argues that no policy should undertake explicit age-based rationing except as part of reforming and building a more just system of healthcare delivery, "where a fairer and more sensible distribution and use of medical services serves as the quid pro quo *for accepting limits on the total volume and mix of services."*

Harry R. Moody, like Callahan, is a philosopher who seeks to link ethical reflection to policy choices. Accepting scarcity and the consequent need for rationing and also the validity of questions of intergenerational equity, he assumes the task both of criticizing the critics of Setting Limits *and offering his own observations about its shortfalls. Though sympathetic to Callahan's position, Moody challenges its political feasibility. He examines various alternatives generally and suggests that implicit rationing strategies may be more acceptable than the hard and explicit rationing that Callahan proposes. In addition, Moody outlines a number of intermediate steps, short of hard rationing, to address the problem of ever-expanding health-care costs.*

Like Callahan and Moody, Martha Holstein is particularly concerned with bridging ethics and policymaking but sharply questions the strength of Callahan's argument to link the two. Arguing that Callahan seriously misreads what the old want, she challenges his understanding of old age and his critique of aging advocates and their support for the "modernization project." Particularly troubled by the even greater inequality between the rich and poor, men and women, and white and minority elders that Callahan's proposal would introduce, Holstein shifts the focus to systemic problems in health-care financing and delivery. She insists that a discussion of health-care limits, in a fundamentally unjust system, holds the old to a standard of the common good far more stringent than our expectations for any other age group.

Rationing Health Care: Legal Issues and Alternatives to Age-Based Schemes

Marshall B. Kapp

MARSHALL B. KAPP is Professor, Department of Medicine in Society, Wright State University, Dayton, Ohio.

THE POLITICAL and ethical ramifications of the age-based health care rationing concept have received a fair amount of commentary. Conversely, extensive discussion of the legal issues raised by a broad, official public policy of discrimination against the elderly in access to medical services (as opposed to literature speculating about the potential liability of physicians and hospitals that *de facto* scrimp on care to particular older individuals under present cost containment pressures like prospective payment according to Diagnosis Related Groups)[1] has been late in coming.

This analytical void is at least partially explicable by the paucity of specific detail that the philosophical promoters of age-based rationing provide in describing how they would practically implement their general policies of formal medical discrimination. Since good legal analysis always begins

Marshall B. Kapp's "Rationing Health Care" from *Issues in Law and Medicine* (Vol. 5, No. 3; Winter 1989). Reprinted by permission of the author and the National Legal Center for the Mentally Dependent and Disabled, Inc.

with a mastery of facts, the factual abyss that characterizes the arguments of Callahan *et al.* deters speculation about the legal implications of those arguments. Nonetheless, and taking into account the generality of this effort, a few brief surmises about the probable legal challenges to a public policy embodying age-based health care rationing are offered here.

First, the Fifth and Fourteenth Amendments to the United States Constitution guaranty that no individual may be deprived by the government of life, liberty, or property without due process of law. In both substantive and procedural terms, this means that persons are entitled to be treated in a "fundamentally fair" way by their government. A governmental scheme to utilize reimbursement policy to consciously and officially deprive older persons, solely because of their age, of access to potentially beneficial health services raises two sorts of due process questions.

For one thing, aging is an immutable, involuntary, uncontrollable contingency of life. Predicating a public benefits rationing scheme upon chronological age, therefore, is arguably an arbitrary and capricious exercise of governmental authority, drawing distinctions among people that are not adequately supported by a reasonable relationship to a legitimate government interest.

Another version of the due process challenge to age-based health care rationing by the government could be based on the phenomenon that many older persons are institutionalized, under explicit or implicit government sanction. They are in mental hospitals or long-term care facilities that are either owned and operated by the government or are heavily supported by public funds. Many older persons have had decisionmaking power removed from them under guardianship or conservator appointments by the courts; and other kinds of limitations on the liberty of older persons may be imposed by government. Should not the elderly be entitled, as a due process *quid pro quo* for these deprivations of freedom by the government, to something in return, namely, to be provided with the basics of life, including potentially beneficial medical care?[2] The courts have accepted a closely analogous treatment-as-*quid-pro-quo*-for-deprivation-of-freedom argument as a constitutional principle in the contexts of involuntary mental hospitalization[3] and imprisonment.[4]

The elderly might also attack an official age-based health care rationing program as a deprivation of the Equal Protection rights that the Fourteenth Amendment guarantees to all citizens. Without doubt, the kind of policy that Callahan and his supporters advocate entails actual and intentional discrimination by the government against a particular category of people based exclusively on their membership in that category. The constitution, however, condones official inequality in some circumstances. The key inquiry is whether an age-based health care rationing policy could be justified as an exception to the general equal protection mandate.

The ordinary equal protection analysis asks whether the government can demonstrate a rational relationship between its differential treatment of different groups and a legitimate public interest. Even under this test, it is debatable whether government's choice of age as the distinguishing characteristic for rationing health care would pass constitutional muster.

Moreover, an official age-based health care rationing scheme ought to be subjected to a higher level of equal protection analysis, that of "strict scrutiny."[5] Under the strict scrutiny test, the government bears the burden of proving that its policy of discriminating among citizen groups is necessary (not just rationally related) to accomplish a compelling (not just a legitimate) public interest. The courts have engaged in strict scrutiny analysis when either a fundamental (not just an important) right is the subject of deprivation or the group being discriminated against is a "suspect class."

Arguably, beneficial health care is a fundamental right, at least as encompassed in the Medicare program. Additionally, although the courts have not yet recognized old age as a "suspect class" for equal protection purposes, they should.[6] In this vein, a lawsuit has recently been filed challenging the excessive taxation of the elderly under the 1988 Medicare Catastrophic Coverage Act.[7] Age-based rationing proposals are an excellent example of the vulnerability of the elderly *qua* elderly to the adverse effects of discriminatory public policy decisions. It is unlikely that a comprehensive, inflexible age-based health care rationing program of the sort Callahan envisions could withstand a strict scrutiny analysis.

Even if an official policy of rationing health care by age were able to withstand a rational relationship or strict scrutiny analysis, such a policy would still need to satisfy the equal protection principle that it be the least invasive, least restrictive alternative reasonably available and that it is likely to be effective in achieving a justifiable aim.[8] Thus, proponents of an age-based health care rationing scheme shoulder difficult if not impossible burdens. They must establish that their scheme was adopted only as a last resort after other, less invasive and restrictive cost containment measures were properly rejected as ineffectual. In addition, they must prove that an age-based rationing program is likely to be effective in achieving the goals of effective cost containment and otherwise improving quality and access within the health care system.

We can expect other constitutional challenges to age-based health care rationing. The constitutional prohibition against governmental interference with freedom of contract[9] that the courts have read into the Fourteenth Amendment's liberty protection surely would be asserted against any law purporting to outlaw altogether the provision of certain services to the elderly, on the grounds of impermissible interference with the physician/patient relationship. A similar attack might be mounted against the Callahan-type proposal (rationing based on payment restrictions) since, even where (as in Medicare) the government is paying the bills, the contractual (as well as fiduciary) relationship is one that exists between the patient and the private health care provider.

The same reasoning may support a challenge to age-based health care rationing under the constitutional right of privacy that the courts have recognized as incorporating the freedom to make personal health care decisions without governmental interference.[10] While establishing an affirmative entitlement to government-funded health care benefits might be difficult to accomplish under the right to privacy rubric, at the least the privacy claim should protect the right of an older individual to pay out-of-pocket for desired services if willing and able.

ALTERNATIVES TO AGE-BASED RATIONING

Age-based health care rationing proposals are objectionable on political, legal, and ethical dimensions. Given that health care resources are or at some point will become scarce, creating an inevitable disparity between demand for health services and ability to satisfy that demand, what policy alternatives are more palatable?

One possibility is a continuation of the status quo of implicit or "soft" rationing. Despite its shortcomings, this system has allowed Americans to wink at each other while providing high quality care to most of our citizens as we maintain a decent level of social tranquility. As one astute observer of American health care has noted, where nonallocation of resources causes harm or risk of harm, this policy is more likely to be deemed popularly acceptable where the negative consequences are imposed by chance (rather than by choice), indirectly (through omission rather than commission), through latent (rather than overt) decisionmaking, by an unidentified rationer, and on a rationee who is individually

263

unidentified at the time the risk is created (a statistical life instead of an actual one).[11]

Whichever rationing policy we choose (or fall into), better prospective health planning ought to be more carefully assimilated into standard medical practice for reasons of both patient autonomy and cost containment. Older patients are not anxious to greedily hoard expensive but futile or unduly burdensome medical interventions, and many would welcome the opportunity to express their preferences and control their medical futures through such mechanisms as living wills and durable powers of attorney. No person should be coerced into executing an advance planning document or forfeiting any medical intervention for which he or she has a right, and certainly not for financial reasons. To the extent, though, that one voluntarily and knowingly elects, as a matter of expressing personal autonomy, to forego particular medical interventions, society should facilitate such an opportunity and accept the cost savings as an incidental but positive byproduct.

Another alternative, although not a promising one, is further tinkering with incremental changes in the health care financing and delivery system of the sort that have destabilized the industry in the past dozen years. The pessimism of Callahan and colleagues on this score is well-founded.

Calls for a program of health care rationing according to age reflect a perception—largely well-founded—of a crisis situation. The most effective and tolerable alternative to age-based rationing may rest with basic, radical reformation of the health care system, namely, the development of a comprehensive, universal National Health Insurance program with built-in, integral, tight cost controls based on evidence of a medical service's efficacy. The private medical marketplace is far preferable to a National Health Service where government delivers as well as subsidizes health care, but a private delivery system where government acts as the single payor or guarantor of payment can and must incorporate tough cost controls (learning to say "no") based on the proven effectiveness and value of an intervention rather than the age or disability *per se* of the patient. We should not consider explicit rationing except as part of reforming and building a more just, larger system of health care delivery, where a fairer and more sensible distribution and use of medical services serves as the *quid pro quo* for accepting limits on the total volume and mix of services.[12]

Finally, we should not focus discussion purely on questions relating to the distribution of medical benefits. Someone must pay for those benefits that are distributed and rationed, and thoughtful contemplation about the shape of the larger health care system commands attention to a more equitable distribution of costs. If the elderly have a political, legal, and ethical claim to participate in the benefits of our health care system on the basis of individual needs, preferences, and capacities to benefit, then there is a correlative social obligation to expand the mandatory resource contributions of those older persons who, judged as individuals, possess the capacity to expand their contributions. Means testing of health care benefits would open a whole other can of political and ethical worms at this point in time, but even the staunchest of generational equity opponents now concede that a true social insurance scheme—especially one with an effective cost containment component assuring equitable distribution of services—should compel high income elderly to pay their fair share of the social burden.[13]

Callahan and his supporters have proposed a serious social policy for dealing with a health care resource scarcity problem that is real and ominous. Both the resource scarcity crisis and the age-based rationing proposals it has generated deserve to be taken seriously. While these proposals are objectionable on political, legal, and ethical grounds, opponents of this approach have an obligation to suggest and help implement social policies of their own that do a better job of promoting social harmony, protecting the legal liberties and entitlements of individuals, and honoring the ethical precepts of autonomy, beneficence, and distributive justice. The concept of health care rationing by age, in setting up a very thoughtful and difficult target, challenges us all and presents us with an opportunity for creative and honest social policymaking.[14]

NOTES

1. Marshall B. Kapp, "Legal and Ethical Implications of Health Care Reimbursement by Diagnosis Related Groups," *Law, Medicine and Health Care* 12 (December 1984): 245–53, 278.

2. Nat Hentoff, "The Pied Piper Returns for the Old Folks," *Human Life Review* 14 (Summer 1988): 108–12.

3. *O'Connor v. Donaldson,* 422 U.S. 563, 95 S. Ct. 2486, 45 L.Ed2d 396 (1975) (State could not involuntarily hospitalize person on the grounds of mental illness "without more." The "without more" language has been interpreted to mean "without adequate treatment"); William J. Curran, " 'The Class Action' Approach to Protecting Health-Care Consumers—The Right to Psychiatric Treatment," *New England Journal of Medicine* 286 (January 6, 1972): 26.

4. *West v. Adkins,* 56 U.S.L.W. 4664 (U.S. Supreme Court, No. 87-5096, June 20, 1988).

5. Cf. Wendy K. Mariner, "Access to Health Care and Equal Protection of the Law: The Need for a New Heightened Scrutiny," *American Journal of Law and Medicine* 12 (1986): 345–380.

6. Hentoff, "The Pied Piper," p. 112.

7. "News at Deadline," *Hospitals* 63 (February 1989): 18.

8. Margaret A. Somerville, " 'Should the Grandparents Die?': Allocation of Medical Resources With an Aging Population," *Law, Medicine and Health Care* 14 (September 1986): 158–63.

9. *Allgeyer v. Louisiana,* 165 U.S. 578 (1897).

10. *In re Quinlan,* 355 A.2d 647 (N.J. 1976).
11. Somerville, " 'Should the Grandparents Die?'," p. 158.
12. Larry R. Churchill, "Should We Ration Health Care By Age?" *Journal of the American Geriatrics Society* 36 (July 1988): 644–47.
13. Eric R. Kingson, "Generational Equity: An Unexpected Opportunity to Broaden the Politics of Aging," *Gerontologist* 28 (December 1988): 765–72.
14. This paper was excerpted from a presentation at a conference on "Current Controversies in the Right to Live, the Right to Die" sponsored by the Law and Religion Program, the Columbus School of Law of The Catholic University of America, and the National Legal Center for the Medically Dependent and Disabled, Inc., April 14, 1989.

"Natural" Limits to Health Care

Harry R. Moody

HARRY R. MOODY is Deputy Director, Brookdale Center on Aging, Hunter College, New York, New York.

Setting Limits asks us to reassess the obligations that society and the elderly owe to one another. It is both a courageous and a disturbing book because it demands a radical shift in thinking and a new look at fairness or equity in the distribution of burdens and benefits across generations. In contrast to those who speak only of the rights of the aged, Callahan explicitly links rights to duties. High among the duties of the old, he argues, is concern for the welfare of succeeding generations.

Setting Limits hopes to inaugurate a debate and finally fashion a consensus around a communitarian principle of living within limits: in effect, a repudiation of the modernizing approach to old age itself. Before looking in detail at this argument, I will dispose of several misguided responses to Callahan that seem to me to entirely miss the point of his book.

Harry R. Moody's " 'Natural' Limits to Health Care" adapted from *Medical Humanities Review* 2(2) (July 1988). Reprinted by permission of the author and *Medical Humanities Review*.

One of the worst of these responses is the assertion that in today's climate of budget cutting, Callahan's book is mischievous because it will be used as a pretext to cut health care funding for the aged, whatever the author's intentions. This assertion amounts to imposing a gag rule on public debate. On the contrary, Callahan's book is a welcome and courageous contribution to an important debate, even if one feels in the end, as I do, that his proposal for an age-based cutoff is unworkable and unwise. Callahan is to be commended for writing this book, not chastised for giving aid and comfort to know-nothing budget cutters, of which he is certainly not one.

There are others who are offended by any justification for letting some people die as a matter of deliberate policy. Those who believe in the absolute sanctity of life see health care as fundamentally different from other goods. Setting limits on access, they argue, means making life-and-death decisions; who are we to say whose life is worth saving? Still others argue that "setting limits" is a dangerous slippery slope, a cost-benefit standard evoking the spectre of Nazi-like elimination of unproductive groups in society. But in fact Callahan does not offer cost-benefit arguments, nor is he "ageist" as one might mistakenly assume. He proceeds from premises about equality, individual worth, and justice, and he is concerned with how one might fashion a health-care system that is humane and sensitive to changing needs at different ages.

Let me turn now to what I take to be some of the serious arguments that can be raised against Callahan's general framework and his specific proposals. These include an attack on his assumption of scarcity, questions about the so-called "natural" life course, and the prospect of further injustices created by an age-based cutoff.

One line of criticism challenges whether there is a scarcity problem at all. Critics doubt that harsh choices about allocating resources are necessary. Some suggest taking more

269

money from other sectors of the economy (e.g., cutting the defense budget). Or perhaps, as some have urged, there would be no scarcity if only we could "cut the fat" from health care in the future. But Callahan believes this line won't succeed. DRGs and recent attempts at cost controls have not worked. And anyway, he believes, incremental steps just postpone the day of reckoning. *Setting Limits* asks us to face up to the problem now, before things get out of hand.

Another line is to acknowledge that the United States spends eleven percent of its gross national product on health care, but to question whether any specific amount is too high. Maybe we should spend more on health care: why not fifteen percent? Further, increases in health care costs have not come about chiefly because of medical technology. Instead, population aging, malpractice and overtreatment, poor reimbursement incentives, and high salaries for medical practitioners have been the real culprits. We should attack these first. And even if we do restrain the growth in costs, let's be prepared for a higher price tag that goes with bigger benefits.

Critics also point out that Callahan's negative image of medical technology itself is misleading. True, some medical technologies—the artificial heart, kidney dialysis—have been expensive and produced poor quality of life. But others—hip replacement, L-dopa therapy for Parkinson's Disease—have improved quality of life. Geriatric medical research is still new and may make great progress in the future. Why be pessimistic about costs of as-yet-uninvented technologies? It would be a terrible mistake to cut off life-extending technologies for people today based purely on projections about possible future cost trends.

A final attack on Callahan's assumption about scarcity is to suggest that his legitimate concerns can be addressed in less dramatic ways right now. By using a more sensitive "need" standard in advanced age we could in fact limit life-extending technology through more appropriate clinical decisions. In contrast to Callahan's assumption, medicine for the elderly may not be an "endless frontier" after all. It is more like an asymptotic function of diminishing returns and inevitable death as we approach the bounds of biologically maximum lifespan. Most very old geriatric patients say they would refuse life-extending technologies anyway. It is the system that promotes over-treatment by ignoring their autonomy. We could achieve significant changes, and perhaps big savings, by voluntary means without an age-based cutoff.

It is hard to see whether Callahan, on his own premises, should be persuaded by this line of argument, which is based largely on empirical and pragmatic judgments about what the scarcity problem actually amounts to. More philosophically interesting is a second line of attack, which I will consider next.

Callahan argues for a "natural" human life course as the standard for thinking about geriatric health care policy. But many would argue that any assumption about a "natural" life course represents a sentimental, pre-modern view of the life course. Any scheme to withhold resources after a fixed chronological age does violence to individual differences in how people age. It seems to go against the great progress that has occurred in improving quality of life in the later years, recently opening up new avenues for growth and freedom. Past normative definitions of old age and the "normal" life course now seem to be in rapid flux.

A further objection to Callahan's age-based cutoff is that it applies to public programs like Medicare, although he hopes that the elderly will voluntarily curtail their use of life-extending technology for the sake of the common good and future generations. But under his framework wealthy people could still buy out of any public system, thus creating intolerable inequity. Implementing Callahan's scheme would seem to introduce or accentuate a two-class health care system.

Others question why Callahan's far-reaching quality-of-life standard doesn't reach any further than the elderly—for example to include neonates or other age groups. In short, why pick on the elderly to start the rationing policy? If cost is the chief guideline, and not the natural life course alone, then would we reject cheap, easy medical technology simply on grounds of age? For example, are we prepared to withhold penicillin or other low-cost acute-care interventions for an eighty-five-year-old with pneumonia? But what if cheap interventions lead to greater expenses down the road? A penicillin shot doesn't cost much. But if the patient survives to live out years in a nursing home, then we are faced with long-term care, which Callahan favors, but which will cost big money. Woody Allen once joked that death is the best way of cutting down on expenses. Is this really what Callahan has in mind?

Callahan urges chronological age as a clear, simple criterion for the (negative) allocation of health care resources. But it is not so easy as one might think to say what this actually implies in practice. There are various ways in which chronological age might be used as an allocation criterion. For example, we can distinguish between an *overt* use (e.g., putting the eskimoes out on the ice floe) and a *covert* use (e.g., the British policy on kidney dialysis, never publicly proclaimed). We can also distinguish between a *direct* use (e.g., no heart transplants for patients over age seventy-five) and an *indirect* use (e.g., not putting an ICU in a nursing home). Finally, we can distinguish between a *distributive* use of an age criterion (e.g., deciding about Medicare coverage for organ transplantation) and a *developmental* use (e.g., deciding how much research funding to provide for specific diseases, such as sickle cell vs. stroke, or AIDS vs. Alzheimer's). In the latter case, we are deciding not how to distribute present goods but about what sort of goods we want to create in the future. Thus, research on stroke or Alzheimer's will benefit the elderly, just as research on sickle cell or AIDS tends to benefit younger people.

The importance of these distinctions is evident as soon as we consider rules of political prudence that might give guidance on what age-based criteria, if any, could be adopted in practice. For example, it is easier to use age in a covert, indirect, or developmental way than it is to use age in an explicitly negative way—as in consciously allowing people over a certain age to die, as Callahan asks us to take seriously. A parallel can be seen in debates about active versus passive euthanasia. Regardless of the ultimate justification of this distinction, no one doubts that pragmatically it's easier to approve omissions rather than to endorse outright killing. Similarly, it would be easier *not* to start a new program (e.g., research on the artificial heart) than it is to get rid of an existing entitlement (e.g., kidney dialysis under Medicare in the United States). The same point holds as true in defense appropriations (e.g., introducing new weapons systems) as in medical technology; it is always easier to stop a project before it gets under way. This is probably the way to introduce an age-based allocation principle.

If one is persuaded that the idea of a natural life course is defensible on grounds of social justice, then it makes a great deal of difference how this principle is introduced. Callahan's ideas sound alarming to many people. But to see that he has a valid point, simply look at our current Medicare budget and then ask yourself, is this how you would spend $80 billion if you were trying to do the best by our aging population? Even if one accepts the broad principle that some kind of age-based allocation is reasonable, as I for one am prepared to do, then we need to look at the prudential principles cited above: for example, the distinctions of overt/covert, direct/indirect, and distributive/developmental. Crude images of an age-based cutoff sound alarming but actually miss the point.

It is intermediate-level values and rules of prudence that are needed here. These would include equity (individual, inter age-group, or inter-cohort); adequacy (treatment of the least advantaged); efficiency (ratio of input to output, cost of administering system, success or failure in achieving stipulated goals); stability (predictable performance of the system over time); legitimacy (perceived fairness, public support); public confidence (perceived future stability of the system); and, not least of all, solidarity (tendency of systems to create divisiveness vs. cohesiveness in the body politic). The position I am urging here is a prudential or pragmatic standpoint that takes seriously conflict among competing values and urges the case for legitimate compromise, which is the essence of politics.

Callahan is extremely pessimistic about the medical outlook for an aging society. He does not consider more optimistic scenarios, nor does he consider prudential judgments that might depend on what sort of pessimistic scenario comes to pass. Whether he is right or wrong in his pessimism is very difficult to say. But even if his pessimistic appraisal turns out to be correct, a gradual, voluntarist approach is clearly preferable to divisive age-based cutoffs. And prudential judgments necessarily take account of politics and historical circumstance. It is here that Callahan is weakest. For example, Callahan fails to give serious attention to inter-cohort equity issues such as the future of the Medicare Trust Fund or the distribution of burdens for financing health care. He ignores the historical dimensions of equity problems.

On the positive side, Callahan's book calls our attention to the need to discuss *priorities,* which is very different from the spectre of "rationing" health care in an aging society of the future. It's a mistake to treat this problem as hypothetical or futuristic. Clearly, there's something wrong *right now* with a health care system that finds money to pay for organ transplants under Medicare but can't seem to provide even minimal child health care. Whatever a "natural" life course means, it ought to mean shifting those priorities. Instead of talking as if we can do everything for everyone, Callahan's book has the merit of focusing debate on a different set of priorities for the health care system right now.

Also on the positive side, Callahan's argument has the advantage of calling for a wider debate about the "ends of medicine," which is what he is really concerned about. This debate implies a deeper discussion about the good and even the meaning of life. It also implies the need for some framework in which notions of "entitlement" and "limit," access and obligation, can be correlated with one another in a perspective of social justice.

There is a final point worth making and that concerns Callahan's call for widespread public debate about his proposal for age-based rationing. In this call, he is reminiscent of Rawls, who argues for a strong criterion of publicity in the adoption of basic principles of justice. In other words, we aren't allowed to propose or act on principles or rules that we are not prepared to defend publicly.

Interestingly, the rules of political prudence proposed above seem to point in exactly the opposite way. If we introduce age-based allocation by means of covert, indirect, or developmental measures, then there may be no widespread public debate about these measures. As in the British dialysis case, it is far easier to do things by subterfuge, particularly when it involves life-and-death decisions. Here we come to an ironic point. Has Callahan proposed a strategy of public debate that virtually guarantees that his rationing proposal will not be adopted, precisely because of the bitterness it engenders? Or again, does covert adoption of age-based cutoffs somehow fatally contaminate the idea, because of the publicity criterion that Rawls would insist upon? It is hard to be sure about what Callahan would say on this point. His book does not contain much discussion about prudential political judgments or about permissible compromises in an imperfect world.

If I am right in my judgment that Callahan's proposal stands virtually no chance of ever being adopted in American public policy, at least through the debate he hopes for, then how is it that Callahan seriously offers the proposal for consideration? The answer, I believe, is that Callahan has grievously underestimated the problem of "translating" theory into practice. I am reminded of Jonathan Schell's book, *The Fate of the Earth*, where, after presenting horrifying conclusions about nuclear war, the author argues that the only solution is the abolition of nuclear weapons and the creation of world government. Then, on the last page of the book, he tells us that he "leaves the details" of implementing this proposal to others. But this conclusion is simply inadequate. Whether on nuclear weapons or on allocation of health care resources, we need a more serious treatment of what practice demands and what political prudence makes possible. We need, in short, a better understanding of the relation between theory and practice.

This question about the relation between theory and practice can be traced back to Kant's essay on the subject, and the locus classicus is found earlier in Aristotle's notion of *phronesis* as the essence of moral judgment or practical wisdom. Why do I cite these classical sources? Because Callahan's "modest proposal" flies in the face of any practical sense of what is possible in American society. At bottom, it is lacking in practical wisdom. His key policy recommendation—cutting off some types of health care for people over a specific age—is one which it is impossible to imagine ever being officially adopted in the United States, whatever one's opinion about the merits of the proposal. The proposal comes like a bombshell in his book, although admittedly as a logical consequence of his general position. Nevertheless it is a conclusion that many readers will take as a *reductio ad absurdum* of his entire argument. Hence, one wonders if there are not other schemes of allocation or priority-setting that might allow us to promote fairness or quality-of-life for the old without the dismaying spectre of an age-based cutoff. Even if tough choices must be made, is age-based rationing the only option available?

Unfortunately, Callahan does not examine any short-run, incremental policy options. But ordinary citizens and policy-makers alike need guidance on what kinds of trade-offs and compromises are actually ethically acceptable, whether at the clinical level or at the policy level. The absence of prudential or pragmatic judgments in Callahan's book is a serious problem. As a result, the book is not likely to serve us well as we face serious cost containment problems in the years ahead. In fact, he has failed to address the most serious unresolved issues of generational equity: namely, burden-sharing, inter-cohort equity, and prudential judgments about incremental political actions in real historical time.

However, those readers who judge Callahan and his book solely by his age-based cutoff proposal are making a serious mistake. Its impracticability in no way refutes the idea of a "natural" life course as a basis for either clinical or policy judgments. It is most unfortunate that people who have not read the rest of Callahan's book will be tempted to dismiss his argument simply because they disagree with his final proposal. But dismissing the book would be a great mistake. One has the impression that not only Britain but Sweden and most other mature welfare states use age-based criteria in allocating scarce resources, although they do so in covert and indirect ways. They "permit" it rather than "approve" it. Yet they do it just the same. In doing so, they may well be justified by principles of justice. In any case, the ethical dilemmas addressed by Callahan are likely to be with us in the future.

DEBATING *SETTING LIMITS*

MARTHA HOLSTEIN

I STARTED on the journey that ended with *A Good Old Age?* quite unexpectedly in the fall of 1986 as the result of an early morning phone call from a friend who asked me to replace her in a panel discussion. So on a foggy San Francisco morning I met Dan Callahan and initiated my own passionate intellectual engagement with him and his ideas.

Although we met again when he spoke at the American Society on Aging's Annual Meeting in March 1987, our next debate was equally unexpected. This time, again in the last minute, I replaced a speaker at a conference in Miami (where I happened to be for other reasons). Dan Callahan and I seemed fated to confront each other—each time with growing respect and warmth but not agreement.

After that Miami meeting I found myself increasingly challenged, but no less angered, by his ideas. These feelings made me eager to probe ever more deeply into the roots of my opposition, since I knew that I shared his deep commitment to community but was profoundly disturbed by what he was saying. I also recognized that those roots were far more complex than my being an "aging advocate," the correct camp he placed me in when we first met.

Callahan's intellectual rigor, honesty, and intensity de-

278

manded, I felt, at least equal attempts on my part; so I talked and wrote, but mostly I thought, trying to sift through my reactions to his assumptions, his arguments, and his conclusions. Soon my own views—with their intellectual and emotional underpinnings—began to take shape, and they still evolve and deepen today.

Now, four years later, I still do not share his views, but each time I've thought about them—as we worked on this collection, as I prepared for my first formal debate with him, as I heard him speak, as my students read and critiqued his work—I've been energized, forced always to ask and re-ask why and what would I do. As we continue our discussions— now, happily, as friends—whenever we meet, he always pushes me to think a little harder, to justify my beliefs, and to talk to him as he sorts through his own thinking.

As I think about the issues, several questions arise at the confluence of reason and emotion:

- Is it worth the threat to our fragile sense of community and to our gradually evolving recognition that old age does not necessarily symbolize inevitable uselessness to deny some medical care categorically?
- Will such categorical denial not, despite argument to the contrary, endanger social regard for the old, rendering them disposable?
- Does an adversarial framework (the old are consuming too many resources at the expense of children) not defeat a call for solidarity in a richly reciprocal society?
- And, finally, though access to health care may not be the most significant social good, it is indisputably necessary to the enjoyment of all other goods. Can we, then, without ethical uneasiness, call upon the old to accept limits in the name of their own and the social good when we allow defense contractors to disgracefully inflate costs for questionable weapons systems? Can we ask them to

accept limits and also ignore America's patently unjust, inefficient, and even occasionally corrupt health-care system?

How can these concerns not be the primary subject of our national agenda? Even if Callahan's arguments were unassailable, the sociopolitical context in which his policy prescriptions would be enacted make them unacceptable. To say, as Callahan does, that we must ask fundamental questions about the meaning of growing old without asking equally fundamental questions about the society we live in and the values it enshrines is at the heart of this moral discomfort. Saying this, however, does not deny the significance of Callahan's effort to force a confrontation, in the starkest possible terms, with difficult questions, for his concerns—about broader communal well-being and the meaning of old age—are profoundly important.

SOCIETAL CONSENSUS ABOUT OLD AGE AND PUBLIC POLICY

Callahan wisely notes that public policy for elders must rest on clearly articulated beliefs about old age. In contemporary America the inchoate and implicit nature of these beliefs contributes to the seeming inconsistency of our public policies. Callahan, however, would take us beyond making beliefs explicit; he would also insist that they be shared, that a consensus be formed around a socially accepted view of what old age ought to be about. Although he is most concerned about health policy, adoption of his beliefs would also influence other policy arenas. To initiate public dialogue (and to ground his policy proposals), Callahan proposes his own understanding of what the meaning and social significance of old age ought to be. Since that understanding shapes his conclusions, they demand critical attention.

Callahan asks us to adopt the view that there is a "natural life span" and hence a "tolerable death" that together provide sufficient justification for age-based limits to certain kinds of health care even when conditions of scarcity do not exist. (See essays in this volume by Brock, Jecker, and Singer for discussions of the "natural life span.") Embedded in the "natural life span" concept are Callahan's premises about what constitutes the good life in old age for the individual older person and the social conditions necessary to make a policy of limits morally acceptable. To understand his arguments fully, these premises deserve separate attention.

The first of these premises is that a policy of limits may be adopted only in a society that richly values old age. For such valuing to occur, Callahan insists that a conception of old age different from that advocated by the modernizing physicians and aging advocates must prevail. The "modernization project," as he perceives it, fails either to give a valued social role to elders as elders or to allow the emergence of a deep sense of personal meaning. He turns instead to an updated version of the "disengagement theory," which becomes not a way that psychologists once described "successful aging" but rather an explicit guide to what constitutes virtue or excellence in the practice of old age. According to Callahan, consensual agreement about this philosophy of old age would give elders a valued place in the social order, thereby providing one underpinning for a public policy of limits.

But this social esteem and significance—the rich understanding of the place of old age in human life—is only one condition for morally justifiable policies. The second premise is that they must also benefit the old intrinsically and not deprive anyone of life for the good of another. Any rationing scheme is objectionable if it doesn't offer "a justification based upon some intrinsic benefit for the elderly themselves" (*SL*, 153). Indisputably, he believes that a person is better off accepting limits—even if public policy imposes them and even if their own personal vision of growing old differs from the view adopted through broad social consensus. He also says that "individual human life [must be] respected for its own sake . . . and that individuals may not be deprived of life to serve the welfare . . . of others" (*SL*, 116). These then are the additional underpinnings of his argument for limits.

Clearly, Callahan's measures are, even by his own admission, very tough. He argues for rationing not as a tool of distributive justice in times of scarcity but rather as something valuable for the lives of elders even when resources are abundant. It is the denial—not the acceptance—of limits, in his view, that leaves elders worse off. Thus, his policy of rationing must stand or fall on the premises of inherent goodness for elders in a society replete with a rich appreciation of old age. Through the evolution of a communal consensus, reached through a generation or more of public discussion, Callahan's view of the good life will come to be shared by most, if not all, elders and successor generations. Although they may have further dreams and aspirations, their deeper obligations to communal well-being and future generations—the flourishing of society—and their own welfare would allow them to face limits without resentment. If Callahan is right, we will adopt his policies because they are just, wise and better for older people in some absolute sense—not only compared to current, less desirable forms of rationing.

Callahan recognizes that this point of view will evolve slowly, if at all. Yet, without these necessary conditions for a richly lived old age, the foundations for the "natural life span" and a policy of limits would slip dangerously. They, therefore, raise a number of questions. Is he convincing that the acceptance of limits, enforced by public policy, really is good for older people? How likely is it that adoption of his vision will substantially improve the social context of growing old? Does he correctly interpret the "modernizing project" and its implications, and do his interpretations inadvertently blame the old? And, last, even if his questions and answers may be deeply attractive to individuals facing the last years of their life, what, if any, are the risks of reaching cultural consensus about a virtuous old age so powerfully held that it justifies the denial of any societal obligation to those who think and feel differently?

ARE LIMITS INTRINSICALLY GOOD FOR OLDER PEOPLE?

What Callahan proposes denies quite intentionally the great varieties of ways that people might choose to grow old, many of which require the support of public or social policies. Although at this time Callahan's attention is specifically directed at medical care at the end of life, if his vision becomes pervasive, it could influence a number of other policies. Thus, the risks of its adoption are compounded. What, then, would be the result of limiting choice-enhancing policies? At the end of life, when physical or cognitive decrements, marginal incomes, societal disregard, the death of family and friends, and the awareness of one's own impending mortality naturally and inevitably limit choices, it becomes ever more imperative to honor what makes a life coherent for the individual. Choice is particularly important when loss can erode both self-esteem and a sense of personal control and independence. For some elders, particularly women and minorities, old age may finally free them from many obligations and allow them, often for the first time, to make explicit choices about their lives; their independent stories may open in old age. Yet another set of norms may be the very thing that destroys old age's uniqueness. (See the Fahey essay in this volume.) Many older people may thus experience Callahan's coherent vision of old age as not in their best interests, as too limited and thereby insufficient to provide them with a suitably rich old age. The denial of rich opportunities may be the very thing we ought to disallow as something inimical to meaning social significance. And, there is a reasonable doubt that Callahan's vision is of intrinsic benefit to the old.

SOCIAL SIGNIFICANCE AND A POLICY OF LIMITS

Callahan, however, is rightly concerned about the lack of social significance for the old. Ironically, years of effort to combat ageism have resulted not in enhanced esteem for elders but often in blame for their overconsumption of social resources. Although the underlying premises of policies such as Medicare and Social Security, the hallmarks of twentieth-century efforts on behalf of older Americans, were never precisely defined, they located the "problem" within the older person, assuming dependency and need (with a touch of merit or desert). Hence the solutions were highly individualistic. Government rarely used public policy to address, at their root, such socially grounded problems as lifelong patterns of inequality, exclusion from significant community and work roles, and the predominance of monetary definitions of productivity. When government ignores old age's social embeddedness, its solutions are incremental, particularized, partial, and generally age segregated. For many, these unspoken assumptions, the resulting design of policies, and the avoidance of any efforts to modify the social conditions of growing old triggered substantial concern. This concern—about the premises and sometimes the policies—resulted in persistent efforts to modify what was felt to be a demeaning view of aging and an insufficient response to the real problems. The partial success of these challenges, combined with an improvement in elders' material well-being because of these policies, provided unanticipated kindling for voices of discontent. With alarming budgetary deficits and a new political movement (Americans for Generational Equity) that chose as its initial image the old holding the young hostage, it became easy to blame elders for a number of social problems but most particularly the poverty of the young. (See the Minkler essay in this volume for a discussion of the intergenerational equity framework.) This newly constructed view of old age simply traded one negative image for another and compounded America's ageist past without solving the problems of children.

Unfortunately, Callahan's surprisingly uncritical acceptance of a framework dependent upon competition between the generations and his call not for social but for individual change plays into this image and locates his policies in an adversarial and victim-blaming context. Although he is rightly concerned about a significant and persistent social ill— the lack of sustained societal regard and respected roles for America's elders—his analysis of the problem and his proposed solutions may have precisely the reverse effect. Why set limits to the lives of greatly valued members of society? Further, his analysis, either by choice or by accidental omission, ignores the social and institutional origins of disregard for elders. Instead, he places considerable trust in the responsiveness of the political and social environment to what is, in reality, a call to older people to find meaning and achieve social significance through self-sacrifice and behavioral change. This individualistic approach, from a political economy perspective, leaves harmful social institutions undisturbed. According to Callahan, individual and not societal and/or institutional change will establish the conditions that make his policies acceptable. By leaving institutions untouched, except indirectly, he sets up the conditions for two negative outcomes: that the old will be even further stigmatized and alienated from a central place in American society and that exploration of the larger questions, which have heretofore conditioned life for the old, will be bypassed in the name of simpler solutions. For example, America's insensitivity to and lack of respect for elders may rest less on our failure to ascribe value to them as a link of past, present, and future, as Callahan proposes, than in the American system with its denial of opportunities to older people, its superannuation, its commodification of need, and its continued creation of dependency. It is perplexing that Callahan fails to ask probing questions about how our history, value system, language, economy, educaton, and institutions impede the development of a socially valued place for old age and allow ageist attitudes to flourish. The restriction of criticism to one value—personal individualism in health-care decision-making—without a comparable criticism of the institutions that structure health care—seems particularly shortsighted.

THE "MODERNIZATION PROJECT"

In part, what Callahan names the "modernization project" calls for policy changes based on a redefinition of old age. His wholehearted disapproval of it—focusing most particularly on what he perceives to be a resistance to death at all costs—discounts many of its virtues while ignoring some fundamental understandings of being old in contemporary America. The language of autobiography and poetry, and the reflections and experiences of family, friends, and service providers suggest that most older people clearly accept death as a vital part of old age; they do not require a policy of limits to assure their recognition of life's finitude. Loss is a part of their daily lives; it is others' avoidance of the subject that is often distressing. Neither older people nor their advocates are passionately committed to the "modernization project," as Callahan understands it, and to the preservation of life at all costs. The decision about high-cost end-of-life treatment generally—despite advance directives—lies less with the elderly than with a medical-care establishment that decides to use the armamentarium of available equipment. Fear of litigation and the highly individualistic nature of medicine may undergird such decisions. Callahan's argument comes dangerously close to scapegoating the old for problems they did not create. It also fails to acknowledge that social regard has not yet flowed from an awareness that most elders express a desire to halt treatment, often advocating for assisted suicide and the right to maintain control over what happens in their last years.

He also misunderstands the reasons for the "modernization project's" desire to confront ageism and negative stereotyping. It does not necessarily translate into a view that old age is merely an extension of middle age. In part, responsibility for the cult of youth rests less with older people and aging advocates than with the nature of America's consumer-driven society. Although the relationship between the newly discovered "aging market" and the efforts of aging advocacy organizations to change the negative image of aging is complex, it suggests that the sudden visibility of the old has less to do with valuing them, as such, than with the fact that they now have the potential to consume costly goods and services. The goal of the "modernization project" (which I think is a far less consistent, coherent effort than Callahan suggests) was not to assure that old would become young or that death could be eliminated but to open appropriate opportunities for elders to use their continued health and vigor productively. It also asks that the old must be as deeply valued for their differences as younger people. It asks us to accept that some are vigorous and some frail; some love kids and others are delighted to finally have some time for adult pursuits that years of child rearing or care giving for elder parents forbade. And, in part, it may ask that we recognize that the "problem" of old age lies less in the individual than in a society that excludes the elderly from any significant roles.

CONSENSUS AND THE
EXACERBATION OF INEQUALITIES

But even if we could somehow justify the desirability of consensus—and consensus around Callahan's vision—the fact that some, but not all, would have to accept the policies that flow from this consensus about old age makes it particularly troublesome. Ultimately, Callahan's proposals give more affluent elders an option that others do not have—of not phasing out, disengaging, and contemplating mortality and decline, or assisting the next generation—because they can buy the life-extending technologies that Medicare would deny. Although Callahan does not argue from justice, his proposals so magnify the differences between the haves and the have-nots that they create an intolerable problem of justice. Although, in time, all may adopt his vision, in the meanwhile the affluent—or the desperate—will get what others cannot. This discrepancy makes it very difficult to accept his premise that "I do not believe a society would be made morally intolerable by that kind of imbalance" (SL, 157). Medical treatment, contrary to the current metaphors of the "healthcare industry" and the patient as consumer, is not simply another consumer good. Although he correctly notes that it is inevitable that those with an abundance of resources will always be able to buy care unavailable to others, to advocate for a public policy based on such class differences would inescapably harm any foundering sense of community that may evolve. Such class differences are painful enough when the stakes are education or housing or clothing. In addition to class biases, his proposals also reinforce racial and gender biases. They will affect women and minorities most seriously—both because they tend to be the poorest of older Americans and women because they are the dominant group among the very old. They are the population groups who will die as a result of his policy of limits.

288

By these imbalances, Callahan's proposals fail the test that Albert Jonsen proposes—allowing the old to live out their history without resentment. At all other stages of our lives, public and social policies may stimulate certain choices or regulate our behavior more directly, but the outcome is rarely death. In the end, this policy of limits, as Callahan describes it, will reinforce existing inequalities and lead to a rationing policy based on ability to pay and not an age standard.

THE QUALITY-OF-LIFE ARGUMENT AND ITS DANGERS

Callahan's concern for assuring a rich context for old age rests not only on his particular understanding of the social significance of old age but also on a responsiveness to quality-of-life concerns. In that wish, he would find support among most elders. Yet, assuring a decent quality of life for those with chronic illness has serious economic consequences. What category of "rights" ought to be included? If we are to house the elderly and provide the sustained attention that chronic illness requires, it will take an enormous social commitment. Will the recognition of these costs place his proposal on the famous "slippery slope"? When will society decide, if we ever take on this responsibility to assure "quality of life," that these costs are also too high? To date, our record in this area has been less than honorable. The fear is a future in which we deny both end-of-life treatment and other forms of essential care.

THE "NATURAL LIFE SPAN," LIMITS, AND OLD AGE

So the question of whether or not Callahan's proposals will contribute to a good old age remains debatable, at best. His proposals indirectly blame the old for wanting life-extending technologies; they deny them a sense of individual purpose, self-respect, or autonomy; they create an image (contrary to his assumptions) of the disposable old; they demand of the old what we ask of no one else—to give up something very precious in the name of their own—but not necessarily freely chosen—good and the common good; they ask the old to adopt a certain manner of being old without challenging the institutions that are likely to corrupt the most virtuous practices. And they would fail a test of justice, since they would harm, even further, the most disadvantaged. Thus, Callahan cannot meet his own tough standards—that the value of any individual life means no deprivation for the good of another—for, in the end, his arguments tilt toward utilitarianism and the social utility of denying end-of-life treatment.

THE COST ISSUE

If the argument that Callahan's proposals are good for older people fails, he can fall back on costs—his secondary concern—and a social efficiency argument. The economic argument provides both initial motivation and collateral support for the entire thesis of *Setting Limits*. Technological change and skyrocketing costs force this "new reckoning with old age and its meaning" (*SL*, 200). Although he refuses to base his case for mandatory limits on the grounds of resource scarcity, costs are a recurrent and dominant theme; he uses them to engage attention and discounts all current cost-containment strategies. And, in his arguments he keeps returning to them: bypass surgery for the ninety-year-old or organ transplants for the very old. But because costs are not pivotal to his argument, he does not try to prove systematically that his proposals are the best ways to save money. Further, by justifying limit setting on the basis of the "natural life span," he automatically excludes limits on high-cost, but perhaps marginally useful, care for younger people.

Though it is a rhetorical question, I think we must ask how firm Callahan's insistence on his policy limits would be if it were not for his profound anxiety about health-care costs over time. So while acknowledging that, for Callahan, costs are not the primary reason for his policy prescriptions, I think we must still ask a number of questions. What effect will his proposals have on costs? Is his insistence correct that his policy is the final redoubt, that we, as a society, are cornered and have no other reasonable options but to redefine medical goals based on a new understanding of old age? Can his proposals do fundamental harm to elders and to our society by detracting attention from more deeply rooted problems?

He recognizes that in today's world his proposals would save very little money; his fear is for the future when the technological imperative will regularly redefine health needs. His preference is for a radical modification in the way we think about old age rather than for a comparable, if not so radical, modification in the way this nation delivers and finances medical care.

THE SOCIAL, POLITICAL, AND HISTORICAL CONTEXT

To answer these questions, we must locate *Setting Limits* in today's political and social environment, when, for the first time in almost twenty years, retrenchment, rather than expansion, in special programs for the old dominates the political agenda. Congress, facing enormous budget deficits and hearing arguments that set the old against the young, designed the Medicare Catastrophic Health Protection Act, the first of this nation's "generationally neutral" programs. Newspaper editorials called on the old to join in deficit-reduction efforts. In many cases the old are becoming the scapegoat for deep social ills.

To provide some common understanding, I would like to

turn briefly to the background of the current crisis. In 1965 Congress enacted the Medicare program. Intending it to be the first step toward a national health-care plan, Congress selected an age-based entitlement program, which they believed was more palatable to the American public than a plan guaranteeing universal access to health care. But Congress was cautious even in the design of this limited program. Reluctant to alienate powerful interest groups, Congress left the basic fee-for-service delivery system essentially intact. Medicare's design also left open a significant area of risk as a result of copayments, deductibles, and Part B-balanced billing for which private insurance could offer protection. So, though designed as an entitlement program for all older Americans, from the beginning it had a differential effect on people based on their income. At the same time, an assured source of government funding, the lack of significant cost controls, and a retrospective reimbursement policy stimulated corporate participation in health care and also accelerated cost escalation. Deregulation and other political accommodations to dominate institutions such as insurance companies, hospitals, and medical associations further accelerated the process of the privatization and the corporatization of health care.

Since 1980, as the public and private commitment to health-care access retrenched and the monopoly control of hospitals and other health-care facilities expanded, the divide between the haves and the have-nots widened. Cost-containment strategies, by increasing beneficiary cost sharing, simply furthered the process that Medicare's initial design initiated. So *Setting Limits* appeared when concern about costs was already eclipsing any conversation about access to care and quality of that care. In this new medical marketplace, the quantity and quality of medical care elders receive is related directly to their income and wealth. For example, their out-of-pocket costs rose by 49 percent for physician visits and 31 percent for other outpatient services between 1981 and 1985. In this context, health-care rationing is rampant but implicit. Callahan is quite right in calling our attention to the fact that rationing based on the ability to pay is rationing nonetheless.

THE LIMITS OF *SETTING LIMITS*

This background is important because it suggests why Callahan's failure to examine institutions that govern the provision of medical care is so significant and why his proposals simply extend the growing inequality that already dominates the health-care "marketplace." His narrow focus fails to account for the vast injustices in our existing system.

America's profound reluctance to admit the effects of class eases the acceptance of health-care services as marketable commodities. Despite the rhetoric that heralded "mainstream" services regardless of one's income, poor elders, dependent upon Medicaid or unable to afford Medigap policies, fare poorly when contrasted to those who can pay directly for services or supplement benefits from entitlement programs. Privatization—often a euphemism for decreased federal spending in both entitlement and means-tested programs and its correlate, profit—triggers no moral uncertainty among those who see the problems of old age as primarily individual and as unrelated to class distinctions or privileges, opportunities, or life circumstances. The emphasis on freedom of consumer choice (i.e., expression of market preferences) and the fact that income implicitly serves as an effective constraint on service utilization means that the resulting inequality in access can be attributed to chance and not to public policy. There is no explicit policy which denies anyone access to health-care services.

Though Callahan is correct—that we must reexamine the goals of medicine and not permit health care to trump other social goals—he may be guilty of putting the proverbial cart before the horse. A renewed emphasis on reforming the entire health-care system may make the problem of costs much less significant. I would add just a few comments to the detailed suggestions about reforming the American health-care system that Binney and Estes offer in their essay and that Kapp suggests in his. By looking only at public entitlements, Callahan ignores the substantial subsidy (in terms of dollars lost to the Treasury) for employer-based private health-care benefits, which are inherently class biased. And by arguing in defense of his position, that even countries with national health plans are concerned about setting limits, he ignores the vastly different starting place: a system that guarantees fair and universal access to care. In such a system a policy of rationing some care for some groups of people also means control over the transfer of those resources to elsewhere in the health-care system. Such assurance is lacking in America's fragmented nonsystem.

Hence, before we invoke the lifeboat ethic, we have to assess our alternatives and examine, once again, Callahan's assumptions. We may not be at our final fortress, as Callahan suggests. The call for limits as a way of solving our national problems deflects attention from systemic concerns. It incorrectly assumes that the costs of health care for elders directly and explicitly compromise the well-being of those whose work and life is essential to the common good, for society to flourish. It assumes that there is no other way of meeting important social needs than by denying treatment to some older people. If we cannot be certain that these assumptions are correct, then we must wonder, quite vigorously, if we are unfairly asking the old to make sacrifices, which are of questionable benefit to them, in a vastly unjust system, when these sacrifices cannot even assure more money for the young or for other purposes. Can the most committed communitarian feel comfortable with a common vision of the good life which is limited to only one generation and linked to only one aspect of our political lives with life and death implications for some but not all? At this time, can there be a defensible scheme for age-based rationing when our health-care delivery mode is so contingent upon whom we work for, what age we are, who our insurer is, or how much money we have?

A last concern with Callahan's narrow perspective on costs is the resistance to look deeply into the federal budget for resources to support health care. Since scarcity, except perhaps for organ availability, is ultimately socially constructed, can we allow a single older person to be denied antibiotic treatments or advanced cancer treatment when we spend over $50 million on a new Stealth bomber and not face a crisis in national values?

CONCLUSION

In conclusion, Callahan's proposals are unlikely to benefit the old and, in fact, may harm them. They won't do much good for the young and society and, in fact, may harm them by oversimplifying the problem and hence the solution. Simultaneously, his proposals encounter some very serious problems of justice. And though the knowledge of death offers a particular authenticity to life, it is not only what older people are about. We should learn to accept and deal with death. But we do not need the policy he is proposing to make that happen. Certainly, if his primary goal is to provoke discussion and not to set down a final agenda, it is regrettable that this part of his task is often lost when his harshest critics see only a punitive approach to the old. It is also regrettable that his solution offers an easy escape from addressing some of the pervasive problems of American society.

PART IX

AFTERWORD: DANIEL CALLAHAN RESPONDS TO HIS CRITICS

I HAVE been asked many times since I wrote *Setting Limits* whether I have changed my mind. My general answer to that question is no, if it is meant to apply to my proposal that we eventually use age as a standard to limit health-care entitlements. I have certainly heard many penetrating objections to that proposal, both of a theoretical and practical kind, and I am quite prepared to admit to their force in many respects. There are moral and social hazards in using age as a limiting standard, and political and pragmatic obstacles in actually implementing it.

What I have not heard, however, is a coherent *alternative* strategy, one that addresses simultaneously (1) the broad question of the meaning of old age and the place of the aged in our society; (2) the necessity of a broader and more coherent range of services for the elderly; and (3) the need eventually to set some kind of limits to health-care expenditures. Even some of my strongest critics concede that these are valid issues, though they may differ with me about how such questions are best addressed. However, they rarely take the next step, that of offering even the rudiments of a rounded alternative approach to the problems—a well-grounded perspective on aging with specific policy proposals.

My proposal is usually compared with some ideal or utopian world and thus easily found wanting (for who wants limits of any kind?); concerns about future financial burdens are too often shrugged aside with speculative hopes about reducing waste and increasing treatment choice and efficiency. The broad thrust of my argument is that because of current and impending financial crises, we will have to fundamentally change the way we think about age, health care, and the allocation of resources to the elderly. Most of my critics, by contrast, are intent to hold on to the same conventional values, trusting that with them we can find our way out of the woods. I remain convinced that we cannot, even though I am acutely aware that my own proposal, together with the values it embodies, has many problems. But won't any alternative have serious drawbacks? My approach needs to be compared with other rationing and limitation policies, not simply with an ideal world where all problems are solved without pain, sacrifice, or a change in practice. My proposal may not look so bad in a comparative context. I came to it out of a sense that given the magnitude of the problems before us, no other course will be as reasonable and effective, even if many others will seem, initially, more palatable, less threatening.

Let me reconstruct, in brief compass, the nature of our present situation, to bring out why it seems to carry with it a kind of unavoidable necessity, pushing us into a corner. I begin with the assumption that the allocation of health-care resources to the elderly is now beginning to create some serious problems: the greatly increased projected costs in the decades ahead, the disparity between resources going to old and young, and—most importantly—the lack of any good evidence that simply improving life-extending curative medicine for the elderly will inherently improve their happiness or well-being. At the same time, I assume that many important needs of the elderly are now unmet, especially those that bear on their daily quality of life and sense of security (for example, long-term care and drugs). I conclude that we must both improve some forms of care for the elderly and, over time, find ways to restrict decisively the intrinsically open-ended frontier of life extension; that is, we must find a way to set some firm limits. Not only will it be impossible for us to meet all needs on that endless frontier, but we can do ourselves great financial and social harm by even trying to do so.

But how can we set limits? Four steps are necessary. First we have to devise, or re-create, a rich theory of the meaning and significance of aging, decline, and death; and, with it, a no less rich theory of the ends of medicine in the face of aging. We need a view of medicine embedded in a view of old age, in turn embedded in a view of the individual life cycle and the cycle of the generations.

The second step is to rethink our priorities in health care, in particular shifting away from the excessive weight given curing and life extension over caring and life improvement; those new priorities should reflect our convictions about the meaning and significance of old age.

The third step is to consider the idea of limits, both out of practical necessity and out of a perception that any coherent system will require some kind of limits; it cannot be open-ended in all directions.

The fourth step is to entertain the idea of using age as a means of setting limits. It would offer the possibility of effectively restricting the endless frontier, of being public and visible, of treating all alike, and of making possible improvements for the elderly in other areas. It will be neither fair nor effective to allocate resources on a case-by-case basis, particularly by physicians working at the bedside. Categorical standards will be needed, and age is the most compelling and feasible candidate.

These are the bare bones of my argument:

- My goal is a long-term change in our thinking, not immediate application. I envision a time span of at least twenty to thirty years to bring that change about, and I am interested in influencing the thinking of younger rather than older age groups.
- I am proposing an approach by stages: an effort to rethink the meaning of old age and health care, a shift of priorities from curing to caring, a significant improvement in long-term and home care for the elderly (as well as other improved social services), a national health insurance plan—and then, *and only then,* the setting of an age limit for life-extending technologies.
- No consensus now exists on the meaning of aging or the ends of medicine, much less on the validity of an age-based restriction on health-care entitlement; the purpose of my book is to see if we can, in the coming decades, create such a consensus.
- We can at present pay for high technology medicine for the elderly, but the combination of a growing number of elderly and the expanding application of technology is an ominous trend. It is that technological application that must be arrested. We will not be able to afford it, and it does not even assure a better old age in the future.
- My focus is on the limitation of entitlement programs for the elderly—publicly financed programs such as Medicare—not on overall health care. The elderly should be permitted to buy any care they want beyond the entitlement limit but should understand that there cannot be an *unlimited* entitlement to public support.
- My concern is by no means exclusively with the economics of health care for the elderly, though the economic issues are real and important. The most challenging task is to use the pending economic crisis as an occasion to think more deeply about the ends of health care and the genuine needs of the elderly.

302

- I meant the second half of the book, and its practical suggestions, to be taken seriously but not literally; that is, as a form of speculation, not as hard and fast prescription. The details matter far less than devising a fresh way to think about policy in the future; the details would properly be left to the political process.

If it was a failure to attend to some of those qualifications that created confusion about the general purposes of the book (and probably my fault for not making them clearer), the more important objections turned on broader and deeper issues. In many quarters there was outright anger and unbridled hostility. Why? I believe I have challenged one of the most central beliefs of contemporary thinking about the elderly, the belief that people should be considered only as individuals, not singled out because of their age for special discrimination, especially a limitation on entitlements. I was accused of ageism, of unfairly stereotyping the elderly and putting forward policies and attitudes that neglect and demean them. I touched, then, not simply on a practical matter of policy but on a highly symbolic issue—and did so in a way that seemed to threaten to unravel decades of work toward improving the status of, and respect due, the elderly. It also turned out, I believe, that the justification I developed for a limit on entitlements embodied a number of other objectionable and offensive features. At least ten major criticisms were leveled against my approach, represented well by the various essays and reviews assembled in this volume. Since it is impossible here to address in detail all individual critiques, I will respond more generally to ten themes that recurrently emerge.

1. *A proposal to set limits on health-care entitlements for the elderly is unnecessary and morally wrong.* As a practical matter, the projection of the costs of health care for the elderly

303

in the future points decisively to the need for some limits, if not now, then within a decade or so. A 1987 Urban Institute study projected deficits in the Medicare program in the range of $27 billion to $60 billion by the year 2000 and $77 billion to $210 billion by 2010.[1] Deficits of that kind approximate the size of the entire federal deficit at present. A Medicare deficit of that magnitude would be an intolerable and unmanageable burden. We can afford to spend a large amount of money on health care for the elderly (and we should be prepared graciously to spend it), but we cannot afford to spend an *unlimited* amount, by which I mean *any* cost of such care created by open-ended technological progress. Not only would it be imprudent for any society to make that kind of a promise, but our present resources are already strained trying to meet present demands. Whether or not the eventual use of age to set those limits would be wise, we would do well to agree at once that *some* method of setting limits will be necessary; that is the imperative first step to any coherent solution.

In saying that we will eventually have to set limits, I do not want to deny that our current system is wasteful, inefficient, needlessly expensive, and full of injustice. On the contrary, those real and grievous shortcomings need immediate attention and they demand widespread and deep change: limits on profits and on high fees and salaries, as well as limits on unnecessary diagnostic tests and unneeded treatment. Yet I do not see the reforming of the present system and the limiting of health care to the elderly as mutually exclusive alternatives.

We should in any case consider and value limits for more than economic reasons. There is no evidence to suggest that the welfare and happiness of the elderly will be advanced by an unlimited commitment to health care. My own observation of human life is that both individuals and societies do better if they understand the value of limits and the curbing of

304

excessive aspirations. There is no direct correlation between the size of health-care budgets and human happiness, or between a longer life and a more satisfying life. The acceptance of our mortality, and a willingness to live within some boundaries to desire, will enhance our human dignity and help us live prudently within our means.

2. *Proposals to limit health care and technological innovation are premodern and antiscientific.* The desire to create a new and transformed old age, one that embodies a distinction between becoming old and becoming sick, is both understandable and hazardous. At most, we can forestall death and perhaps reduce the length of illness prior to death. But to pursue that goal obsessively, or to think that we can and should make of old age a time of indefinitely extended middle age, is to incur excessive financial costs as well as ultimate disappointment. We have modernized old age in many respects, but we have not succeeded—nor will we ever succeed—in banishing the debilities it inevitably brings and the fear it engenders. Indeed, the very extension of life expectancy brings with it an increase in chronic illness. We should reflect on that phenomenon, which may not be, as some would have it, a correctable accident. The desire to modernize old age distorts our perception of the life cycle, threatening to lead the old to seek resources that ought justly to be reserved for the young, those who have their lives to live and who need themselves to have the opportunity to become old. Science can offer great benefits when used wisely; it can be a hazard if used imprudently.

3. *The data used to justify setting limits are too pessimistic and too uncertain to be of compelling force.* Though I believe that I made use of the best data available—which show mounting problems in paying for and satisfying the health demands of the elderly—I was nonetheless thought by many to be too "pessimistic." Why should we believe studies that

305

show Medicare running deficits in the range of hundreds of billions of dollars in twenty to thirty years? How do we know that the projections will turn out to be true? Have not past projections often been false? How can I be certain that cost-containment efforts will continue to fail? Those are pertinent and reasonable questions. But in the absence of any counterinformation (which I could not locate), it is not enough simply to invoke such questions, as if they answer themselves, provide us with grounds to act as if no serious problem exists, or reassure us that any problems can be solved in some more acceptable fashion.

Common sense, I believe, suggests that we must build our policy and our thinking around what we now know or project—not around what we hope will be true, or around our desire to avoid unpleasant policies. If the projections I use turn out to be false, then we may never (at least for economic reasons) have to set an age limit on entitlement to care. If we can find some way to make cost containment work without setting the kind of stringent limits I envision, then that will relieve the pressure to find an economic solution. Yet I will be amazed if that happens. The logic of growing numbers of the elderly and a continued commitment to technological progress works against it.

The elderly do not *now* use a heavy proportion of high-technology medicine—but present usage is not my concern. It is the powerful *trend* to apply to the elderly medical procedures originally developed for younger patients that threatens a grave future crisis. Recent studies of dialysis and organ transplants, of general surgery and open-heart surgery, show a steady increase in patient age, with a sharp increase in the use of such procedures for those over the ages of seventy-five and eighty.[2] Trends of that kind mean that even if we could achieve every cost-containment reform now proposed, we would still have a serious problem in the long run. That is now what is taking place in countries that have already adopted precisely the reforms being sought (as the supposed solution) in our country.

Will not my own proposals for reform in the system—especially the need for better long-term care and home care—increase the costs of elderly health care? They surely will, and I would foresee an increase in costs over the next decade or so as a result of those improved benefits. But an age limit on expensive, life-extending medicine would, in the long run, help create a firm, almost impenetrable barrier to unlimited acute-care expenditures. We could then envision a leveling off of costs, but at a stage where there would be a better balance between length of life and quality of life.

4. *To treat the elderly as a group ignores significant differences among them.* While it is obviously true that the elderly are, as individuals, a highly varied group—perhaps even more than other age groups—it is both necessary and legitimate to think of them also as members of a group. They are a highly varied group of *elderly* people, not of children or young adults. The Social Security and Medicare programs were enacted with that perception in mind. Even the most cursory scanning of health-care information or illness incidence shows that the elderly have, as a group, far greater health needs than other groups—even if some elderly are in perfect health, livelier, and more active than some much younger people. But if we must think about allocation decisions, then the needs and costs of groups are highly pertinent.

We must ask what a group can *reasonably* claim of common resources, to avoid a situation in which—in the name of meeting individual need—one group is allowed to consume a disproportionate share of resources. Indeed, to focus only on individual need is highly hazardous; then the life of the disease-threatened ninety-year-old adult is made equal in its claim on resources to that of the ninety-minute-old child. That child is forced to compete against that elderly person, even though the latter has already had the chance to become an elderly person, which is not yet the case with the child. But a logic of meeting individual need with an age-blind eye leads to precisely that kind of unjust outcome. Elderly individuals have a perfect right to develop their own life plans and life goals, but that right cannot include an unlimited demand upon publicly funded programs to support those goals. Individuals can only ask to have their general and reasonable needs met, not those idiosyncratic goals shaped and cultivated as part of some private vision of their personal good; the latter they should pay for out of their own pockets.

I have never believed that the elderly have deliberately sought to take resources from the young; it has happened only inadvertently. But it has happened because the elderly got there first with a strong entitlement program (Medicare), and one that so powerfully consumes a growing share of resources that legislators are loath to add new programs for other groups, particularly children and the poor. The elderly entitlement programs have, in that sense, had a potent blocking function. There is, of course, no guarantee that money saved on health care for the elderly would go to the young, but there is every certainty that with a large amount going to the elderly no large-scale new programs will be enacted for the young. The Medicare program established in 1965 was viewed as a first step toward national health insurance. As it turned out, it has all but guaranteed that there will not be any such insurance in the near future.

5. *Chronological age is an arbitrary and capricious standard for policy formulation.* If limits are to be set to entitlement allocations to the elderly, and *if* we are serious about finding effective limits, and *if* we want to make certain that we can devise a balanced, coherent system of care for the elderly, then only age is likely to be an effective standard. Constant medical progress steadily presses forward the frontier of high-

technology care of the elderly. While it is true that the elderly
are not desperately seeking any and all forms of life-extending
technology, much medical progress does lead to effective
treatment, which the elderly often do want; that is one reason
for an increase in the average age of those who undergo
surgical and other medical procedures. Only useless and burdensome treatment is resisted, not the kind that promises
some success. This kind of success is our problem, and it is
this kind of success we cannot indefinitely afford.

I see this as a frontier of progress that must be powerfully
restricted in the years ahead, and the only barrier likely to
be effective is age itself. If the researchers know that the fruits
of their work will not be rewarded if they lead to expensive
care beyond a certain age, and if manufacturers of expensive
technologies know that the use of their devices will not be
reimbursable (at least under public programs), then a powerful incentive will have been created to radically slow the
progress. As matters now stand, the incentive is to move
ahead, always to move ahead. The argument that we need
more research precisely because we have so many medical
and economic problems with present forms of medical care
is wonderfully optimistic but wholly at odds with recent medical history. Far from reducing costs, research probably helps
to drive costs up. As data from the National Institutes of
Health show, investment in research and increased health-
care costs correlate almost perfectly.[3]

It is simply inconceivable that we can both afford to continue such progress without restraint and at the same time
hope to put into place improved long-term care, home care,
and social services for the elderly, all of which are desperately
needed. The technological progress in saving and extending
life will serve another kind of blocking function, this time
guaranteeing that costly life-extending technologies will use
up money that could have been spent on other kinds of health
needs of the elderly. To use age as a standard—a barrier

against costly unlimited progress—would be to use the only genuinely decisive standard: It is clean, simple, visible, and equitable.

6. *Treatment decisions should be based on individual need and efficacy considerations, not categorical standards.* For well over twenty years there has been a strong effort to find ways to terminate futile treatments, to allow people simply to die when there is no hope for recovery. Categorical standards—that is, formal and impersonal standards applying to all—have been avoided. But no effective way of making individual decisions to terminate treatment has been found—or is likely to be found. Bedside treatment decisions are often technically, emotionally, and morally difficult to make. The argument, therefore, that we can rely on case-by-case treatment decisions for the elderly as a means of fairly allocating resources is utterly implausible. We can hardly do it now, when only the individual welfare of patients, not allocation, is the goal. To expect that individual physicians can serve as rationers is unrealistic as a practical matter and flies in the face of the ethic of medicine, which makes the welfare of the individual patient—not the apportioning of societal resources—the central moral obligation. It is no less utopian to believe that giving patients more choice about their treatment will necessarily save money. Despite the fact that some thirty-eight states have "living will" legislation, there is no evidence that it has saved any money. Only categorical standards, determined by society and not dependent upon subjective or uncertain clinical evidence, can effectively be used for allocating resources. Such standards would, to be sure, have problems of their own—for example, distinguishing between life-extending technologies and those that simply relieve suffering. When that distinction is uncertain, the presumption should be to use the technology.

Yet even if effective individual decisions could be made,

there is no reason to assume that what is the right decision for an individual patient—providing the appropriate efficacious treatment—will in the aggregate be affordable for society. On the contrary, the need to set limits will almost certainly require that we at times find ways of denying individuals beneficial treatments. An artificial heart may well work someday with a ninety-five-year-old patient, and it may be correct for a physician committed to that patient's best interests to recommend it—but that hardly means our society through Medicare could afford to begin paying the costs of artificial hearts for all such patients in that age group.

There is an even more fundamental difficulty. Because of constant medical progress, the demands of individual medical "need" are unlimited. Medical "need" is a function of the state-of-the-art of medicine. No one thought a century ago that someone dying of liver failure "needed" a transplant; only when the technology became available was a need created. Our needs are defined by our desires, by technological possibility, and by cultural expectations; needs so defined have no intrinsic limits. The quest for a set of "essential needs" has been a failure to date as reflected in our inability to define a "minimally adequate" level of health care, or to define "medical necessity," often offered as a standard of care. That is no accident; it is an inherently meaningless concept, one that will never be given a plausible content in the face of medical progress.

I believe that in Chapter 6 of *Setting Limits* I got myself in trouble by suggesting that an exception should be made in the termination of treatment for patients in otherwise good health. I was myself seduced by our natural inclination to look at individual cases. That was a mistake, and my critics were quite right to point that out. I would now say that, to be consistent in the use of age as a standard, no exceptions should be made, particularly exceptions based on the conditions of an individual patient; the whole point of a cate-

311

gorical standard is to avoid having to make judgments of that kind. In the paperback edition, I changed that passage, leaving open the question of whether the use of age could admit of exceptions. I have come increasingly to think that, while theoretically possible, exceptions would not be workable and would, moreover, undermine the very value and use of a categorical standard.

7. *The notion of a biographical "natural life span" is too vague and too insensitive to individual differences.* If it is both theoretically hopeless and practically impossible to effectively allocate resources to the elderly based on individual decisions about need and treatment efficacy, what alternatives do we have? We must develop out of the cultural and social ingredients available to us a standard that could command a consensus. I tried to locate such a standard in the idea of the "natural life span"—a notion of a biographically full life having nothing whatever to do with biological life spans. There are two reasons for doing so. The first is that most cultures, past and present, seem to have some conception of a "full life" and judge a death at that point as more acceptable, less tragic and wrenching, than a premature death; our own government, and much of the literature of preventive medicine, uses the notion of the avoidance of a "premature death" as a goal of the health-care system. It is not an unfamiliar or strange concept even to us.

The other reason for using the notion of the "natural life span" is based on a common observation: The death of an elderly person, after a long life, elicits a different response than the death of a young person; the funeral or memorial service of an elderly person is ordinarily different, marked far less by tears and inconsolable grief. Death is always sad, but not necessarily tragic or outrageous.

But even if there is something to the idea of a "natural life span" and a "tolerable death," can it be used fairly for policy purposes? Is it not too vague and general, and too indifferent to individual biographies to be just and workable? Keep in mind how I propose that it be used. First, as a positive aspiration, it is meant to stimulate us to work to insure that all young people have the opportunity to become elderly people, to avoid a premature death. Everyone should have the chance to live out a full life span. Second, as a way of setting limits, its purpose is to help us answer the question: If we must set limits, what is a *reasonable* standard for doing so? It is reasonable for a society to say that it will help everyone to live a full life, but that it cannot, and will not, promise them a life tailored to their individual wants and aspirations, much less a life that pursues every technological advance that might extend their lives. It is precisely that effort to respond to every individual need that has put us in great trouble; there is no end to the possibilities, and thus no end to the demands on the public purse and the public interest. No one who has been assisted and enabled by a public entitlement program to live out a full life can legitimately claim to have been shortchanged by a public refusal to continue indefinitely to satisfy individual wants and needs. This is especially true when the price of such an effort would jeopardize meeting the legitimate needs of other age groups, and other societal needs besides health.

We will, to be sure, never achieve perfect consensus on these matters. But we can create a new consensus in the future, one that could be sufficiently strong for policy purposes, strong enough to pass legislation that will command the support of the majority of citizens. The proposal that instead of my approach we adopt that of the "prudential life span" strategy may also have merit, but it too would require a new consensus. Since the explicit policy details of that model have never been spelled out, it is hard to tell if it would be a superior approach. In any case, whether the choice be to pursue that approach or my own, a new consensus would be imperative.

313

8. *Limits on public health-care entitlements for the elderly would exacerbate current inequities.* It is not possible in this or any other society—save at the cost of totalitarianism—to guarantee the poor medical benefits precisely identical to those that the rich or powerful can command. No society could pay for such a policy (which would include, for instance, the use of a private jet to obtain medical benefits not available in this country). A more feasible goal is to make certain that the poor are given a decent level of health care such that the disparity between what they and the rich get is not glaring and outrageous. Common sense, moreover, should tell us that any and all allocation plans will involve some trade-offs: What is the best balance of goals when not all can perfectly be achieved?

My contention is that a health-care system that sought to help us avoid premature death, to help us live out a "natural life span," and to help us in our old age to meet our long-term and home-care needs would be a fair and balanced system. It would certainly be fairer and more ample than our present system. The trade-off I am proposing is simply this: A rounded, coherent program designed to meet the full range of elderly health-care needs is better than one that puts its emphasis on acute-care, high technology life-extending medicine. That kind of medicine is a bottomless pit economically, effectively blocking the possibility of responding to all the other needs of the elderly and other groups.

Would it not be unfair to those beyond a certain age to be denied public entitlement to forms of medicine they could not afford? To some extent, yes, if the focus is exclusively on what, at some point, they will be denied. But my answer is no, if the goal is to achieve the more balanced, rounded system that I propose. Nor do I think my system would be legally unacceptable or unconstitutional. There is no constitutional right to health care for those of any age, and Congress—

which created the Medicare program—can set limits if it so chooses. I do not deny that it would be *politically* difficult to do so, and certainly impossible at present; but that is why we need to develop a new political consensus to facilitate future change.

But would it not, finally, be ageist to use age to set a limit on what the elderly can ask from society in its public programs? No. First, the present Medicare program is itself an age-based program, and of a kind available to no other age group; the elderly already start with a great advantage over everyone else. It is not to stereotype or demean the elderly to say that they should have a full and generous program, but not an unlimited one, and to say so because neither our society nor any other can afford to promise to pursue medical progress and individual cure for the elderly as far as it might go—just as it could not make such a promise, say, to save each and every low-birth-weight baby, or each and every young adult who might need an artificial heart. To limit health care to the elderly is to make a statement about the limits of economically affordable medical technology as much as about the elderly.

9. *Death and decline are proper subjects of scientific inquiry and should be fought with public expenditures.* An old age founded on the acceptance of aging, decline, and death as part of human life will be one that is truer to human nature and to the life cycle than to an obsessively modernizing view of aging, for the latter is not prepared to accept limits, to accept death, or to accept aging. It thus seeks to deny the inevitable (not necessarily in principle, but in practice) and would have society spend unlimited resources in trying to change that inevitability. None of us want to die, and none of us want to be sick. Yet we must see that a quest to thwart mortality can carry with it a high price tag: to mislead people

315

about the possibilities of their own lives and to badly skew the use of resources to avoid death rather than enhance the living of life.

The great contribution of the idea of "ageism" is to alert us to the possibility of unfair and inaccurate stereotypes about the elderly, for instance, that they are all frail, senile, and unproductive. We know that to be false. But the danger of pressing the fear of stereotyping the elderly too far is in pretending that age is irrelevant, that only individuality matters. But age is a fact of human life, and aging a part of our biological nature. We can generalize validly about the elderly without stereotyping them, and we can try to work with those generalizations to devise fair policy. The generalization I want to work with is that old age is part of the life cycle, that decline and death can only be forestalled, not defeated, and that old age can only be given meaning and significance if we incorporate those fundamental perceptions in the way we think about the elderly—and think about our own aging. The crusade against "ageism" began as an effort to help us think more clearly about the elderly, but it is now in danger of obscuring our perceptions.

10. *The ends of aging and medicine are questions about which a consensus cannot and should not be forged in a pluralistic society.* Much of morality in America is now dominated by an individualism and pluralism that would deny the possibility of coming to any serious common moral consensus, and that would leave profound and moral questions as much as possible in the hands of individuals. The problem of health care for the elderly, however, shows the limitations of that approach. One way or another, we must have some common moral discussion. The failure of individual need to provide a standard for setting limits means that no option remains but to devise a communal standard. That in turn will require that we ask some fundamental questions, of a kind that makes us uncomfortable in a pluralistic society. What ought to be the meaning and significance of old age? What do we owe to different age groups in our society? What are the limits of the demands that we can, as individuals, make on our fellow citizens? What is our deepest good as human beings, and our deepest good as a society? To what extent does constant medical progress serve our deepest good as human beings, and serve our deepest good as a society?

Those are inescapably moral questions, the kind that forces us to raise questions about our basic values and moral principles. What has been called a "thin theory" of the good would have us avoid such questions, at least in our public life. Yet I do not see how we can work our way out of the health-care problem for the elderly without some "thick theory," one that tries to envision what best serves the highest human ends and best serves as the basis for a fair, and sensible, health-care system. The elderly must give some thought to their obligations to younger age groups and ask whether excessive demands on their part could lead to harm to others and themselves. The young must begin asking what they should reasonably want when they become old, and what their present obligations to the elderly are. Inevitably, these questions will be dealt with politically, as we shape and reshape policy. But there can be no good or lasting political solution not based on serious reflection about the underlying moral issues.

A FINAL WORD

Those are my general responses to the major themes touched upon by the critics of *Setting Limits*. What I am looking for, in short, is a future policy well rooted in a coherent, and deep, view of the place of aging in our lives. My critics have doubtless scored a number of points against my argument, but I think it disappointing that many go to great lengths to object to my proposals without offering an alternative long-term, deep vision. The primary counterresponse seems to have been that we should try other less drastic ways to make our health-care system more efficient and less costly. That is true, and I fully support all efforts in that direction. But I see no reason to believe that these efforts can cope with the crisis that is now emerging, one that is fueled by the desire for unlimited medical progress for the elderly and a large and growing number of elderly. Efficiency alone cannot get us out of that dilemma.

I see much of the resistance to my viewpoint not simply as an objection to the use of age limits—certainly understandable—but as an objection to *any* significant limits. Once we have come to accept the inevitability of such limits—as reality will force us to do—and reflect seriously on what would truly benefit the elderly, then we will be in a better position to compare the choices open to us. My guess is that when that happens, age as a standard will not look nearly so threatening as it now does. We will find that there are few viable options open to us, and all of them will bring some degree of distress and limitation. In the meantime, we can all hope that we will, as we think and debate together, come to treasure the elderly and to better understand how we might all best age and, at the same time, be responsible citizens, concerned not only with our own welfare (rightly enough) but with the welfare of all.

NOTES

1. John Holahan and John L. Palmer, "Medicare's Fiscal Problems: An Imperative for Reform," *Journal of Health Politics, Policy and Law* 13:1 (1988), 53–81.

2. See Gregory de Lissovoy, "Medicare and Heart Transplants: Will Lightning Strike Twice?," *Health Affairs* 7:4 (1988): 61–72; L. Henry Edmunds, Jr., et al., "Open-Heart Surgery in

Octogenarians," *New England Journal of Medicine* 1319:3 (1988): 131–36; Michael Hosking et al., "Outcomes of Surgery in Patients 90 Years of Age and Older," *Journal of the American Medical Association* 261:13 (1989): 1909–15.

3. National Institutes of Health, *NIH Data Book* (Bethesda, MD: 1988), p.1.